Spelling Connections

J. Richard Gentry, Ph.D.

ZB **Zaner-Bloser**

Author

J. Richard Gentry, Ph. D.

Reviewers

Paula Boales, Killeen ISD, Killeen, TX

Sherry Durham, Ed. D., Lufkin ISD, Lufkin, TX

Karyn L. Huskisson, Klein Instructional Center, Spring, TX

Carmen Ramos, San Benito CISD, San Benito, TX

Susan Shogan, Round Rock ISD, Round Rock, TX

Linda Stout, Crawford ISD, Crawford, TX

ELL and Spanish Consultants

Ellen Riojas Clark, Ph.D., Professor, College of Education
and Human Development, Division of Bicultural-Bilingual
Studies, The University of Texas at San Antonio, TX

Bertha Pérez, Ed.D., Professor Emeritus of Literacy,
College of Education and Human Development,
The University of Texas at San Antonio, TX

Rocio Reyes-Moore, Spanish Language Productions,
Alexandria, OH

ISBN 978-0-7367-6868-9

Zaner-Bloser, Inc., P.O. Box 16764, Columbus, Ohio 43216-6764

1-800-421-3018

www.zaner-bloser.com

Printed in the United States of America   11 12 13 14 15 997 6 5 4 3 2

Certified Chain of Custody
SUSTAINABLE FORESTRY INITIATIVE Promoting Sustainable Forest Management
www.sfiprogram.org

This SFI label applies to the text paper.

Table of Contents

Writer's Handbook

Spelling Dictionary

Writing Thesaurus

Index

Word Sorting

A word sort helps you become a Word Detective. When you sort, you look for patterns in your spelling words. You see how words are the same and how they are different. Word sorting can help you remember how to spell words.

Buddy Sort using the word sort cards

Word sort on an interactive whiteboard

There are different kinds of word sorts you can use with your spelling words.

- **Individual Sort**—Use word sorting to practice your spelling words.
- **Buddy Sort**—Do a word sort with a partner.
- **Speed Sorts on Your Own**—Time yourself as you sort your spelling words. Then do it again and try to improve on the number of seconds it takes to complete the word sort.
- **Speed Sorts With a Team**—See which team can complete the sort in the shortest time and with the greatest accuracy.

Spell Check

Most computers have a spell checker. Spell check is a tool that can find many spelling mistakes, but it can't find them all!

Sometimes a writer types the wrong word. For example, if you type **there** instead of **their**, the spell checker will not catch your mistake because the word you typed is spelled correctly. The spell checker does not know you meant to write a different word.

Spell check can help you find and correct mistakes in your writing. But you still must proofread everything you write!

Look, Say

1 **Look** at the word.

2 **Say** the letters in the word. Think about how each sound is spelled.

Cover, See

3 **Cover** the word with your hand or close your eyes.

4 **See** the word in your mind. Spell the word to yourself.

Write, Check

5 **Write** the word.

6 **Check** your spelling against the spelling in the book.

Spelling Strategy
Taking a Test

1. **Get** ready for the test. Make sure your paper and pencil are ready.

2. **Listen** carefully as your teacher says each word and uses it in a sentence. Don't write before you hear the word **and** the sentence.

3. **Write** the word carefully. Make sure your handwriting is easy to read. If you want to print your words, ask your teacher.

4. **Use** a pen to correct your test. Look at the word as your teacher says it.

5. **Say** the word aloud. Listen carefully as your teacher spells the word. Say each letter aloud. Check the word one letter at a time.

6. **Circle** any misspelled parts of the word.

7. **Look** at the correctly written word. Spell the word again. Say each letter out loud.

8. **Write** any misspelled words correctly.

Connections to THINKING

Read the spelling words and sentences.

1.	land	*land*	The farmer planted corn on his **land**.
2.	stick	*stick*	Kayla used a big **stick** as a bat.
3.	plan	*plan*	Dad will help us **plan** our vacation.
4.	trip	*trip*	Our class went on a **trip** to the zoo.
5.	stand	*stand*	Please **stand** in this line.
6.	act	*act*	My sister likes to **act** in plays.
7.	thing	*thing*	What is that **thing** on your desk?
8.	last	*last*	John spent his **last** dollar on pizza.
9.	lift	*lift*	This box is too heavy to **lift**.
10.	band	*band*	The **band** plays music at games.
11.	grand	*grand*	Lisa won the **grand** prize.
12.	swim	*swim*	Shana likes to **swim** in the pool.
13.	stamp	*stamp*	Please put a **stamp** on this letter.
14.	list	*list*	Write the words in a short **list**.
15.	sand	*sand*	Many beaches are covered by **sand**.

Think & Sort the spelling words.

1–9. Write the words that have the **short a** sound.

10–15. Write the words that have the **short i** sound.

Remember

The **short a** sound you hear in **plan** is spelled **a**. The **short i** sound you hear in **trip** is spelled **i**.

 TEKS 3.24A Use knowledge of letter sounds, word parts, word segmentation, and syllabication to spell.
3.24C Spell high-frequency and compound words from a commonly used list.

Match Ending Sounds

1–4. Write the spelling words that rhyme with **stand**. Circle the consonant blends (two consonants together) in each word.

Identify Word Structure

Follow the directions and write the spelling word. Then circle the letter that makes the short vowel sound you hear in the word.

5. Take away the first sound of **fact**.

6. Change the first sound of **fast**.

7. Change the first sound of **mist**.

8. Change the first two letters of **sting**.

9. Change the first sound of **drip**.

Blend Sounds

Write the spelling words for each set of letter sounds you blend. Write a word with:

10. the **sw** consonant blend and the **short i** sound.

11. the **short i** sound and the **ft** consonant blend.

12. the **pl** consonant blend and the **short a** sound.

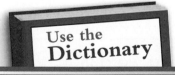

Use the
Dictionary

13–15. A dictionary lists words in alphabetical order. Write the three spelling words that begin with the letters **st** in alphabetical order.

Dictionary Check Be sure to check your answer in your **Spelling Dictionary**.

TEKS 3.24A Use knowledge of letter sounds, word parts, word segmentation, and syllabication to spell.
3.24C Spell high-frequency and compound words from a commonly used list.

Connections to READING

land	stick	plan	trip	stand
act	thing	last	lift	band
grand	swim	stamp	list	sand

Complete the Analogies

Write a spelling word to complete each analogy.

1. **Beginning** is to **end** as **first** is to _____.
2. **Ship** is to **water** as **car** is to _____.
3. **Song** is to **sing** as **play** is to _____.
4. **Insect** is to **crawl** as **fish** is to _____.
5. **Small** is to **tiny** as **large** is to _____.

Make Inferences

Write the spelling word that fits each clue.

6. You should do this and place your hand over your heart for the Pledge of Allegiance.
7. This is how Tim and Lin pick up a gift.
8. Sandy sticks this on a letter before she sends it.
9. Vin needs this for roasting marshmallows.
10. This group can play loud music.

Use Context Clues

Read this paragraph. Write the spelling word that completes each sentence.

After school let out, the Lee family decided to __11.__ a vacation. Kim and Nucha made a __12.__ of places they wanted to visit. They each wrote down one __13.__ they hoped to do. All of the Lees wanted to build __14.__ castles. Where do you think the Lees will go on their __15.__?

 TEKS 3.24C Spell high-frequency and compound words from a commonly used list.

Proofread a Letter

To show where changes are needed, you can use proofreading marks. The symbol ≡ means make a capital letter. The symbol / means make a small letter. Proofread the letter below for eight misspelled words. Then rewrite the letter. Write the spelling words correctly and make the corrections shown by the proofreading marks.

Dear Parents,

Come help Çlean up the lan at Grannd Park. We plann to take a tripp there on the lasst day of school at 10:00 a.m. there is a lisst of things to do. You can pick up Éach big stik and lift up every heavy theng.

Mr. Bell's Third grade Class

Proofreading Marks

≡	Capital Letter
/	Small Letter
∧	Add
ℓ	Delete
⊙	Add a Period
⁋	Indent

PERSUASIVE Writing Prompt
Write a Letter

Think of a project you would like to do with a parent. Write a letter inviting your parent to help you with the project. Use as many spelling words as you can.

- Use the writing process: prewrite, draft, revise, edit, and publish.
- Use language that will persuade, such as *please*. Explain why you need your parent's help.
- Include a greeting, closing, and signature.
- Use complete sentences with correct capitalization, punctuation, grammar, and spelling.
- Read your work. Circle three words you are unsure about, and check their spellings in a dictionary.

Transfer

Think of three words that rhyme with **trip** and three words that rhyme with **last**. Write the words in your Spelling Journal and circle the letter that makes the short vowel sound.

TEKS 3.24A Use knowledge of letter sounds, word parts, word segmentation, and syllabication to spell. **3.24C** Spell high-frequency and compound words from a commonly used list. **3.24G** Use print and electronic resources to find and check correct spellings.

bat	trip	land	sand	magnet
fan	act	stand	brick	packet
miss	thing	last	dancer	slim
win	grand	lift	gadget	whiskers
stick	stamp	band	skill	
plan	list	swim	grasp	

Syllables and Sounds

1–5. Write the words with two syllables. Circle the **short a** or **short i** sound in each word. Make sure to check your **Spelling Dictionary**. Some words may have more than one **short a** or **short i** sound.

Pattern Power

Add, drop, or change one letter in each word below to make a spelling word.

6. bend
7. swam
8. art

9. stump
10. left
11. send

Meaning Mastery

Write words from the list to match each meaning. Circle the **short a** or **short i** sound.

12. any object
13. to be on your feet
14. the ability to do something
15. to hold with your hand

 TEKS 3.24A Use knowledge of letter sounds, word parts, word segmentation, and syllabication to spell.
3.24C Spell high-frequency and compound words from a commonly used list.

Science

Word Hunt

Read the paragraphs below and look for words with **short a** or **short i**.

Vegetables need sun, water, air, and food to grow. They get food and water from the soil.

Bugs can eat the vegetables farmers grow. Farmers can spray poison to get rid of the bugs, but poison harms the land. Many farmers use good bugs to fight bad bugs.

Some flowers are like magnets for good bugs. Farmers plant these flowers near their vegetables so good bugs will come.

Ladybugs and wasps are good bugs that act like heroes by eating the bad bugs. A praying mantis eats a lot of bugs. A mantis looks like a walking stick. It's a great bug for a garden.

If you plan to grow vegetables, put good bugs on your list. Then take a trip to a garden store. Many stores sell good bugs. You can buy good bugs through the mail, too.

WORD SORT

Follow the directions. Write each word once.

1. Write the two-syllable word that contains both a **short a** sound and a **short i** sound.

2–4. Write the one-syllable words that have more than three letters and contain the **short a** sound.

5–8. Write the one-syllable words that have more than three letters and contain the **short i** sound.

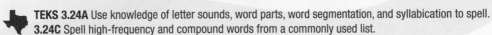
TEKS 3.24A Use knowledge of letter sounds, word parts, word segmentation, and syllabication to spell.
3.24C Spell high-frequency and compound words from a commonly used list.

Read the spelling words and sentences.

1.	crop	*crop*	Ms. Lutz is harvesting her bean **crop**.
2.	test	*test*	Joni passed her spelling **test**.
3.	clock	*clock*	Is the time on this **clock** correct?
4.	spent	*spent*	Dana **spent** her money on books.
5.	drop	*drop*	Ben felt a **drop** of rain on his head.
6.	left	*left*	Mary writes with her **left** hand.
7.	sled	*sled*	The **sled** slid on the ice.
8.	plot	*plot*	He grows peas in his garden **plot**.
9.	spend	*spend*	Juan and Shawn **spend** summers at camp.
10.	west	*west*	The sun sets in the **west**.
11.	block	*block*	He carved a dog from a **block** of wood.
12.	tent	*tent*	Clowns rode on horses in the circus **tent**.
13.	desk	*desk*	Shanita likes to study at her **desk**.
14.	flock	*flock*	The **flock** of birds flew south in the fall.
15.	nest	*nest*	The crow laid an egg in its **nest**.

Think & Sort the spelling words.

1–6. Write the words that have the **short o** sound.

7–15. Write the words that have the **short e** sound.

Remember

The **short o** sound you hear in **drop** is spelled **o**.
The **short e** sound you hear in **desk** is spelled **e**.

TEKS 3.24A Use knowledge of letter sounds, word parts, word segmentation, and syllabication to spell.
3.24C Spell high-frequency and compound words from a commonly used list.

Match Ending Sounds

1–3. Write the spelling words that rhyme with **rock**. Circle the two consonants at the end of each word.

4–5. Write the spelling words that rhyme with **went**. Circle the two consonants at the end of each word.

Segment Words

6. Replace the first letter of **bend** with two consonants to make this spelling word.

Change one letter in each word to create a spelling word.

7. drip

8. crow

9. disk

10. slot

Use the Dictionary

Write the spelling words that have the following words in their definitions.

11. snow

12. examination

13. direction

14. right

15. eggs

Dictionary Check Be sure to check the answers in your **Spelling Dictionary**.

TEKS 3.24A Use knowledge of letter sounds, word parts, word segmentation, and syllabication to spell.
3.24Bv Spell words with more advanced orthographic patterns and rules: complex consonants. **3.24C** Spell high-frequency and compound words from a commonly used list.

21

crop	test	clock	spent	drop
left	sled	plot	spend	west
block	tent	desk	flock	nest

Complete the Analogies

Write a spelling word to complete each analogy.

1. **Practice** is to **game** as **study** is to _____.
2. **Up** is to **down** as **right** is to _____.
3. **Bird** is to **robin** as **direction** is to _____.
4. **Surfboard** is to **wave** as _____ is to **snow**.

Identify Synonyms

Write the spelling word that could best replace each underlined word or words.

5. He carved a horse from a <u>solid piece</u> of wood.
6. The <u>group</u> of birds flew south for the winter.
7. That farmer's main <u>plant</u> is corn.
8. Squirrels collect acorns that <u>fall</u> from trees.
9. This <u>section</u> of land will make a good garden.

Use Context Clues

Write spelling words that fit each category.
- 10–11. house, shelter
- 12–13. buying, expensive
- 14. time, watch
- 15. classroom, chalkboard

 TEKS 3.24C Spell high-frequency and compound words from a commonly used list.

Connections to WRITING

Proofread a Journal Entry

The symbol ∧ means **add**. The symbol ℰ means **take out**, or delete. Proofread the journal entry below for eight misspelled words. Then rewrite the entry. Write the spelling words correctly and make the corrections shown by the proofreading marks.

> **September 10**
>
> amy and I went camping. When we got to the camp,
> ‾‾‾
> we felt a dropp of rain. We set up our tint next to t̶o̶
> a cropp of corn. Next we spint some time fishing.
> Then we watched a flok of crows eat corn. We didn't
> see a nesst. Before we went to sleep, I told a story
>   up
> with a scary plott. finally we set our cluck to get ∧
>   ‾‾‾
> early the next day.

Proofreading Marks

≡	Capital Letter
/	Small Letter
∧	Add
ℰ	Delete
⊙	Add a Period
⌗	Indent

NARRATIVE Writing Prompt
Write a Journal Entry

Think of an event you experienced that was important to you. Write a journal entry about it. Choose descriptive words carefully. Use as many spelling words as you can.

- Use the writing process: prewrite, draft, revise, edit, and publish.
- Write about what happened in the same order as events occurred.
- Use complete sentences with correct capitalization, punctuation, grammar, and spelling.
- Read your work. Circle three words you are unsure about, and check their spellings in a dictionary.

Transfer

Think of three words that rhyme with **drop** and two words that rhyme with **test**. Write the words in your Spelling Journal and circle the letter that makes the short vowel sound.

TEKS 3.24A Use knowledge of letter sounds, word parts, word segmentation, and syllabication to spell. **3.24C** Spell high-frequency and compound words from a commonly used list. **3.24G** Use print and electronic resources to find and check correct spellings.

Word Study

cot	drop	crop	flock	lemon
nod	plot	test	colony	necklace
send	spend	left	kept	pocket
tell	block	sled	letters	welcome
clock	desk	west	socket	
spent	nest	tent	empty	

Consonant Blends

Write words from the list that have these consonant blends.

1–2. sp

3. sl

4. sk

Pattern Power

Use words from the list to complete these exercises.

5–7. Write the spelling words that rhyme with **sock**. Circle the letters that spell /**k**/ at the end.

8–13. Write the words that fit the pattern __ e __ t.

Double the Consonant

Write the base words for these words.

14. nodding **15.** dropping

 TEKS 3.24A Use knowledge of letter sounds, word parts, word segmentation, and syllabication to spell.
3.24Bi Spell words with more advanced orthographic patterns and rules: consonant doubling when adding an ending. **3.24Bv** Spell words with more advanced orthographic patterns and rules: complex consonants.
3.24C Spell high-frequency and compound words from a commonly used list.

Social Studies

Word Hunt

Read the paragraphs below. Look for words with the **short o** and **short e** sounds.

> The Oregon Trail was once the main way to get to the west. Thousands of people traveled on the trail more than 150 years ago. Many wanted to start new lives as farmers. A farmer could grow a fine crop of wheat in the rich Oregon soil.
>
> It took months to make the trip. The people walked all day next to their wagons. They would rest at lunchtime and at night. The oxen that pulled the wagons were strong but slow. Sometimes people had to leave furniture by the road to lighten the wagons. A traveler might see a chair or table by the road.
>
> Life on the trail was hard. Buffalo herds might block the trail. People died from disease. They had to cross mountains and swift rivers.
>
> The people who reached Oregon built new towns. They were proud to be pioneers of the Oregon Trail.

Follow the directions. Write each word only once.

1–5. Write the words that have more than three letters and contain the **short o** sound.

6–8. Write the words that have more than three letters and contain the **short e** sound.

 TEKS 3.24A Use knowledge of letter sounds, word parts, word segmentation, and syllabication to spell.
3.24C Spell high-frequency and compound words from a commonly used list.

Connections to THINKING

Read the spelling words and sentences.

1.	lunch	*lunch*	Domingo ate **lunch** at noon.
2.	until	*until*	We stroked the cat **until** it purred.
3.	cover	*cover*	What is on the **cover** of your book?
4.	buzz	*buzz*	Tamika heard some bees **buzz**.
5.	become	*become*	Joel wants to **become** a teacher.
6.	stuff	*stuff*	We will **stuff** the old pillow.
7.	nothing	*nothing*	The gift she made cost **nothing**.
8.	dull	*dull*	The point on my pencil is **dull**.
9.	month	*month*	February is the shortest **month**.
10.	study	*study*	People **study** to learn.
11.	love	*love*	Karen has a **love** for pets.
12.	uncle	*uncle*	An **uncle** is a parent's brother.
13.	cuff	*cuff*	The **cuff** of the sleeve was dirty.
14.	none	*none*	She ate the apples and left us **none**.
15.	under	*under*	Is the baseball **under** the bed again?

Think & Sort the spelling words.

1–9. Write the words that have the **short u** sound spelled **u**.

10–15. Write the words that have the **short u** sound spelled **o**.

Remember

The **short u** sound can be spelled in different ways:
u as in **lunch** and **o** as in **become**.

TEKS 3.24A Use knowledge of letter sounds, word parts, word segmentation, and syllabication to spell.
3.24C Spell high-frequency and compound words from a commonly used list.

Connections to PHONICS

Identify Beginning Sounds

1–3. Write the spelling words that begin with the **short u** sound.

Segment Words

4–5. Write the spelling words that follow the pattern __ o __ e.

6–7. Write the one-syllable spelling words that end with a consonant digraph. Remember that a consonant digraph is two or more letters that work together to make one sound. Circle the consonant digraphs.

8–11. Write the spelling words with double consonants that make only one sound.

Use the dictionary to find how to divide these words into syllables. Write the words, and use a slash to separate the syllables.

12. cover   **14.** nothing

13. become   **15.** study

Dictionary Check Be sure to check your answers in your **Spelling Dictionary**.

 TEKS 3.24A Use knowledge of letter sounds, word parts, word segmentation, and syllabication to spell. **3.24Bv** Spell words with more advanced orthographic patterns and rules: complex consonants. **3.24C** Spell high-frequency and compound words from a commonly used list. **3.24D** Spell words with common syllable constructions.

lunch	until	cover	buzz	become
stuff	nothing	dull	month	study
love	uncle	cuff	none	under

Complete the Analogies

Write a spelling word to complete each analogy.

1. **Dog** is to **bark** as **bee** is to _____.
2. **Night** is to **day** as **sharp** is to _____.
3. **Out** is to **in** as **over** is to _____.
4. **Mother** is to **father** as **aunt** is to _____.
5. **Morning** is to **breakfast** as **noon** is to _____.
6. **Store** is to **shop** as **school** is to _____.
7. **Ten** is to **zero** as **many** is to _____.

Make Inferences

Write the spelling word to solve each riddle.

8. There's a new one every 28 to 31 days. What is it?
9. You find this at the end of your sleeve. What is it?
10. This gift comes from your heart. What is it?

Use Context Clues

Write spelling words to complete the story.

Dave has **11.** fond of his new black shoes. He lost one shoe and did not want to go to school **12.** he found it. Under his dresser he found socks, toys, and lots of other **13.**, but no shoe. There was **14.** at all under his bed. Finally, he lifted the **15.** off his bed and there it was!

 TEKS 3.24C Spell high-frequency and compound words from a commonly used list.

Connections to WRITING

Proofread a Personal Narrative

The symbol ⊙ means add a period. The symbol ¶ means indent. Proofread the personal narrative below for eight misspelled words. Then rewrite it. Write the spelling words correctly and make the corrections shown by the proofreading marks.

¶One sunny day I had lonch in the park with my friend Jack. We could hear Bees buz as we ate. We decided to cuver up the rest of our food so we could play ball. Jack said he still heard bees, but we saw nune. we played ontil four o'clock and then we went home to studdy. I still heard buzzing so I looked onder the lid of my lunch box⊙I'll never forget what I saw there: a mad bee! I luv bees and I let it go free.

Proofreading Marks

≡	Capital Letter
/	Small Letter
∧	Add
ℓ	Delete
⊙	Add a Period
¶	Indent

NARRATIVE Writing Prompt
Write a Personal Narrative

Write a paragraph about something interesting that has happened to you. Include details to make it come to life for your audience. Use as many spelling words as you can.

- Use the writing process: prewrite, draft, revise, edit, and publish.
- Write about things in the order in which they occurred.
- Use complete sentences with correct capitalization, punctuation, grammar, and spelling.
- Key your narrative in a word-processing program. Use the spell-check feature to check your spelling.

Transfer

Think of four more two-syllable words with the **short u** sound spelled **u** or **o**. Write the words in your Spelling Journal. Circle the letter that makes the **short u** sound.

TEKS 3.24A Use knowledge of letter sounds, word parts, word segmentation, and syllabication to spell. 3.24C Spell high-frequency and compound words from a commonly used list. 3.24G Use print and electronic resources to find and check correct spellings.

cup	become	lunch	cuff	bunch
dust	nothing	cover	button	sponge
jump	study	stuff	hunter	trunk
rub	love	dull	summit	ugly
until	none	month	trust	
buzz	under	uncle	bucket	

Pattern Power

Use words from the spelling list above to complete these exercises.

1–7. Write the words that contain the **short u** sound spelled **o**.

8–9. Write two words that rhyme with **puff**.

10–11. Write two words that rhyme with **munch**.

Word Building

Replace the underlined letter or letters in each word to make a spelling word.

12. <u>f</u>ull   **13.** <u>cy</u>cle

Spelling Rules

Drop the final **e** and add **-ing** to make a new word. (Example: **move, moving**)

14. become   **15.** love

 TEKS 3.24A Use knowledge of letter sounds, word parts, word segmentation, and syllabication to spell. **3.24Bii** Spell words with more advanced orthographic patterns and rules: dropping final "e" when endings are added. **3.24C** Spell high-frequency and compound words from a commonly used list.

Math

Word Hunt

Read the paragraphs below. Look for words with the **short u** sound.

When is nothing very big? When "nothing" is the number zero! People in many ancient cultures liked to study math. For a long time, they did not use the number zero.

Then people in India noticed that a number that meant "none" would help them add. It would help them multiply, too. A math book in India used the number zero about 1,500 years ago. People in India set rules for zero. They said that zero plus zero is zero. A number times zero is zero, too.

The idea of zero spread very slowly. People did not like the idea at first. They did not understand a number that meant "nothing." It took until about the 1600s for zero to become widely used.

Today, math would be impossible without zero. We could not do very simple math problems. We would not know the difference between 11 and 101. We can cheer for zero by saying, "Here's to nothing!"

Follow the directions. Write each word once.

1–6. Write the words with more than one syllable that have the **short u** sound spelled **u**.

7–8. Write the words with more than one syllable that have the **short u** sound spelled **o**.

 TEKS 3.24A Use knowledge of letter sounds, word parts, word segmentation, and syllabication to spell.
3.24C Spell high-frequency and compound words from a commonly used list.

Connections to THINKING

Read the spelling words and sentences.

1. proud   *proud*   I am **proud** of myself for getting an A.
2. boil   *boil*   Water will **boil** when it gets very hot.
3. loud   *loud*   The music was too **loud** for my ears.
4. house   *house*   The Carters live in a large **house**.
5. join   *join*   Roberto wants to **join** the team.
6. cloud   *cloud*   We saw a dark **cloud** in the sky.
7. sound   *sound*   The loud ringing **sound** made me jump.
8. voice   *voice*   The singer had a beautiful **voice**.
9. oil   *oil*   Salad dressing often includes **oil**.
10. round   *round*   Put the dough in the **round** pan.
11. point   *point*   Please sharpen the **point** of this pencil.
12. south   *south*   North is the opposite of **south**.
13. found   *found*   Rosa **found** her missing sock.
14. soil   *soil*   Some plants need rich **soil** to grow well.
15. ground   *ground*   It is hard to dig in the frozen **ground**.

Think & Sort the spelling words.

1–6. Write the words that have the /oi/ sound.

7–15. Write the words that have the /ou/ sound.

Remember

The /oi/ sound you hear in **oil** is spelled **oi**. The /ou/ sound you hear in **loud** is spelled **ou**.

TEKS 3.24A Use knowledge of letter sounds, word parts, word segmentation, and syllabication to spell. **3.24Bvi** Spell words with more advanced orthographic patterns and rules: abstract vowels. **3.24C** Spell high-frequency and compound words from a commonly used list.

Identify Rhyming Words

1–2. Write the spelling words that rhyme with **soil**.

3. Write the spelling word that rhymes with **coin**.

4–6. Write the spelling words that rhyme with **crowd**. Circle the words that begin with a consonant blend.

7–9. Write the spelling words that rhyme with **sound**. Circle the word that begins with a consonant blend.

Understand Word Structure

10. Change one letter in **mouse** to make a spelling word.

11. Change one letter in **paint** to make a spelling word.

12. Change the beginning sound in **choice** to make a spelling word.

Use the Dictionary

13–15. A dictionary lists words in alphabetical order. Write the three spelling words that begin with the letter **s** in alphabetical order.

Dictionary Check Be sure to check your answer in your **Spelling Dictionary**.

TEKS 3.24A Use knowledge of letter sounds, word parts, word segmentation, and syllabication to spell. **3.24Bvi** Spell words with more advanced orthographic patterns and rules: abstract vowels. **3.24C** Spell high-frequency and compound words from a commonly used list.

proud	boil	loud	house	join
cloud	sound	voice	oil	round
point	south	found	soil	ground

Complete the Analogies

Write a spelling word to complete each analogy.

1. **Box** is to **square** as **ball** is to _____.
2. **East** is to **west** as **north** is to _____.
3. **Whisper** is to **quiet** as **yell** is to _____.
4. **Cold** is to **freeze** as **hot** is to _____.
5. **Find** is to **found** as **grind** is to _____.

Understand Idioms

Write a word from the box to complete each idiom.

6. If you _____ forces with someone, you work together to do something.
7. If you sing at the top of your _____, you sing as loudly as you can.
8. If you and a friend like each other very much, then you get along like a _____ on fire.

Use Context Clues

Write spelling words to complete the paragraph.

Eleni was **9.** to be the Science Fair winner. Her model showed how rainwater goes from a **10.** in the sky, to the earth, and back again. She used arrows to **11.** to the water soaking into some sandy **12.**. She rubbed salad **13.** on the grass to make it look wet. She even **14.** a way to make the **15.** of rain!

 TEKS 3.24C Spell high-frequency and compound words from a commonly used list.

Connections to WRITING

Proofread an Article

Proofread the article below for eight misspelled words. Then rewrite it. Write the spelling words correctly and make the corrections shown by the proofreading marks.

¶A tornado is a column of air that is shaped like a ~~a~~ funnel. The funnel dips down from a clout. At the poynt where the funnel touches the gound, it stirs up soyl and other objects⊙ A Tornado can sounnd like a lowd train. A tornado can destroy a howse. Cars have been fownd upside down. Tornadoes are a great Danger.

EXPOSITORY Writing Prompt
Write an Article

Think of an interesting weather event you have experienced or read about. Write an article about the event. Use as many spelling words as you can.

- Use the writing process: prewrite, draft, revise, edit, and publish.
- Include a topic sentence with your central idea, and include supporting sentences with facts and details.
- End with a concluding statement.
- Use complete sentences with correct capitalization, punctuation, grammar, and spelling.
- Read your work. Circle three words you are unsure about, and check their spellings in a dictionary.

Transfer

Think of three more words with the /oi/ sound and three more words with the /ou/ sound. Write the words in your Spelling Journal. Circle the two letters that make each vowel sound.

TEKS 3.24A Use knowledge of letter sounds, word parts, word segmentation, and syllabication to spell. **3.24Bvi** Spell words with more advanced orthographic patterns and rules: abstract vowels. **3.24C** Spell high-frequency and compound words from a commonly used list. **3.24G** Use print and electronic resources to find and check correct spellings.

bounce	join	proud	soil	ointment
coin	voice	boil	aloud	outfit
count	oil	cloud	choice	scout
shout	point	sound	mouth	trout
loud	south	round	noise	
house	ground	found	broil	

Pattern Power

Write the one-syllable words from the list that rhyme with the following words. Circle the vowel spellings.

1–2. loin

3–5. spoil

6–7. plowed

8. boys

9. mouse

Special Consonants

10–12. Write the words from the list with the /**s**/ sound spelled **ce**.

13–14. Write the words from the list with the consonant digraph **th**.

15. Write the word from the list with the consonant digraph **sh**.

TEKS 3.24A Use knowledge of letter sounds, word parts, word segmentation, and syllabication to spell. **3.24Bv** Spell words with more advanced orthographic patterns and rules: complex consonants. **3.24Bvi** Spell words with more advanced orthographic patterns and rules: abstract vowels. **3.24C** Spell high-frequency and compound words from a commonly used list.

Fine Arts

 Word Hunt

Read the paragraphs below. Look for words that have the /oi/ or /ou/ sound.

Did you ever see a painting made with oil paints? Oil paints are made of color joined with oil. These paints take time to dry. That means artists have time to wipe off their mistakes and try again. They can be proud of their final painting.

To paint with oil, an artist needs heavy paper, paintbrushes, and paints. The painter often wears an outfit of old clothes. To mix colors, artists use a piece of wood called a palette. It has a round shape with cutouts that make it easy to hold.

The artist must choose a subject. Beginners often choose something simple, like a tree. A bowl of fruit is a colorful subject. Sometimes an artist wants to paint something that moves, like a cloud in the sky. The artist can take a photograph of the subject and use it as a model.

The point of painting with oils is to have fun mixing colors. If you painted with oils, what would you paint?

WORD SORT

Follow the directions. Write each word once.

1–3. Write the words that contain the /oi/ sound.

4–8. Write the words that contain the /ou/ sound.

 TEKS 3.24A Use knowledge of letter sounds, word parts, word segmentation, and syllabication to spell. **3.24Bvi** Spell words with more advanced orthographic patterns and rules: abstract vowels. **3.24C** Spell high-frequency and compound words from a commonly used list.

Connections to THINKING

Read the spelling words and sentences.

1.	crew	*crew*	The airplane **crew** prepared to land.
2.	loose	*loose*	His **loose** baby tooth fell out.
3.	news	*news*	The good **news** is that he won the race.
4.	school	*school*	Kurt left his books at **school**.
5.	drew	*drew*	Shandra **drew** a picture of Alex.
6.	knew	*knew*	She **knew** that lying was wrong.
7.	smooth	*smooth*	The shirt felt **smooth** and soft.
8.	pool	*pool*	He swam in the deep **pool**.
9.	shoot	*shoot*	Can I **shoot** a picture of you?
10.	threw	*threw*	Michael **threw** the garbage out.
11.	roof	*roof*	A worker fixed the leaking **roof**.
12.	fool	*fool*	A magician likes to **fool** his audience.
13.	chew	*chew*	She asked us to **chew** our food slowly.
14.	balloon	*balloon*	The **balloon** floated into the sky.
15.	choose	*choose*	We will **choose** a color for the walls.

Think & Sort the spelling words.

1–6. Write the words that have /o͞o/ spelled **ew**.

7–15. Write the words that have /o͞o/ spelled **oo**.

Remember

The /o͞o/ sound can be spelled in different ways: **oo** as in **pool** and **ew** as in **chew**.

 TEKS 3.24A Use knowledge of letter sounds, word parts, word segmentation, and syllabication to spell. **3.24Bvi** Spell words with more advanced orthographic patterns and rules: abstract vowels. **3.24C** Spell high-frequency and compound words from a commonly used list.

Connections to PHONICS

Identify Sounds and Letters

1–5. Write the spelling words that end with the /o͞o/ sound. Circle the consonant blend or digraph in each word.

6–8. Write the spelling words that rhyme with **tool**. Circle the letters that spell the /o͞o/ sound.

Segment Words

9. Replace the first letter in **moose** to make a spelling word.

10. Replace the last letter in **root** to make a spelling word.

11. Replace one letter in **short** to make a spelling word.

12. Add one letter to the word **chose** to make a spelling word.

Use the Dictionary

A dictionary has guide words to help you find a word more easily. Guide words are listed at the top of each dictionary page. Write the spelling word that would be found on a dictionary page with the following guide words:

13. almost and **banana**

14. nest and **ocean**

15. smoke and **spin**

TEKS 3.24A Use knowledge of letter sounds, word parts, word segmentation, and syllabication to spell. **3.24Bv** Spell words with more advanced orthographic patterns and rules: complex consonants. **3.24Bvi** Spell words with more advanced orthographic patterns and rules: abstract vowels. **3.24C** Spell high-frequency and compound words from a commonly used list.

crew	loose	news	school	drew
knew	smooth	pool	shoot	threw
roof	fool	chew	balloon	choose

Complete the Analogies

Write a spelling word to complete each analogy.

1. **Dull** is to **sharp** as **rough** is to _____.
2. **Touch** is to **feel** as **select** is to _____.
3. **Eyes** are to **see** as **teeth** are to _____.
4. **Sleep** is to **bed** as **swim** is to _____.
5. **Thick** is to **thin** as **tight** is to _____.
6. **Think** is to **thought** as **know** is to _____.
7. **Clap** is to **cheer** as **trick** is to _____.
8. **Report** is to **wrote** as **illustration** is to _____.
9. **Came** is to **went** as **caught** is to _____.

Make Inferences

Write a spelling word to solve each riddle.

10. You can watch it on TV or read it in the paper. What is it?
11. It is a group of workers on board a boat or plane. What is it?
12. I float above the trees, and I am used for gathering weather data. What am I?
13. I am a group of fish or a place of learning. What am I?
14. You can find me on top of a house. What am I?
15. It is what you can do with a camera or a basketball. What is it?

TEKS 3.24C Spell high-frequency and compound words from a commonly used list.

Connections to WRITING

Proofread a News Story

Proofread the news story below for eight misspelled words. Then rewrite it. Write the spelling words correctly and make the corrections shown by the proofreading marks.

¶In our schol, we had a battle of the books. At the beginning of the year we droo numbers to divide into teams. We knoo we had to read all the books on the list. At the end of the year we held the battle. The gym was Decorated with a balon at each seat. One got loos and drifted up to the roff. The questions were not easy, but my team won! We got to chews a book as a prize. The local paper wrote a nooz story about the battle. Reading is so much fun!

Proofreading Marks

≡	Capital Letter
/	Small Letter
∧	Add
ℒ	Delete
⊙	Add a Period
¶	Indent

NARRATIVE Writing Prompt
Write a News Story

Write a news story about something special that happened at your school. Use as many spelling words as you can.

- Develop your story by explaining the "five Ws and how." Tell what happened, when and where it happened, how and why it happened, and who was involved.
- Use the writing process: prewrite, draft, revise, edit, and publish.
- Use complete sentences with correct capitalization, punctuation, grammar, and spelling.
- Read your work. Circle three words you are unsure about, and check their spellings in a dictionary.

Transfer

Think of two more words with the /o͞o/ sound spelled **ew** and two more words with the /o͞o/ sound spelled **oo**. Write the words in your Spelling Journal. Circle the two letters that make the vowel sound.

TEKS 3.24A Use knowledge of letter sounds, word parts, word segmentation, and syllabication to spell. **3.24Bvi** Spell words with more advanced orthographic patterns and rules: abstract vowels. **3.24C** Spell high-frequency and compound words from a commonly used list. **3.24G** Use print and electronic resources to find and check correct spellings.

Word Study

blew	knew	crew	chew	scoop
boot	pool	loose	dew	mushroom
grew	threw	drew	loop	stew
noon	roof	smooth	proof	toadstool
news	balloon	shoot	toot	
school	choose	fool	kangaroo	

Homophones

Write the words that are homophones for each word. Remember that homophones are words that sound the same but have different spellings and meanings. Circle the consonant blends or digraphs.

1. blue

2. new

3. through

Pattern Power

Write the words from the list with the following patterns. Circle the /o͞o/ spelling in each word.

4–10. __ **oo** __

11–12. the /**ch**/ sound spelled **ch**

13–15. __ __ **oo** __

TEKS 3.24A Use knowledge of letter sounds, word parts, word segmentation, and syllabication to spell. **3.24Bv** Spell words with more advanced orthographic patterns and rules: complex consonants. **3.24Bvi** Spell words with more advanced orthographic patterns and rules: abstract vowels. **3.24C** Spell high-frequency and compound words from a commonly used list. **3.24E** Spell single syllable homophones.

Technology

Word Hunt

Read the paragraphs below. Look for words that have /oo/ spelled **ew** or **oo**.

Did you ever see a weather balloon? These balloons are used by the National Weather Service, or NWS. Twice a day, the NWS sets the balloons loose from spots around the country. They are about six feet wide. Each one carries a special tool. The tool measures wind speed, temperature, and other things.

A crew on the ground studies the data that the tool sends. The information shows the current weather conditions. What will the weather be like in three days? A weather forecaster uses the information to predict the weather. You can hear the weather report on the news.

Gas makes a weather balloon fly. It soars about twenty miles high. It flies for hours. Then its smooth surface bursts, and the tool floats to the ground. Not every tool is found. Imagine if one landed on the roof of your school! You would mail the tool to the NWS. Mailing instructions are printed on the side.

Follow the directions. Write each word once.

1–2. Write the words that have the /oo/ sound spelled **ew**.
3–8. Write the words that have the /oo/ sound spelled **oo**.

TEKS 3.24A Use knowledge of letter sounds, word parts, word segmentation, and syllabication to spell. **3.24Bvi** Spell words with more advanced orthographic patterns and rules: abstract vowels. **3.24C** Spell high-frequency and compound words from a commonly used list.

Units 1–5

Assessment

Each word in the box fits one of the spelling patterns you have studied over the past five weeks. Read the spelling pattern descriptions. Then write each assessment word below the unit number it fits.

Unit 1

1–3. The **short a** sound you hear in **plan** is spelled **a**. The **short i** sound you hear in **trip** is spelled **i**.

Unit 2

4–6. The **short o** sound you hear in **drop** is spelled **o**. The **short e** sound you hear in **desk** is spelled **e**.

Unit 3

7–9. The **short u** sound can be spelled in different ways: **u** as in **lunch** and **o** as in **become**.

Unit 4

10–12. The **/oi/** sound you hear in **oil** is spelled **oi**. The **/ou/** sound you hear in **loud** is spelled **ou**.

Unit 5

13–15. The **/o͞o/** sound can be spelled in different ways: **oo** as in **pool** and **ew** as in **chew**.

Words for Assessment

fund

stout

groom

damp

troop

son

hound

track

ton

coop

bent

shock

toil

lend

trim

Unit 1: Short a, Short i

> plan   stick   grand   stamp
> list   act   trip

Write the spelling word that goes with each clue.

1. Add **l** to **pan**.
2. Add **t** to **sick**.
3. Add **r** to **tip**.
4. Change **e** to **t** in **ace**.
5. Change **nd** to **mp** in **stand**.
6. Change **n** to **s** in **lint**.
7. Change **st** to **gr** in **stand**.

Unit 2: Short o, Short e

> drop   spend   clock   spent
> nest   desk   block

Add, change, or drop one letter from each word to write a review word.

8. black
9. sent
10. click
11. disk
12. drip
13. next
14. send

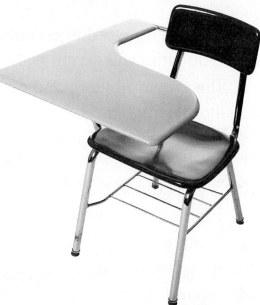

Review

Unit 3: Short u

none	until	love	nothing
study	buzz	under	

Write the spelling word for each clue.

1. This word rhymes with **dove**.
2. This word rhymes with **does**.
3. This word rhymes with **thunder**.
4. This word rhymes with **sun**.
5. This word ends in **ing**.
6. This word rhymes with **muddy**.
7. This word begins with **short u** and has a stress on its second syllable.

Unit 4: ou, oi

point	house	voice	ground
south	loud	join	

Write a spelling word to complete each sentence. The word you write will rhyme with the underlined word.

8. The <u>crowd</u> at the game gave a _____ cheer for their team.
9. "Please make your <u>choice</u>," said the clerk with a kind _____.
10. Flip a <u>coin</u> to decide which team you will _____.
11. The doctor asked me to _____ to the <u>joint</u> that hurt.
12. Can I go _____ to reach the <u>mouth</u> of the river?
13. A <u>mouse</u> had made its _____ in the woodpile.
14. I <u>found</u> my book lying on the _____.

Unit 5: ew, oo

| threw | school | knew | choose |
| balloon | roof | news | |

Write a spelling word to complete each sentence. The word you write will be a homophone of the underlined word.

1. He _____ that the shoes he was wearing were not <u>new</u>.
2. Marisol <u>chews</u> her food very quickly, but we _____ to eat more slowly.
3. Ted just _____ the baseball <u>through</u> the window!

Write the spelling word for each clue.

4. This word rhymes with **spool**.
5. This word has the /$\overline{oo}$/ sound in its second syllable.
6. This word rhymes with **goof**.
7. This word rhymes with **crews**.

Spelling Study Strategy

Circle Dot

Find a partner. Each of you should write a list of 15 spelling words. Then trade lists. Your partner should read aloud one word from your list. You write that word.

When you finish, your partner should spell the word aloud. Make a dot on your paper under each correct letter. If a letter is not correct, draw a circle around it. Make a little circle to show where a letter has been left out. The circles will show where you have trouble. Write the word again and check the spelling. Take turns.

Standardized Test Practice

Directions: Read the introduction and the passage that follows. Then read each question and fill in the space in front of the correct answer on your answer sheet.

Julio took a trip with his uncle. He wrote this story about how the trip turned out to be different than what he expected. He wants you to review his paper. As you read, think about ways Julio can improve his story.

Adventure at Round Lake

(1) Last month my uncel Ramon offered to take me on a trip to Round Lake. (2) I thought it sounded like fun, figuring I could swimm and build things in the sand. (3) But the trip was not what I expected.

(4) We left home early and drove wist toward the lake. (5) I felt excited, but I worried about the clowds in the sky. (6) "Those are not rain clouds," said Uncle Ramon. (7) "They're fair-weather cumulus clouds. (8) You can tell because they look like puffy cotton balls."

(9) I wanted to swim as soon as we arrived, but Ramon said it would be the best time to go bird watching. (10) "Birds?" I croaked. (11) Ramon pointed to a large nest in a nearby willow tree. (12) He said many birds make their nests from grasses that grow near ponds and lakes.

(13) Just then a loud sound overhead startled us, as a flok of geese flew low across the water. (14) It was awesome! (15) Ramon spent lots more time pointing out other amazing stuf on our walk. (16) We saw a hawk, a beaver dam, and a prowd white swan floating through water lilies.

(17) Thanks to Uncle Ramon, I now know that nature is not dul. (18) Plus, we went for a great swim before lonch.

GO ON

1 What change, if any, should be made in sentence 1?

- ○ Change *month* to **munth**
- ○ Change *uncel* to **uncle**
- ○ Change *Round* to **Rownd**
- ○ Make no change

2 What change should be made in sentence 2?

- ○ Change *sounded* to **sonded**
- ○ Change *swimm* to **swim**
- ○ Change *things* to **thengs**
- ○ Change *sand* to **sannd**

3 What change, if any, should be made in sentence 4?

- ○ Change *left* to **laft**
- ○ Change *wist* to **west**
- ○ Change *lake* to **lak**
- ○ Make no change

4 What change, if any, should be made in sentence 5?

- ○ Change *felt* to **feelt**
- ○ Change *about* to **abowt**
- ○ Change *clowds* to **clouds**
- ○ Make no change

5 What change, if any, should be made in sentence 11?

- ○ Change *pointed* to **poynted**
- ○ Change *nest* to **nast**
- ○ Change *tree* to **trea**
- ○ Make no change

6 What change, if any, should be made in sentence 13?

- ○ Change *just* to **jest**
- ○ Change *loud* to **lowed**
- ○ Change *flok* to **flock**
- ○ Make no change

7 What change, if any, should be made in sentence 15?

- ○ Change *spent* to **spint**
- ○ Change *pointing* to **poynting**
- ○ Change *stuf* to **stuff**
- ○ Make no change

8 What change, if any, should be made in sentence 16?

- ○ Change *beaver* to **beever**
- ○ Change *prowd* to **proud**
- ○ Change *swan* to **swon**
- ○ Make no change

9 What change, if any, should be made in sentence 17?

- ○ Change *Thanks* to **Tanks**
- ○ Change *Uncle* to **Uncel**
- ○ Change *dul* to **dull**
- ○ Make no change

10 What change, if any, should be made to sentence 18?

- ○ Change *went* to **wint**
- ○ Change *swim* to **swem**
- ○ Change *lonch* to **lunch**
- ○ Make no change

STOP

Grammar, Usage, and Mechanics
Kinds of Sentences

There are four kinds of sentences. Each ends with a special mark.

- **Telling Sentence:** My friend will come, too.
- **Command:** Move over, please.
- **Sentence That Shows Strong Feeling:** This is fun!
- **Asking Sentence:** Have you met her?

Practice Activity

Read the different kinds of sentences. Write a spelling word to complete each sentence.

grand	trip	spend	clock	buzz
nothing	voice	house	choose	news

Telling Sentences

1. We are planning a _____ to Florida.
2. Each student will _____ a book to read.
3. I saw that story on the evening _____ program.

Commands

4. Do not _____ all your money.
5. Please speak in a soft _____ here.
6. Make sure you leave _____ behind.

Asking Sentences

7. What is the time on that _____?
8. Which _____ on this street is yours?

Sentences That Show Strong Feeling

9. The bowling party is a _____ idea!
10. That bee has a very loud _____!

The Writing Process: Narrative
Writing a Personal Narrative

PREWRITING

Sometimes people write true accounts about experiences they have had. Think about a special time you've had with your friends. What did you do? What made it important or special to you? As you think about your topic, make an outline of your ideas. You can find personal narratives at the library. An adult can help you search for personal narratives on Internet sites.

DRAFTING

Use your outline to write a personal narrative. Use as many spelling words as possible. If you don't know how to spell a word, make a guess. You will be able to revise your narrative later.

REVISING

When you have finished writing, read your narrative from beginning to end. Have you included all of the points in your outline? Now write your final draft.

EDITING

Use the **Editing Checklist** to proofread your narrative. Be sure to use proofreading marks when you make corrections. Circle at least two words that might be misspelled. Use a dictionary or electronic resource to check the spelling.

PUBLISHING

Write or print a final copy of your personal narrative, and share it with your readers.

EDITING CHECKLIST

Spelling

✓ Circle words that contain the spelling patterns and rules learned in Units 1–5.

✓ Check the circled words in your **Spelling Dictionary**.

✓ Check for other spelling errors.

Capital Letters

✓ Capitalize important words in the title.

✓ Capitalize the first word in each sentence.

✓ Capitalize proper nouns.

Punctuation

✓ Use commas, apostrophes, and quotation marks correctly.

Grammar, Usage, and Mechanics

✓ End each sentence with the correct punctuation.

TEKS 3.24A Use knowledge of letter sounds, word parts, word segmentation, and syllabication to spell.
3.24G Use print and electronic resources to find and check correct spellings.

Connections to THINKING

Read the spelling words and sentences.

1.	state	*state*	In which **state** do you live?
2.	close	*close*	Please **close** the door as you leave.
3.	slide	*slide*	The boy went down the water **slide**.
4.	face	*face*	Tanja drew a happy **face**.
5.	globe	*globe*	A **globe** is a round map of the world.
6.	pave	*pave*	The workers will **pave** the street.
7.	size	*size*	Mary's shoes are the wrong **size**.
8.	smoke	*smoke*	My eyes tear when I smell **smoke**.
9.	flame	*flame*	The **flame** set the grease on fire.
10.	broke	*broke*	The glass **broke** into pieces.
11.	prize	*prize*	Carla won first **prize** at the fair.
12.	skate	*skate*	Juanita learned to **skate** on ice.
13.	smile	*smile*	A baby will **smile** when it is happy.
14.	plane	*plane*	David went to New York by **plane**.
15.	stone	*stone*	The **stone** in her shoe hurt her toe.

Think & Sort the spelling words.

Write the words that have:

1–6. the **long a** sound spelled **vowel-consonant-e**.

7–10. the **long i** sound spelled **vowel-consonant-e**.

11–15. the **long o** sound spelled **vowel-consonant-e**.

Remember

The long vowel sounds in **pave, size,** and **globe** are spelled **vowel-consonant-e**.

 TEKS 3.24A Use knowledge of letter sounds, word parts, word segmentation, and syllabication to spell. **3.24C** Spell high-frequency and compound words from a commonly used list. **3.24D** Spell words with common syllable constructions.

Understand Vowel Sounds

Each word below has a short vowel sound. Change or add letters to write a spelling word that has a long vowel sound.

1. glob
2. smock
3. plan
4. stat
5. slid

Identify Rhyme

Write the spelling word or words that rhyme with each word below.

6. lace
7. cave
8. blame
9. phone
10–11. rise

Use the Dictionary

Look at these dictionary letters and symbols for words with long vowel sounds. Say each word, then write the spelling word. Use the pronunciation key and check your spellings in your **Spelling Dictionary**.

12. /brōk/
13. /smīl/
14. /skāt/
15. /klōz/

 TEKS 3.24A Use knowledge of letter sounds, word parts, word segmentation, and syllabication to spell.
3.24C Spell high-frequency and compound words from a commonly used list.

53

state	close	slide	face	globe
pave	size	smoke	flame	broke
prize	skate	smile	plane	stone

Complete the Analogies

Write a spelling word to complete each analogy.

1. **Black** is to **white** as **open** is to _____.
2. **Toes** is to **foot** as **nose** is to _____.
3. **Jet** is to **model airplane** as **Earth** is to _____.
4. **Water** is to **swim** as **ice** is to _____.
5. **Land** is to **car** as **air** is to _____.

Make Inferences

Write a spelling word for each clue.

6. I flicker at the top of a candle.
7. I rise through a chimney.
8. I can also be called a rock.
9. I am given as a reward.
10. I am something your face can do.
11. I am often found on a playground.

Use Context Clues

Write spelling words to complete the paragraph.

state	broke	pave	size

Workers came to the road to fill and __12.__ a hole. The __13.__ of the hole was large. Heavy trucks had used the road so much that the surface __14.__ up. Our __15.__ government pays for road repair.

 TEKS 3.24C Spell high-frequency and compound words from a commonly used list.

Connections to WRITING

Proofread Interview Questions

Proofread the interview questions below for eight misspelled words. Then rewrite the questions. Write the spelling words correctly and make the corrections shown by the proofreading marks.

1. How did you learn to skayt so well?
2. did you slid often when you practiced?
3. Did you hit a stoan when you broak your leg?
4. Did you ever fall on your fase?
5. how did you feel when you lost the prise at the stat meet?
6. Do you travel to Meets by car, bus, or plain?

Proofreading Marks

≡	Capital Letter
/	Small Letter
∧	Add
ℒ	Delete
⊙	Add a Period
⌿	Indent

EXPOSITORY Writing Prompt
Write Interview Questions

Pretend you are going to interview one of your heroes. Write a list of five interview questions you would like to ask the person. Use as many spelling words as you can.

- Use the writing process: prewrite, draft, revise, edit, and publish.
- Consider including questions about your hero's background and achievements. You might also ask what advice he or she has for young people.
- Number your questions and use complete sentences with correct capitalization, punctuation, grammar, and spelling.
- Read your work. Circle three words you are unsure about and check the spelling in a print or online dictionary.

Transfer

Write new words that have the same **vowel-consonant-e** pattern as six of the spelling words.

TEKS 3.24A Use knowledge of letter sounds, word parts, word segmentation, and syllabication to spell. **3.24C** Spell high-frequency and compound words from a commonly used list. **3.24D** Spell words with common syllable constructions. **3.24G** Use print and electronic resources to find and check correct spellings.

cake	face	slide	skate	grace
dime	size	globe	alive	ripen
joke	broke	pave	scene	shone
mule	smile	smoke	scrape	
state	plane	flame	tube	
close	stone	prize	erase	

Compound Words

Compound words are formed by joining two smaller words. Write the spelling word that is used in each compound word below.

1. prizewinner
2. skateboard
3. airplane
4. closeout
5. downsize

Word Building

The words below have short vowel sounds. Replace the underlined letters to write a word from the list that has a long vowel sound spelled **vowel-consonant-e**.

6. p<u>a</u>t<u>h</u>
7. t<u>u</u>c<u>k</u>
8. sm<u>i</u>t<u>h</u>
9. c<u>a</u>s<u>t</u>
10. gr<u>a</u><u>ss</u>

Homophones

Homophones are words that sound the same but have different spellings and meanings. Write a word from the list that is a homophone for each word.

11. seen
12. plain
13. clothes
14. shown
15. sighs

TEKS 3.24A Use knowledge of letter sounds, word parts, word segmentation, and syllabication to spell. **3.24C** Spell high-frequency and compound words from a commonly used list. **3.24D** Spell words with common syllable constructions. **3.24E** Spell single syllable homophones.

Science

Word Hunt

Read the paragraphs below. Look for words with the **vowel-consonant-e** pattern.

Picture a volcano that is as tall as a twelve-story building. It is as wide as a city block. It has been erupting for the last five years. Next find a place on the globe called Guam. It is a small island that lies in the North Pacific Ocean, west of Hawaii. The big volcano is near Guam, but it is not on land. It's under the sea.

Now scientists can watch this undersea volcano erupt. This volcano does not throw out smoke and flame. It pushes gas, rocks, and ash into the ocean.

Not many fish can survive near the gas, but scientists know that a few shrimp and other animals like living in this harsh area. These odd animals like hot spots!

Follow the directions. Write each word once.

Write the words that have:

1–2. the **long a** sound spelled **vowel-consonant-e**.
3–6. the **long i** sound spelled **vowel-consonant-e**.
7–8. the **long o** sound spelled **vowel-consonant-e**.

 TEKS 3.24A Use knowledge of letter sounds, word parts, word segmentation, and syllabication to spell. **3.24C** Spell high-frequency and compound words from a commonly used list. **3.24D** Spell words with common syllable constructions.

57

Connections to THINKING

Read the spelling words and sentences.

1.	aid	*aid*	A map is a useful **aid** on a trip.
2.	pay	*pay*	How much did you **pay** for the pen?
3.	chain	*chain*	Tina wears a golden **chain**.
4.	mail	*mail*	Did you **mail** my letter?
5.	tray	*tray*	Put the glasses on the **tray**.
6.	paint	*paint*	We will **paint** my room yellow.
7.	maybe	*maybe*	If we try, **maybe** we will win.
8.	plain	*plain*	I like to wear **plain** shirts.
9.	lay	*lay*	Please **lay** my crayons down.
10.	main	*main*	We went to the **main** building.
11.	always	*always*	Is he **always** late?
12.	pail	*pail*	Another word for **pail** is bucket.
13.	laid	*laid*	The hen **laid** an egg.
14.	away	*away*	Please throw **away** the empty box.
15.	paid	*paid*	Did you get **paid** for the work?

Think & Sort the spelling words.

1–9. Write the words that have the **long a** sound spelled **ai**.

10–15. Write the words that have the **long a** sound spelled **ay**.

Remember

The **long a** sound can be spelled in different ways: **ai** as in **paint** and **ay** as in **tray**.

➤ **TEKS 3.24A** Use knowledge of letter sounds, word parts, word segmentation, and syllabication to spell.
3.24C Spell high-frequency and compound words from a commonly used list.

Connections to PHONICS

Change the Vowel Sound

Two vowels together often make a long vowel sound. Add the letter **a** or **i** to make a new word with the **long a** sound.

1. chin
2. plan
3. ad
4. man
5. lid
6. pad

Identify Ending Sounds

7–8. Write the spelling words that rhyme with **rail**.

9–11. Write the one-syllable spelling words that end with the **long a** sound.

12. Write the two-syllable spelling word that ends with the **long a** sound.

Use the Thesaurus

Use your **Writing Thesaurus** to find the spelling word entries that include the synonyms below.

13. color
14. possibly
15. forever

TEKS 3.24A Use knowledge of letter sounds, word parts, word segmentation, and syllabication to spell. **3.24C** Spell high-frequency and compound words from a commonly used list.

aid	pay	chain	mail	tray
paint	maybe	plain	lay	main
always	pail	laid	away	paid

Replace the Words

Write the spelling word that could best replace the underlined word or words in each sentence.

1. She wore a <u>simple</u> dress, but her earrings were fancy.
2. <u>Perhaps</u> my mom will take us to the movies tonight!
3. Brushing every day is the <u>most important</u> way to keep your teeth healthy.
4. Ana carried our sandwiches and fruit on a <u>platter</u>.
5. Let's fill this <u>bucket</u> with sand and shells.
6. Travis is <u>constantly</u> telling funny stories.
7. Mr. Lodge is moving <u>somewhere else</u>.

Understand Verb Tense

Verbs have present, past, and future tense. Write the present and past tense of each verb below.

	laying	paying
Present Tense	8. _____	10. _____
Past Tense	9. _____	11. _____

Use Nouns and Verbs

Many words can act as both a verb and a noun. Write the spelling word that could be used as the noun and the verb in each sentence.

12. The artist will _____ with that _____.
13. Will you _____ this _____ at the post office today?
14. We can use this _____ to _____ the load to the truck.
15. The Red Cross will _____ the flood victims with food and other _____.

TEKS 3.24C Spell high-frequency and compound words from a commonly used list.

Proofread a Poem

Proofread the poem below for eight misspelled words. Then rewrite the poem. Write the spelling words correctly and make the corrections shown by the proofreading marks.

Chores for Two

Dad: Shay, I have some chores for you.

Shay: What would you like me to do?

Dad: Will you please bring in the mal?

Then fill up the yellow payl.

We will mop this messy floor.

Maybee we will pant the door.

Shay: I don't like to whine or pout.

I'm alwees Happy to help out.

Dad: Thanks for coming to to my ayd.

Now it's time that you were pade.

Shay: I was not expecting pa.

Thank you, dad. You made my day!

Proofreading Marks

≡	Capital Letter
/	Small Letter
∧	Add
ℯ	Delete
⊙	Add a Period
¶	Indent

DESCRIPTIVE Writing Prompt
Write a Poem

Use spelling words to write a poem about your chores. Use the writing process: prewrite, draft, revise, edit, and publish.

- Use language that will help readers experience your poem through their senses. Every two lines or every other line should rhyme.
- Read your work. Circle three words you are unsure about and check their spelling in a dictionary.

Transfer

Write three more words with **long a** spelled **ay** and three words with **long a** spelled **ai**.

 TEKS 3.24A Use knowledge of letter sounds, word parts, word segmentation, and syllabication to spell. **3.24C** Spell high-frequency and compound words from a commonly used list. **3.24G** Use print and electronic resources to find and check correct spellings.

braid	mail	aid	paid	drain
play	maybe	tray	holiday	sprain
spray	main	paint	railway	stray
train	always	plain	remain	tailor
pay	laid	lay	waist	
chain	away	pail	delay	

Meaning Mastery

Homophones are words that sound alike but have different spellings and meanings. Write a word from the box that matches each clue. Then write a word from the box that is a homophone for that word. Use a dictionary to check the meaning of the new word.

| pale | mail | mane | pail | plane | main | male | plain |

1–2. packages or letters

3–4. a round bucket with a handle

5–6. clear or simple

7–8. most important

Word Building

Add **ai** or **ay** to make a spelling word.

9. br __ __ d

10. tr __ __

11. m __ __ be

12. l __ __

13. del __ __

14. ch __ __ n

15. aw __ __

TEKS 3.24A Use knowledge of letter sounds, word parts, word segmentation, and syllabication to spell. **3.24C** Spell high-frequency and compound words from a commonly used list. **3.24E** Spell single syllable homophones.

Social Studies

Word Hunt

Read the paragraphs below. Look for words with **long a** spelled **ai** or **ay**.

In 1940 in France, four boys went to play in the woods. They saw a hole in the ground and started to dig in it. Under the hole was a large cave. Inside on the cave walls, the boys saw big paintings. There were pictures of cows, horses, and bulls. Yellow, black, and red color seemed to make the animals come alive.

Scientists studied the cave art. They thought it was made about 17,000 years ago! Hundreds of painted caves have been found. Many are in Spain and France.

Nobody knows why early people painted on cave walls. Most of the pictures show animals that people hunted. Some show humans. Maybe the painters thought the pictures would help them hunt better. The answer may always be a mystery. The point is that since thousands of years ago, people have known that art is important.

Follow the directions. Write each word once.

1–4. Write the words that have the **long a** sound spelled **ai**.

5–8. Write the words that have the **long a** sound spelled **ay**.

 TEKS 3.24A Use knowledge of letter sounds, word parts, word segmentation, and syllabication to spell. **3.24C** Spell high-frequency and compound words from a commonly used list.

63

Connections to THINKING

Read the spelling words and sentences.

1.	sheep	*sheep*	Farmers raise **sheep** for their wool.
2.	dream	*dream*	All people **dream** during sleep.
3.	street	*street*	The **street** has much traffic.
4.	east	*east*	The sun rises in the **east**.
5.	treat	*treat*	Do you **treat** your pet dog well?
6.	mean	*mean*	Scaring the child was a **mean** trick.
7.	wheels	*wheels*	Bicycle **wheels** vary in size.
8.	peace	*peace*	The treaty brought **peace** to the land.
9.	real	*real*	The book is about a **real** event.
10.	cheese	*cheese*	Milk is used to make **cheese**.
11.	leave	*leave*	Sometimes I **leave** early for school.
12.	stream	*stream*	A river is a large **stream**.
13.	sweet	*sweet*	This candy tastes **sweet**.
14.	teacher	*teacher*	My **teacher** helps me learn.
15.	heat	*heat*	Fire creates **heat**.

Think & Sort the spelling words.

1–5. Write the words that have the **long e** sound spelled **ee**.

6–15. Write the words that have the **long e** sound spelled **ea**.

Remember

The **long e** sound can be spelled in different ways: **ea** as in **treat** and **ee** as in **street**.

 TEKS 3.24A Use knowledge of letter sounds, word parts, word segmentation, and syllabication to spell.
3.24C Spell high-frequency and compound words from a commonly used list.

Connections to PHONICS

Replace the Vowels

Substitute the vowel in each word below with **ee** or **ea** to write a spelling word. Circle the vowel that is silent in each word.

1. ship
2. hit
3. pace
4. trot
5. strum
6. chose
7. men
8. drum
9. strut
10. love

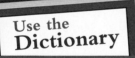

Use the
Dictionary

Write the spelling word that has the word below in its definition. Look up each word to check.

11. sun
12. true
13. sugar
14. person
15. turns

Dictionary Check Be sure to check your answers in your **Spelling Dictionary**.

TEKS 3.24A Use knowledge of letter sounds, word parts, word segmentation, and syllabication to spell.
3.24C Spell high-frequency and compound words from a commonly used list.

65

sheep	dream	street	east	treat
mean	wheels	peace	real	cheese
leave	stream	sweet	teacher	heat

Use Antonyms

Write the spelling word that has the opposite meaning of the underlined word so the sentence makes sense.

1–2. The <u>kind</u> sheep finally made <u>war</u> with the other sheep.

3–4. Kareem will <u>come to</u> the picnic and travel <u>west</u> along the stream.

5–6. The <u>cold</u> melted the <u>sour</u> treat.

7. The cheese is made with <u>imaginary</u> milk.

Understand Meaning

Write a spelling word that matches each clue.

8. These are round parts of a bicycle.

9. This word names a farm animal.

10. We do this while we are asleep.

11. I like to eat crackers with this.

12. This person explains things to us at school.

Categorize the Words

Add a spelling word to each of the word groups below.

13. river, creek, brook, _____

14. dessert, snack, sweet fruit, _____

15. road, avenue, drive, _____

 TEKS 3.24C Spell high-frequency and compound words from a commonly used list.

Proofread a Recipe

Proofread the recipe below for eight misspelled words. Then rewrite the recipe. Write the spelling words correctly and make the corrections shown by the proofreading marks.

tomato Sandwich

- bread
- tomato
- sweat butter
- 1 slice cheeze

1. Have an adult slice the tomato and toast the bread. Be careful of the heet.

2. Put tomato on a slice of buttered Toast.

3. add reel cheese, salt, and pepper.

4. Put the second slice of buttered toast on top⊙

Now enjoy your dreem treet in pease. Don't leeve the sandwich alone or someone might eat it!

Proofreading Marks

≡	Capital Letter
/	Small Letter
∧	Add
℘	Delete
⊙	Add a Period
⌗	Indent

EXPOSITORY Writing Prompt

Write a Recipe

Write step-by-step directions for making your favorite snack. Use as many spelling words as you can.

- Use the writing process: prewrite, draft, revise, edit, and publish.
- Name your snack and list the ingredients. Then number the steps.
- Use complete sentences with correct capitalization, punctuation, grammar, and spelling.
- Read your work. Circle three words you are unsure about and check their spelling in a dictionary.

Transfer

Write four more words with **long e** spelled **ee** and four words with **long e** spelled **ea**.

TEKS 3.24A Use knowledge of letter sounds, word parts, word segmentation, and syllabication to spell. **3.24C** Spell high-frequency and compound words from a commonly used list. **3.24G** Use print and electronic resources to find and check correct spellings.

Word Study

bean	east	dream	sweet	peacock
clean	wheels	treat	beetle	peanut
need	real	mean	degree	scream
seem	stream	peace	reason	sleeping
sheep	teacher	cheese	steam	
street	heat	leave	greet	

Meaning Mastery

These sentences use incorrect homophones. Write a spelling word that is a homophone for the boldfaced word.

1. When the dog stopped barking, there was **piece** on my street.
2. Our new neighbors **seam** to be very kind.

Base Words

Write the base word for each word below.

3. sleeping
4. sheepish
5. really
6. leaving
7. heater
8. eastern

Pattern Power

Write the spelling words that end with the same three letters as:

9–11. beet.

12–15. cream.

Circle the consonant blend in each word.

TEKS 3.24A Use knowledge of letter sounds, word parts, word segmentation, and syllabication to spell. **3.24Bii** Spell words with more advanced orthographic patterns and rules: dropping final "e" when endings are added. **3.24Bv** Spell words with more advanced orthographic patterns and rules: complex consonants. **3.24C** Spell high-frequency and compound words from a commonly used list. **3.24E** Spell single syllable homophones.

Math

Word Hunt

Read the paragraphs below. Look for words with **long e** spelled **ee** or **ea**.

A Greek writer named Euclid is often called the "Father of Geometry." We should know a lot about this man. He wrote some of the most useful math books of all time. We don't know much about his life, though. We know he lived around 300 B.C. At some point, he decided to leave Greece. He went south and east to Egypt. There, he was a math teacher. Those are almost all the facts we have about him.

We do not need to know about Euclid's life to understand what his ideas mean. Euclid wrote about lines, shapes, angles, and other important math concepts. One of his books was so popular that it was studied for more than 2,000 years. Abraham Lincoln said it helped him reason and prove ideas. Did Euclid ever imagine that his books would be so famous? We will never know.

WORD SORT

Follow the directions. Write each word once.

1–3. Write the words that have the **long e** sound spelled **ee**.

4–8. Write the words that have the **long e** sound spelled **ea**.

 TEKS 3.24A Use knowledge of letter sounds, word parts, word segmentation, and syllabication to spell. **3.24C** Spell high-frequency and compound words from a commonly used list.

Read the spelling words and sentences.

1. night — *night* — We sleep during the **night**.
2. bright — *bright* — I like to wear **bright** colors.
3. find — *find* — Can you **find** my lost keys?
4. light — *light* — The **light** helps us see in the dark.
5. wild — *wild* — Deer are **wild** animals.
6. high — *high* — The kite flew **high** in the sky.
7. blind — *blind* — Some **blind** people use dogs as guides.
8. fight — *fight* — People who **fight** get hurt.
9. sight — *sight* — The glasses improved her **sight**.
10. kind — *kind* — The **kind** boy helps sick birds.
11. sign — *sign* — We will cross at a stop **sign**.
12. knight — *knight* — A **knight** fought for his king.
13. mild — *mild* — I eat only **mild** cheese.
14. right — *right* — He draws with his **right** hand.
15. sigh — *sigh* — A **sigh** is a long, deep breath.

Think & Sort the spelling words.

1–6. Write the spelling words that have the **long i** sound spelled **i**.

7–15. Write the spelling words that have the **long i** sound spelled **igh**.

Remember

The **long i** sound can be spelled in different ways: i as in **kind** and igh as in **sigh**.

 TEKS 3.24A Use knowledge of letter sounds, word parts, word segmentation, and syllabication to spell. **3.24C** Spell high-frequency and compound words from a commonly used list.

Connections to PHONICS

Use Sound and Letter Patterns

Add **gh** to each word below to write a word with the **long i** sound.

1. nit
2. fit
3. sit
4. lit
5. knit

Match Ending Sounds

6–7. Write the spelling words that end with the **long i** sound.

8–10. Write the spelling words that rhyme with **mind**.

11. Write the spelling word that rhymes with **line**.

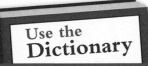

Use the **Dictionary**

Write the spelling word that would appear on a dictionary page with the following guide words.

12. meter • more

13. west • wishes

14. bridge • busy

15. return • rush

TEKS 3.24A Use knowledge of letter sounds, word parts, word segmentation, and syllabication to spell.
3.24C Spell high-frequency and compound words from a commonly used list.

71

night	bright	find	light	wild
high	blind	fight	sight	kind
sign	knight	mild	right	sigh

Use Antonyms

Write the spelling word from the box that is opposite in meaning to each of these words.

1. low
2. dim
3. day

4. seeing clearly
5. tame
6. spicy hot

Use Idioms

Write a spelling word to complete each sentence.

7. If your dad is your _____ in shining armor, he is your hero.

8. If something is a _____ for sore eyes, you are happy to see it again.

9. If two dogs _____ over a bone, they battle to decide who gets to have it.

Use Context Clues

Write spelling words to complete the story.

"I'm lost," Riley said with a long, deep **10.** . "Can you help me **11.** the library?"

The police officer replied, "Sure. Go to the first traffic **12.** . Turn **13.** and drive for five blocks. When you get to High Street, you should see a **14.** for Knight Library."

"Thank you for your help!" Riley said. "You have been very **15.** ."

 TEKS 3.24C Spell high-frequency and compound words from a commonly used list.

Connections to WRITING

Proofread a Friendly Letter

Proofread the letter below for eight misspelled words. Then rewrite the letter. Write the spelling words correctly and make the corrections shown by the proofreading marks.

Proofreading Marks

☰	Capital Letter
/	Small Letter
∧	Add
ℯ	Delete
⊙	Add a Period
⌗	Indent

Dear Tio Pedro,   November 15

⌗Our scout troop went on a nite hike! Our parents drove us rite to the nature preserve. It was at the top of a hi hill. it was easy to fined our troop leader. The liht from the moon was not very brite, so we used our flashlights⊙We saw a young Deer sleeping. we also found a brown turkey feather. It was a sine that a wild turkey was was nearby. It was a real site!

Love,

Miguel

NARRATIVE Writing Prompt
Write a Friendly Letter

Write a friendly letter to a friend or relative about a trip you have recently taken with family or friends. Use as many spelling words as you can.

- Use the writing process: prewrite, draft, revise, edit, and publish.
- Write today's date and a greeting such as "Dear Papa."
- Clearly describe the events in the order they happened.
- Include who went on the trip, where you went, and what happened.
- Use complete sentences with correct capitalization, punctuation, grammar, and spelling.
- Read your work. Choose three words you are unsure about and check their spelling in a dictionary.

Transfer

Write three more descriptive words with the **long i** sound spelled **i** or **igh.** Write the words in your Spelling Journal and circle the letters that make the **long i** sound.

TEKS 3.24A Use knowledge of letter sounds, word parts, word segmentation, and syllabication to spell. **3.24C** Spell high-frequency and compound words from a commonly used list. **3.24G** Use print and electronic resources to find and check correct spellings.

ivory	light	find	sigh	highlight
lion	high	wild	libraries	nightmare
shiny	kind	blind	might	rewind
tiger	sign	fight	slight	wildcat
night	mild	sight	title	
bright	right	knight	grind	

Pattern Power

For each word below, change the short vowel sound to a long vowel sound and write the spelling word.

1. willed   **2.** milled

Meaning Mastery

Remember that homophones are words that sound the same but have different spellings and meanings.

3–4. Write the two words in the list that are homophones.

Write a homophone from the list for each word below.

5. hi   **7.** fined   **9.** rite
6. mite   **8.** site

Base Words

Look up each word in a dictionary to confirm the spelling of its base word. Write the base word.

10. blinding   **13.** shinier
11. brighten   **14.** sighing
12. slightly   **15.** fighter

 3.24A Use knowledge of letter sounds, word parts, word segmentation, and syllabication to spell. **3.24Biii** Spell words with more advanced orthographic patterns and rules: changing y to i before adding an ending. **3.24C** Spell high-frequency and compound words from a commonly used list. **3.24E** Spell single syllable homophones.

Fine Arts

Word Hunt

Read the paragraphs below. Look for words with **long i** spelled **i** or **igh**.

Have you ever heard the sound of a recorder? Chances are you have heard this popular woodwind instrument. You can find recorders in many schools.

The recorder is not easy to play! It can sound squeaky. When it is played right, it makes a sweet, light sound. It is used to play every kind of song, from Japanese music to jazz.

The recorder is similar to a flute. A player blows into it to make a sound. The player puts fingers over the holes to change the sound. It plays both high and low notes. A soprano recorder plays higher pitches than an alto recorder.

Recorders have been played for hundreds of years. Kings and queens of old played them. A king may have played a recorder made of ivory. Today most recorders are made of shiny wood or plastic.

 WORD SORT

Follow the directions. Write each word once.

1–4. Write the words that have the **long i** sound spelled **i**.

5–8. Write the words that have the **long i** sound spelled **igh**.

 TEKS 3.24A Use knowledge of letter sounds, word parts, word segmentation, and syllabication to spell.
3.24C Spell high-frequency and compound words from a commonly used list.

Connections to THINKING

Read the spelling words and sentences.

1. snow	*snow*	The new **snow** is white and fresh.
2. load	*load*	The mule has a heavy **load** on its back.
3. almost	*almost*	I am **almost** nine years old.
4. row	*row*	We **row** the boat across the lake.
5. soak	*soak*	I **soak** my sore foot in hot water.
6. window	*window*	The **window** lets in a lot of light.
7. foam	*foam*	Wind makes **foam** appear on the water.
8. most	*most*	We had the **most** points.
9. flow	*flow*	Does this river **flow** into the ocean?
10. goat	*goat*	We get milk and cheese from a **goat**.
11. throw	*throw*	Please **throw** me the ball.
12. float	*float*	I can **float** on the water.
13. blow	*blow*	The guards will **blow** their trumpets.
14. below	*below*	Your coat is **below** mine in the pile.
15. soap	*soap*	Wash with warm water and **soap**.

Think & Sort the spelling words.

1–7. Write the words with the **long o** sound spelled **ow**.

8–13. Write the words with the **long o** sound spelled **oa**.

14–15. Write the words with the **long o** sound spelled **o**.

Remember

The **long o** sound can be spelled in different ways:
ow as in **row, oa** as in **goat,** and **o** as in **most**.

 TEKS 3.24A Use knowledge of letter sounds, word parts, word segmentation, and syllabication to spell.
3.24C Spell high-frequency and compound words from a commonly used list.

Understand Word Structure

Replace the underlined letter or letters with
o, oa, or **ow** to write a spelling word.

1. r<u>ed</u>
2. fl<u>ee</u>t
3. fla<u>g</u>
4. g<u>ri</u>t
5. thr<u>ee</u>
6. bl<u>ue</u>
7. sna<u>p</u>
8. m<u>a</u>st

Identify Rhyme

Write a spelling word that belongs
in each rhyming group.

9. hope, scope, _____
10. home, roam, _____
11. mowed, toad, _____
12. joke, broke, _____

Use the Dictionary

Your **Spelling Dictionary** shows how words are divided
into syllables. Find the words below in the Spelling
Dictionary. Write each word and use a slash to divide
it between the syllables.

13. almost   14. below   15. window

Dictionary Check Be sure to check your answers in
your **Spelling Dictionary**.

TEKS 3.24A Use knowledge of letter sounds, word parts, word segmentation, and syllabication to spell.
3.24C Spell high-frequency and compound words from a commonly used list.

77

snow	load	almost	row	soak
window	foam	most	flow	goat
throw	float	blow	below	soap

Use Synonyms

Write the spelling word that is a synonym for the underlined word.

1. We are <u>nearly</u> ready for the spelling bee.
2. Please put these desks in a <u>straight line</u>.
3. We stood <u>under</u> the bridge.
4. Tim will <u>pitch</u> the trash into the can.
5. Maria helped <u>pile</u> the wood into the truck.
6. The sink was filled with soapy <u>bubbles</u>.

Use Alliteration

Complete each sentence with a spelling word. The sentences should make sense.

7. Five ferries _____ on Flower Lake.
8. The Fig and Fox Rivers _____ from Fargo.
9. The slippery _____ slid in the sink.
10. On Grandpa's farm, the _____ gobbled green grass.
11. Sissy and Susie had to _____ their smelly socks in soap and hot water.

Solve the Riddles

Write a spelling word to solve each riddle.

12. I often fall when it is cold.
13. Winds do this.
14. I am many, but not all. What am I?
15. You can see through me.

 TEKS 3.24C Spell high-frequency and compound words from a commonly used list.

Connections to WRITING

Proofread Directions

Proofread the directions below for eight misspelled words. Then rewrite the directions. Write the spelling words correctly and make the corrections shown by the proofreading marks.

¶Jumping in a wave is fun. to have the moast fun, do it right. Wait until the wave Is almoast ready to crash. Then dive into it. To do this, thro yourself into the wave just belo its top. Make sure you go against the flowe of the water. keep your mouth shut and bloe air out through your nose. Then just flote as you soke in the water⊙

Proofreading Marks

☰	Capital Letter
/	Small Letter
∧	Add
℘	Delete
⊙	Add a Period
¶	Indent

EXPOSITORY Writing Prompt
Write Directions

Write directions for how to do something you do well, such as floating in the water or giving your dog a soapy bath. Use as many spelling words as you can.

- Use the writing process: prewrite, draft, revise, edit, and publish.
- Before writing your draft, think about your audience. What are your reasons for giving these directions?
- Write all the steps in the correct order.
- Use complete sentences with correct capitalization, punctuation, grammar, and spelling.
- Read your work. Circle three words you are unsure about and check their spelling in a dictionary.

Transfer
Write three more words that tell about how to do something and have the **long o** sound spelled **ow, oa,** or **o**. Write the words in your Spelling Journal and circle the letters that make the **long o** sound.

TEKS 3.24A Use knowledge of letter sounds, word parts, word segmentation, and syllabication to spell.
3.24C Spell high-frequency and compound words from a commonly used list. **3.24G** Use print and electronic resources to find and check correct spellings.

Word Study

coat	row	load	blow	potato
follow	window	soak	coast	swallow
grow	goat	foam	fold	toast
road	float	most	pillow	tomato
snow	below	flow	solo	
almost	soap	throw	loaf	

Pattern Power

An open syllable ends with a vowel sound. A closed syllable ends with a consonant sound. Complete the exercises below. Write an **O** next to each word that is an open syllable, and a **C** next to each word that ends with a closed syllable.

1. Write the word that rhymes with **hope** but is spelled with **oa**.
2–7. Write the one-syllable words that rhyme with **tow**.
8–10. Write the words that rhyme with **boat**.

Meaning Mastery

Write the spelling word that matches each definition. Use your **Spelling Dictionary** to check your answers.

11. anything that is carried
12. a glass-covered opening in a house
13. a reddish fruit that is commonly grown
14. a quantity of small bubbles
15. the greatest in amount

TEKS 3.24A Use knowledge of letter sounds, word parts, word segmentation, and syllabication to spell. **3.24C** Spell high-frequency and compound words from a commonly used list. **3.24D** Spell words with common syllable constructions.

Technology

Word Hunt

Read the paragraphs below. Look for words with **long o** spelled **ow, oa,** or **o**.

Did you ever watch a driver use a GPS? GPS stands for *global positioning system.* Using satellite data, GPS units can find anyone's location. They are very useful to drivers, but were you aware that sailors use them, too?

Imagine that a sailor wanted to make a solo sail along the coast. First he or she would map the route using charts on the GPS unit. During the trip, GPS shows exactly where the boat is on the chart. That makes the trip safer. Fog does not throw the sailor off course. Other features, such as a buoy or an island, can be seen on the chart.

A GPS is waterproof, too. A wave can wash right over a GPS unit, and it will still work.

 **WORD SORT**

Follow the directions. Write each word once.

1–2. Write the words that have the **long o** sound spelled **ow**.

3–4. Write the words that have the **long o** sound spelled **oa**.

5–8. Write the words that have the **long o** sound spelled **o**.

 TEKS 3.24A Use knowledge of letter sounds, word parts, word segmentation, and syllabication to spell.
3.24C Spell high-frequency and compound words from a commonly used list.

81

Units 7–11

Assessment

Each assessment word in the box fits one of the spelling patterns you have studied over the past five weeks. Read the unit descriptions. Then write each assessment word under the unit number it fits.

Unit 7

1–3. The long vowel sounds in **pave, size,** and **globe** are spelled **vowel-consonant-e**.

Unit 8

4–6. The **long a** sound can be spelled in different ways: **ai** as in **paint** and **ay** as in **tray**.

Unit 9

7–9. The **long e** sound can be spelled in different ways: **ea** as in **treat** and **ee** as in **street**.

Unit 10

10–12. The **long i** sound can be spelled in different ways: **i** as in **kind** and **igh** as in **sigh**.

Unit 11

13–15. The **long o** sound can be spelled in different ways: **ow** as in **row, oa** as in **goat,** and **o** as in **most**.

Words for Assessment

stripe

bail

cream

bind

groan

sold

thigh

bead

bait

brave

fellow

rind

creep

sway

grove

Review

Unit 7: Vowel-Consonant-e

broke	smile	close	state
face	stone	size	

Write a spelling word by taking the **-ing** off each word below and adding the final **e**.

1. smiling   **3.** facing

2. closing   **4.** sizing

Change the word with a short vowel sound to a spelling word with a long vowel sound.

5. brick

6. stat

7. stun

Unit 8: Long a: ai, ay

always	chain	laid	maybe
mail	pay	main	

Write the spelling word that rhymes with each word.

8. day   **9.** braid   **10.** baby

Find the word that is misspelled in each sentence. Write the word correctly.

11. I alwaze try to help a friend in trouble.

12. The magazine was delivered with our male.

13. The mane gate of the garden was locked.

14. The swing fell when the chian broke.

Review

Unit 9: Long e: ee, ea

real	teacher	street	wheels
east	heat	stream	

Rearrange the letters of each underlined word to write a spelling word with **long e**.

1. The sun comes up in the <u>teas</u>.

2. I could see many fish in the clear <u>master</u>.

3. That moving truck has many <u>hewels</u>.

4. In front of my school is a wide <u>tester</u>.

5. The fruit in that picture looks almost <u>aler</u>.

6. The reading <u>cheater</u> gave them each a book.

7. The fire gave out a lot of <u>eath</u>.

Unit 10: Long i: i, igh

bright	mild	kind	right
night	sign	high	

Write the spelling word that rhymes with the underlined word and completes the sentence.

8. The <u>child</u> likes his chili hot and spicy, not _____.

9. There is a <u>vine</u> growing on the "For Sale" _____.

10. <u>I</u> am not afraid to jump off the _____ diving board.

11. The _____ clerk tried to <u>wind</u> up the clock.

12. The cat got a <u>fright</u> in the middle of the _____.

13. Warren <u>might</u> get every test question _____.

14. The _____ <u>light</u> of the moon lighted the path.

Unit 11: Long o: ow, oa, o

almost	snow	float	window
below	goat	soap	

Write a spelling word to match each description.

1. Two syllables; accent on first syllable; ends with a closed syllable

2. Two syllables; accent on first syllable; ends with an open syllable

3. One open syllable

4. Two syllables; accent on second syllable; ends with an open syllable

5–7. One closed syllable

Spelling Study Strategy

Sorting by Vowel Spelling Patterns
Write spelling words on small cards. Then sort the words by spelling pattern. Share your words with a partner.

1. Make stacks of words with **long o** spelled **ow** or **oa**.

2. Make stacks of words with **long a** spelled **ai** or **ay**.

3. Make stacks of words with **long e** spelled **ee** or **ea**.

4. Make stacks of words with **long i** spelled **i** or **igh**.

5. Make stacks of words with **vowel-consonant-e** spellings for **long a, long i,** or **long o**.

Directions: Read the introduction and the passage that follows. Then read each question and fill in the space in front of the correct answer on your answer sheet.

Dwayne wrote this story about a boy who can't find one thing he can do well. He wants you to review his paper. As you read, think about ways Dwayne can improve his story.

Dion's Dream

(1) Standing in the outfield, Dion watched his close friend Chad thro the ball to third base. (2) The runner tried to slied but was out by a mile. (3) Dion let out a sigh. (4) He and Chad were alwais on the same team. (5) Chad was a great player and the best at whatever he did. (6) He could roller skate faster than kids twice his size, he had already won a prize, and he brok the record for a race he ran. (7) Dion couldn't think of one thing he was good at.

(8) He lay awake that night, trying to dreem up something he could do well, but his mind was a total blank. (9) "Guess I should quit trying to find something," he thought. (10) "Maybe it's just not there." (11) He knew how to count sheep, though, and soon fell asleep.

(12) The next morning, Dion's teacher asked Dion for help. (13) She needed someone to make a sine about the summer reading program, Stories from Around the Globe. (14) Dion put some paint in a tray and got busy. (15) First he painted a chain of books in bright colors that circled the glob. (16) Then he added the words telling about the program. (17) When he handed his teacher the sign, her face lit up. (18) "It's wonderful!" she said. (19) His dream had come true.

GO ON

1 What change, if any, should be made in sentence 1?

- ⬭ Change *close* to **clos**
- ⬭ Change *thro* to **throw**
- ⬭ Change *base* to **bays**
- ⬭ Make no change

2 What change, if any, should be made in sentence 2?

- ⬭ Change *slied* to **slide**
- ⬭ Change *out* to **owt**
- ⬭ Change *mile* to **mil**
- ⬭ Make no change

3 What change, if any, should be made in sentence 4?

- ⬭ Change *alwais* to **always**
- ⬭ Change *same* to **saym**
- ⬭ Change *team* to **teme**
- ⬭ Make no change

4 What change, if any, should be made in sentence 6?

- ⬭ Change *skate* to **skat**
- ⬭ Change *prize* to **pries**
- ⬭ Change *brok* to **broke**
- ⬭ Make no change

5 What change should be made in sentence 8?

- ⬭ Change *lay* to **la**
- ⬭ Change *night* to **nigth**
- ⬭ Change *dreem* to **dream**
- ⬭ Change *mind* to **mined**

6 What change, if any, should be made in sentence 11?

- ⬭ Change *count* to **cuont**
- ⬭ Change *sheap* to **sheep**
- ⬭ Change *asleep* to **asleap**
- ⬭ Make no change

7 What change, if any, should be made in sentence 13?

- ⬭ Change *make* to **maik**
- ⬭ Change *sine* to **sign**
- ⬭ Change *Globe* to **Glob**
- ⬭ Make no change

8 What change, if any, should be made in sentence 14?

- ⬭ Change *some* to **sum**
- ⬭ Change *paint* to **pant**
- ⬭ Change *tray* to **tra**
- ⬭ Make no change

9 What change should be made in sentence 15?

- ⬭ Change *painted* to **panted**
- ⬭ Change *chain* to **chayn**
- ⬭ Change *bright* to **brite**
- ⬭ Change *glob* to **globe**

10 What change, if any, should be made to sentence 17?

- ⬭ Change *teacher* to **teecher**
- ⬭ Change *face* to **fase**
- ⬭ Change *sign* to **sine**
- ⬭ Make no change

STOP

Grammar, Usage, and Mechanics
Singular and Plural Nouns

A singular noun names one person, place, or thing.

> The **girl** has a **cat**.
> The **boat** has a **sail**.

A plural noun names more than one person, place, or thing.

> The **girls** own many **cats**.
> These **boats** have many **sails**.

Many plural nouns are formed by adding an **-s** to the end of the singular noun.

Practice Activity

A. Write the singular form of each plural noun below.

1. teachers
2. stones
3. nights
4. windows
5. streets
6. prizes

B. Change the plural noun to a singular noun so each sentence makes sense.

7. The baby had a big **smiles** for her mother.
8. My bicycle **chains** is broken.
9. The farmer has six sheep but just one **goats**.
10. You can cool your feet off in that **streams**.

The Writing Process: Narrative
Writing a Friendly Letter

PREWRITING
Writing a friendly letter is a fun way to share information. You can write a letter to a friend or a family member. Think about some exciting news you could share with this person. Make a list of the events in order.

DRAFTING
Use your list of events to write a friendly letter. Make sure your letter has all five parts: heading, greeting, body, closing, and signature. Use as many spelling words as possible.

REVISING
When you have finished your first draft, read your letter from beginning to end. Check to see if you have included all of the events on your list. Did you include all five parts of a friendly letter? Now write your final draft.

EDITING
Use the **Editing Checklist** to proofread your letter. Be sure to use proofreading marks when you make corrections. Read your writing. Circle at least two words that may be misspelled. Use a dictionary or electronic resource to check the spelling.

PUBLISHING
Write or print a final copy of your friendly letter. Ask an adult to help you address and mail it.

EDITING CHECKLIST

Spelling
- ✓ Circle words that contain the spelling patterns and rules learned in Units 7–11.
- ✓ Check the circled words in your **Spelling Dictionary**.
- ✓ Check for other spelling errors.

Capital Letters
- ✓ Capitalize important words in the title.
- ✓ Capitalize the first word in each sentence.
- ✓ Capitalize proper nouns.

Punctuation
- ✓ End each sentence with the correct punctuation.
- ✓ Use commas, apostrophes, and quotation marks correctly.

Grammar, Usage, and Mechanics
- ✓ Make sure each singular noun names one person, place or thing.
- ✓ Make sure each plural noun has the correct ending.

 TEKS 3.24A Use knowledge of letter sounds, word parts, word segmentation, and syllabication to spell.
3.24G Use print and electronic resources to find and check correct spellings.

89

ch, sh, tch, th, wr, ck

Connections to THINKING

Read the spelling words and sentences.

1.	shape	*shape*	A square is a **shape** with four sides.
2.	church	*church*	Many people go to a **church** or temple.
3.	watch	*watch*	Let's **watch** the game on television.
4.	father	*father*	My **father** taught me to throw a ball.
5.	wrap	*wrap*	We **wrap** the gifts in pretty paper.
6.	check	*check*	Put a **check** mark next to each word.
7.	finish	*finish*	I will **finish** the book tonight.
8.	sharp	*sharp*	That knife has a very **sharp** edge.
9.	mother	*mother*	My **mother** showed me how to bat.
10.	write	*write*	I will **write** an e-mail message to you.
11.	catch	*catch*	Throw the ball, and I will **catch** it.
12.	chase	*chase*	Do not let the dog **chase** the cat.
13.	shall	*shall*	I **shall** call you in the morning.
14.	thick	*thick*	This **thick** coat will keep you warm.
15.	wrote	*wrote*	Nan **wrote** me a letter yesterday.

Think & Sort the spelling words.

Write the words that have:

    1–2. /k/ spelled **ck**

    3–5. /r/ spelled **wr**

    6–9. sh

  10–11. th

  12–13. ch

  14–15. tch

Remember

Two consonants together can spell a single sound: **wr (wrap)**, **ck (thick)**. Two or three consonants together can spell new sounds: **ch (chase)**, **sh (shape)**, **th (thick)**, and **tch (watch)**. Some of these patterns, including **wr, ck, ch,** and **tch,** are sometimes called complex consonants.

TEKS 3.24A Use knowledge of letter sounds, word parts, word segmentation, and syllabication to spell. **3.24Bv** Spell words with more advanced orthographic patterns and rules: complex consonants. **3.24C** Spell high-frequency and compound words from a commonly used list.

Connections to PHONICS

Identify Sound and Letter Patterns

Write the spelling word by adding the missing letters.

1. __ __ ick

2. fa __ __ er

3. mo __ __ er

Use Word Structure

Say each spelling word. Listen carefully for both the beginning and ending sounds. Write the spelling word or words that have the same beginning and ending sounds as the words below. Circle the letters that work together to make a single sound.

4–5. ship

6–7. rate

8. rope

9. coach

10. witch

11. fish

12. shell

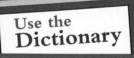
Use the Dictionary

13–15. A dictionary lists words in alphabetical order. Write these spelling words in alphabetical order:

check   chase   church

Dictionary Check Check the order in your **Spelling Dictionary**.

TEKS 3.24A Use knowledge of letter sounds, word parts, word segmentation, and syllabication to spell.
3.24Bv Spell words with more advanced orthographic patterns and rules: complex consonants.
3.24C Spell high-frequency and compound words from a commonly used list.

shape	church	watch	father	wrap
check	finish	sharp	mother	write
catch	chase	shall	thick	wrote

Complete the Analogies

Write a spelling word to complete each analogy.

1. **Oak** is to **tree** as **triangle** is to _____.
2. **Punctuation** is to **comma** as **mark** is to _____.
3. **Toss** is to **grab** as **throw** is to _____.
4. **Leapfrog** is to **jump** as **tag** is to _____.
5. **Narrow** is to **wide** as **thin** is to _____.
6. **Letter** is to **envelope** as **gift** is to _____.
7. **Computer** is to **typed** as **pencil** is to _____.

Use Context Clues

Write a spelling word to complete the story.

"What time **8.** I meet you on Sunday?" Jimmy asked. Mike said, "I forgot to tell you. My **9.** and **10.** will drop me off at your house after **11.**."

"Great!" said Jimmy. "That will give me time to **12.** my morning chores. I also have to **13.** my little cousin for a while."

Mike said, "I will be there at 10 o'clock **14.**. I will **15.** it down so that I don't forget!"

 TEKS 3.24C Spell high-frequency and compound words from a commonly used list.

Proofread a Poem

Proofread the poem below for eight misspelled words. Then rewrite the poem. Write the spelling words correctly and make the corrections shown by the proofreading marks.

to Chas a Fish

I rap a worm around hook.

I drop it in the babbling brook

My wach says that it's 9 a.m.

I hope I get a catsh by 10.

Is that a charp tug Shal i chek?

No, my line's caught on the deck.

Big, thik fish, please don't be slow.

If you just bite, I'll let let you go.

Proofreading Marks

☰	Capital Letter
/	Small Letter
∧	Add
℘	Delete
⊙	Add a Period
⌐⌐	Indent

DESCRIPTIVE Writing Prompt
Write a Poem

Write a poem about a sport or hobby you enjoy. The lines of the poem do not have to rhyme. Use as many spelling words as you can.

- Use the writing process: prewrite, draft, revise, edit, and publish.
- Be sure to tell when, where, why, and how you enjoy the hobby. Include details about what you see, do, taste, touch, hear, or smell.
- Use complete sentences with correct capitalization, punctuation, grammar, and spelling.
- Read your work. Circle three words you are unsure about and check their spellings in a dictionary.

Transfer

Write four more describing words with consonant digraphs **wr, ck, ch, sh, th,** or **tch.** Write the words in your Spelling Journal and underline the consonants that work together to spell a single sound.

TEKS 3.24A Use knowledge of letter sounds, word parts, word segmentation, and syllabication to spell. **3.24Bv** Spell words with more advanced orthographic patterns and rules: complex consonants. **3.24C** Spell high-frequency and compound words from a commonly used list. **3.24G** Use print and electronic resources to find and check correct spellings.

bench	father	shape	wrote	depth
chin	check	wrap	chuckle	hatch
shine	finish	sharp	scratches	seashore
thank	mother	catch	shower	shipwreck
church	write	chase	wrinkle	
watch	shall	thick	chance	

Spelling Rules

You must use the correct spelling rules when adding endings to words. Write the spelling words that follow the rules below.

1–7. drop the final **e** before adding **-ed** or **-ing**

8–9. double the final consonant before adding **-ed** or **-ing**

10. Write the word that is the irregular past tense form of another spelling word and does not follow a rule.

Compound Words

Write the spelling word that is part of each compound word below.

11. housemother

12. churchyard

13. grandfather

14–15. Write the spelling words that are already compound words.

 TEKS 3.24A Use knowledge of letter sounds, word parts, word segmentation, and syllabication to spell. **3.24Bi** Spell words with more advanced orthographic patterns and rules: consonant doubling when adding an ending. **3.24Bii** Spell words with more advanced orthographic patterns and rules: dropping final "e" when endings are traded. **3.24C** Spell high-frequency and compound words from a commonly used list.

Science

WordHunt

Read the paragraphs below. Look for words with five or more letters in which the consonants **wr, ck, ch, sh, th,** and **tch** spell a single sound.

> Did you ever build and race your own toy car? Toy car races, called derbies, are fun for the whole family. Everyone in the family can join in the fun by helping build the car. Kids can learn a lot about force and motion, too.
>
> Usually a child starts with a block of soft wood, two axles, and a set of four plastic wheels. First a piece of wood is carved into the shape of a car. If it is too thick, it will not fit on the track.
>
> Kids put a lot of effort into decorating the cars with paint and stickers. Next comes the fun part. The car is placed at the top of a sloping track. Gravity causes a change in motion and makes the car roll down. Friction causes it to stop at the bottom of the track. Judges watch and time the cars. The first car to cross the finish line with the fastest speed wins!

 **WORD SORT**

Follow the directions. Write each word only once.

1. Write the word that is spelled with both **th** and **ck**.
2. Write the word that begins with **sh**.
3–5. Write the words that are spelled with **ch** or **tch**.
6–8. Write the words that are spelled with **ck**.

 TEKS 3.24A Use knowledge of letter sounds, word parts, word segmentation, and syllabication to spell.
3.24Bv Spell words with more advanced orthographic patterns and rules: complex consonants.
3.24C Spell high-frequency and compound words from a commonly used list.

95

Connections to THINKING

Read the spelling words and sentences.

1.	change	*change*	I will **change** into my baseball clothes.
2.	fence	*fence*	There is a **fence** around the pool.
3.	space	*space*	We use this **space** as a gym.
4.	age	*age*	Letifa is now ten years of **age**.
5.	center	*center*	My desk is in the **center** of the room.
6.	large	*large*	We ordered a **large** pizza.
7.	since	*since*	I have been able to swim **since** I was five.
8.	price	*price*	The **price** of the book is ten dollars.
9.	page	*page*	Read to the bottom of the **page**.
10.	ice	*ice*	The **ice** will melt when it warms up.
11.	dance	*dance*	Mom and Dad **dance** at the party.
12.	pencil	*pencil*	This **pencil** has no eraser.
13.	slice	*slice*	Please cut a **slice** of bread for me.
14.	place	*place*	This is a nice **place** to visit.
15.	city	*city*	We take the bus into the **city**.

Think & Sort the spelling words.

Write the words that have

1–4. the /j/ sound spelled with **soft g + e**.

5–13. the /s/ sound spelled with **soft c + e**.

14–15. the /s/ sound spelled with **soft c + i**.

Remember

The **soft g** sounds like /j/. The **soft g** in **age** is spelled **g** followed by **e**. The **soft c** sounds like /s/. The **soft c** can be spelled **c** followed by **e** (**ice**) or **c** followed by **i** (**city**).

TEKS 3.24A Use knowledge of letter sounds, word parts, word segmentation, and syllabication to spell. **3.24Bv** Spell words with more advanced orthographic patterns and rules: complex consonants. **3.24C** Spell high-frequency and compound words from a commonly used list.

Identify Vowel Sounds

1–3. Write the one-syllable spelling words that have **n** followed by /s/ spelled with **soft c**. If the word has a short vowel sound, circle the word.

4–8. Write the other one-syllable spelling words that have /s/ spelled with **soft c**. If the word has a short vowel sound, circle the word.

Use Rhyme

Write the spelling words that rhyme with each word below.

9–10. cage

11. barge

12. range

Use the Dictionary

You can use a dictionary to find out how to divide a word into syllables. Look for the following words in your **Spelling Dictionary** in this book or online. Write each word, and use a slash mark to show where to divide the word.

13. center   **14.** city   **15.** pencil

TEKS 3.24A Use knowledge of letter sounds, word parts, word segmentation, and syllabication to spell.
3.24Bv Spell words with more advanced orthographic patterns and rules: complex consonants.
3.24C Spell high-frequency and compound words from a commonly used list. **3.24D** Spell words with common syllable constructions.

change	fence	space	age	center
large	since	price	page	ice
dance	pencil	slice	place	city

Understand Meaning

Write a spelling word that matches each clue.

1. This word can describe an elephant.
2. This is where to find the planets and stars.
3. This names one piece of bread.
4. This can mean "because."
5. This is a small part of a book.
6. This names a very large town.
7. This is in a bar code on a package for sale.
8. This word might be a waltz or a tango.
9. This can be a noun meaning "location" or a verb meaning "put."

Make Inferences

Write a spelling word to answer each riddle.

10. What runs all around a field but never moves?
    a f_____
11. What goes up but never comes down?
    your a_____
12. What is the hardest thing about learning to skate?
    the i_____
13. What makes a point but never says a word?
    a p_____
14. Why did the woman have her purse open?
    She was expecting some c_____ in the weather.
15. Why is a nose always in the middle of a face?
    It's the c_____.

 TEKS 3.24C Spell high-frequency and compound words from a commonly used list.

Connections to WRITING

Proofread a Letter

Proofread the letter below for eight misspelled words. Then rewrite the letter. Write the spelling words correctly and make the corrections shown by the proofreading marks.

Proofreading Marks

≡   Capital Letter

/   Small Letter

∧   Add

✊   Delete

⊙   Add a Period

¶   Indent

Dear neighbors,

¶Let's make the playground a better plase for Children! We can chang this larje spase into a great park for the sity. The fens needs to be Fixed also, sinse it fell down in May. We'll meet in the senter of the playground on Sunday.

yours truly,
Mark Jackson

PERSUASIVE Writing Prompt
Write a Letter

Write a letter inviting someone to help you make a change in your town. Explain what needs to change, what your plans are, and why the person might want to help. Use as many spelling words as you can.

- Use the writing process: prewrite, draft, revise, edit, and publish.
- To make your letter as persuasive as possible, give details about why the change is necessary.
- Use complete sentences with correct capitalization, punctuation, grammar, and spelling.
- Read your work. Circle three words you are unsure about and check their spellings in a dictionary.

Transfer

Write two more words with /j/ spelled **g** and two words with /s/ spelled **c**. Write the words in your Spelling Journal and circle the letter that spells /j/ or /s/ in each word.

TEKS 3.24A Use knowledge of letter sounds, word parts, word segmentation, and syllabication to spell. **3.24Bv** Spell words with more advanced orthographic patterns and rules: complex consonants. **3.24C** Spell high-frequency and compound words from a commonly used list. **3.24G** Use print and electronic resources to find and check correct spellings.

nice	large	fence	slice	cider
orange	since	space	bridge	nudge
race	ice	center	cellar	plunge
spice	dance	price	engine	pounce
change	place	page	piece	
age	city	pencil	cedar	

Base Words and Endings

Write each spelling word below. Then drop the final **e** and add **-ing** to write a new word.

1–2. page

3–4. slice

5–6. ice

7–8. price

Plurals

Write each spelling word. Then, if the word ends with a consonant or **e,** add **s** to write the plural. If the word ends with **y,** change **y** to **i** and add **es** to write the plural.

9–10. pencil

11–12. city

13–14. fence

TEKS 3.24A Use knowledge of letter sounds, word parts, word segmentation, and syllabication to spell. **3.24Bii** Spell words with more advanced orthographic patterns and rules: dropping final "e" when endings are added. **3.24Biii** Spell words with more advanced orthographic patterns and rules: changing y to i before adding an ending. **3.24C** Spell high-frequency and compound words from a commonly used list.

Social Studies

Word Hunt

Read the paragraphs below. Look for words with **soft g** spelled **g** and words with **soft c** spelled **c**.

There is a reason to celebrate on May 5th. This day is a holiday called Cinco de Mayo (SEENG-koh da MAH-yoh). It has been popular since 1967.

A group of college students started it. They wanted to honor the Battle of Puebla. This battle happened in Mexico on May 5, 1862. Mexican soldiers were fighting the French army. France wanted to rule their country. The French army was huge, but the Mexicans won the fight. They showed great courage.

The day is a time to enjoy Mexican culture. People have parties. They wear special clothes. They enjoy food, dance, and music. It is fun for any age group. Everyone likes to eat good food and dance!

WORD SORT

Write the English words that answer the directions. Write each word only once.

1–4. Write words with the /j/ sound spelled **g**.

5–8. Write words with the /s/ sound spelled **c**.

TEKS 3.24A Use knowledge of letter sounds, word parts, word segmentation, and syllabication to spell.
3.24Bv Spell words with more advanced orthographic patterns and rules: complex consonants.
3.24C Spell high-frequency and compound words from a commonly used list.

Connections to THINKING

Read the spelling words and sentences.

1. shook — *shook* — I **shook** the juice before pouring it.
2. flash — *flash* — I just saw a **flash** of lightning.
3. speech — *speech* — The mayor made a long **speech**.
4. think — *think* — I like to **think** before I answer.
5. strong — *strong* — We are **strong** enough to lift this.
6. cloth — *cloth* — That coat is made from heavy **cloth**.
7. brook — *brook* — The water in the **brook** is cold.
8. stitch — *stitch* — One **stitch** will not hold the button.
9. string — *string* — The cat chases the ball of **string**.
10. scratch — *scratch* — Please **scratch** my back.
11. fresh — *fresh* — This bread is **fresh** and tasty.
12. spring — *spring* — I will play baseball in the **spring**.
13. switch — *switch* — Use the **switch** to turn on the light.
14. stretch — *stretch* — We want to **stretch** if we sit for too long.
15. splash — *splash* — Jim made a big **splash** in the pool.

Think & Sort the spelling words.

Write the words that begin with a

   1–2. consonant digraph.

   3–15. consonant blend.

Circle the digraph or blend in each word.

Remember

Consonant digraphs are consonants that work together to make one new sound: **ch, ng, sh, th, tch**. **Consonant blends** are consonants that make more than one sound when they are used together: **br, cl, fl, fr, scr, sp, spl, spr, st, str, sw**. Digraphs and blends are sometimes called complex consonants.

TEKS 3.24A Use knowledge of letter sounds, word parts, word segmentation, and syllabication to spell. **3.24Bv** Spell words with more advanced orthographic patterns and rules: complex consonants. **3.24C** Spell high-frequency and compound words from a commonly used list.

Analyze Complex Consonants

Remember that in a consonant blend, you can hear the sound of each letter. In a consonant digraph, two or more letters work together to make a single sound.

An example of a two-letter consonant blend is **cl** as in **clap**.

An example of a three-letter consonant blend is **str** as in **strike**.

An example of a two-letter digraph is **th** as in **thunder**.

An example of a three-letter digraph is **tch** as in **watch**.

1–15. Write each spelling word. Then follow the directions.

Draw a circle around each two-letter consonant blend.

Draw a box around each three-letter consonant blend.

Underline each two-letter consonant digraph.

Draw a wavy line under each three-letter digraph.

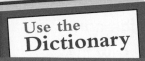

Use the **Dictionary**

Use a dictionary to learn a word's part of speech. An abbreviation for the part of speech follows the entry word; for example, *n.* for noun, *v.* for verb, and *adj.* for adjective. Find the part of speech for each spelling word in your **Spelling Dictionary**. Write its abbreviation next to each word on the list you made for the activity above. If a word has two entries, write both parts of speech for that word.

 TEKS 3.24A Use knowledge of letter sounds, word parts, word segmentation, and syllabication to spell.
3.24Bv Spell words with more advanced orthographic patterns and rules: complex consonants.
3.24C Spell high-frequency and compound words from a commonly used list.

shook	flash	speech	think	strong
cloth	brook	stitch	string	scratch
fresh	spring	switch	stretch	splash

Complete the Analogies

Write a spelling word to complete each analogy.

1. **Evening** is to **morning** as **fall** is to _____.
2. **Tiny** is to **huge** as **stale** is to _____.
3. **Mountain** is to **hill** as **river** is to _____.
4. **Take** is to **took** as **shake** is to _____.
5. **Cloth** is to **fabric** as **yarn** is to _____.
6. **Easy** is to **difficult** as **weak** is to _____.
7. **Sentence** is to **write** as **idea** is to _____.

Use Context Clues

Write a spelling word to complete each sentence.

8. Use a soft _____ to wipe down the car.
9. I heard a clap of thunder just as I saw the _____ of lightning.
10. We should always _____ after we exercise.
11. I got a _____ on my elbow when I fell down.
12. The doctor sewed one _____ in Jimmy's finger.
13. We will _____ schools for sixth grade.
14. I don't get nervous when I have to make a _____ in front of an audience.
15. Please don't _____ me. I don't want to get wet!

 TEKS 3.24C Spell high-frequency and compound words from a commonly used list.

Connections to WRITING

Proofread a Paragraph

Proofread the paragraph below for eight misspelled words. Then rewrite the paragraph. Write the spelling words correctly and make the corrections shown by the proofreading marks.

¶ We hiked up Sugar Mountain on a clear sping day. We walked along the ~~the~~ rushing barook to the top. We saw fish splassh in the water⊙The sun was warm, and there was a storng, fresch breeze. We smelled the deep green Pine trees. We stayed away from the branches so they wouldn't scrach us. after the hike, I thingk we were all ready to strech out for a nap⊙

Proofreading Marks

☰	Capital Letter
/	Small Letter
∧	Add
ℓ	Delete
⊙	Add a Period
¶	Indent

DESCRIPTIVE Writing Prompt
Write a Paragraph

Think of an interesting place you have visited. Write a paragraph describing the place that will help someone else experience what it was like. Use as many spelling words as you can.

- Use the writing process: prewrite, draft, revise, edit, and publish.
- Include details that tell about what you saw, heard, smelled, touched, or tasted.
- Use complete sentences with correct capitalization, punctuation, grammar, and spelling.
- Key your paragraph in a word-processing program. Use the spell-check feature to check your spelling.

Transfer

Write three descriptive words that are spelled with consonant digraphs and three descriptive words that are spelled with consonant blends. Write the words in your Spelling Journal and circle each consonant digraph and blend.

 TEKS **3.24A** Use knowledge of letter sounds, word parts, word segmentation, and syllabication to spell. **3.24Bv** Spell words with more advanced orthographic patterns and rules: complex consonants. **3.24C** Spell high-frequency and compound words from a commonly used list. **3.24G** Use print and electronic resources to find and check correct spellings.

bring	think	flash	switch	hunger
clap	strong	brook	flight	panther
store	cloth	stitch	station	shade
trash	fresh	string	strange	twitch
shook	stretch	scratch	thunder	
speech	splash	spring	crouch	

Word Building

Add one of the following consonant digraphs or blends to make a word from the list: **sh, tch, th, cl, sp**.

1. __ __ ook
2. __ __ eech
3. __ __ oth
4. pan __ __ er
5. swi __ __ __
6. sti __ __ __
7. __ __ ap

Compound Words

Write a word to answer the clue. Then write the compound word.

8–9. This word plus **shoe** is what you use to tie your shoes.

10–11. This word plus **light** means "something that helps you see in the dark."

12–13. This word plus **time** means "a season of the year."

14–15. This word plus **room** means "a place to keep things."

TEKS 3.24A Use knowledge of letter sounds, word parts, word segmentation, and syllabication to spell.
3.24Bv Spell words with more advanced orthographic patterns and rules: complex consonants.
3.24C Spell high-frequency and compound words from a commonly used list.

Math
Word Hunt

Read the paragraphs below. Look for words with five or more letters that have the digraphs **ch, sh,** and **tch** or the consonant blends **cl** and **nk**.

Imagine a clock with a bright, round face that shows the numbers 1 through 12. A small hand points to the three, and a big hand points to the dot just past the three. This is an *analog* clock. Now imagine a *digital* clock. It shows the same time, 3:16, in numerals. Which kind of clock do you think is better?

A digital clock is easy to read. You don't have to look at any clock hands. You see these clocks on cell phones, watches, and many other devices.

An analog clock helps you understand how much time passes. Say, for example, that it is 3:16 and you are going to see a movie at 3:30. On an analog clock you can see that you have less than a quarter of an hour to get ready. You don't have to do any math in your head.

Each kind of clock is useful—and both will help you get to school on time!

Follow the directions. Write each word only once.
Write the words that have five or more letters and contain:

1–5. a consonant digraph **ch, sh, tch,** or **ng**.
6–8. a consonant blend **br, cl,** or **nk**.

TEKS 3.24A Use knowledge of letter sounds, word parts, word segmentation, and syllabication to spell.
3.24Bv Spell words with more advanced orthographic patterns and rules: complex consonants.
3.24C Spell high-frequency and compound words from a commonly used list.

Connections to THINKING

Read the spelling words and sentences.

1.	afraid	*afraid*	Is Cindy **afraid** of that big dog?
2.	around	*around*	Let's run **around** the block.
3.	upon	*upon*	We looked **upon** a strange sight.
4.	never	*never*	You should **never** call people names.
5.	open	*open*	May I **open** my presents now?
6.	animal	*animal*	The **animal** has four legs and a tail.
7.	ever	*ever*	Will we **ever** get there?
8.	about	*about*	This book is **about** a hidden cave.
9.	again	*again*	We will visit Grandpa **again** tonight.
10.	another	*another*	Take **another** look at what you wrote.
11.	couple	*couple*	That **couple** has three children.
12.	awake	*awake*	Are you **awake** at seven o'clock?
13.	over	*over*	I climbed **over** the tall fence.
14.	asleep	*asleep*	My dog is **asleep** on his bed.
15.	above	*above*	The light switch is **above** the desk.

Think & Sort the spelling words.

Write the words that have

1–2. two **schwa** sounds.

3–9. one **schwa** sound spelled **a.**

10–14. one **schwa** sound spelled **e.**

15. one **schwa** sound spelled **u.**

Remember

The **schwa** sound can be spelled **a** as in **about, u** as in **upon,** and **e** as in **over.**

TEKS 3.24A Use knowledge of letter sounds, word parts, word segmentation, and syllabication to spell. **3.24Bvi** Spell words with more advanced orthographic patterns and rules: abstract vowels. **3.24C** Spell high-frequency and compound words from a commonly used list.

Connections to PHONICS

Identify Schwa Spellings

Each syllable in a word has just one vowel sound. The **schwa** sound only occurs in unstressed syllables and can be spelled by different vowels. Add the missing **schwa** spelling to complete a syllable and write a spelling word.

1. __ • pon
2. ev • __r
3. __ • bove
4. __ • noth • __r
5. nev • __r
6. __ • wake
7. o • v__r

Analyze Abstract Vowels

8–12. Write the spelling words that have vowel sounds that are spelled with two letters. Circle the **schwa** spelling, and underline the letters that spell the vowel sound in the stressed syllable.

Use the Dictionary

Look at these dictionary respellings. Say each word. Then write the spelling word for each respelling. Use the pronunciation guide in your **Spelling Dictionary** and check the spelling in the dictionary. Notice that the pronunciation symbol for **schwa** looks like an upside-down **e** (ə).

13. /kŭp′ əl/   **14.** /ăn′ ə məl/   **15.** /ō′ pən/

 TEKS 3.24A Use knowledge of letter sounds, word parts, word segmentation, and syllabication to spell. **3.24Bvi** Spell words with more advanced orthographic patterns and rules: abstract vowels. **3.24C** Spell high-frequency and compound words from a commonly used list. **3.24D** Spell words with common syllable constructions.

Connections to READING

afraid	around	upon	never	open
animal	ever	about	again	another
couple	awake	over	asleep	above

Complete the Proverbs

A proverb is a saying that has a special meaning and is used often. Write the spelling word that completes each proverb.

1. If at first you don't succeed, try, try _____.
2. It's _____ too late to learn.
3. Rain, rain, go away. Come again _____ day.
4. Opportunity is waiting, but you need to _____ the door.
5. Don't cry _____ spilled milk.

Complete the Analogies

6. **Student** is to **school** as _____ is to **farm**.
7. **Under** is to **below** as **over** is to _____.
8. **Interested** is to **bored** as **asleep** is to _____.

Use Context Clues

Write spelling words to complete the story.

Once **9.** a time, there was a silly girl who had fallen **10.** on someone's bed. As she slept, she had a strange dream **11.** a little house and oatmeal and chairs. The girl was enjoying her dream, but she woke up and saw a **12.** of bears looking at her. She was so **13.** that she jumped up, ran **14.** the corner, down the stairs, and out of the house. Don't worry! The little girl lived happily **15.** after!

 TEKS 3.24C Spell high-frequency and compound words from a commonly used list.

Connections to WRITING

Proofread an E-Mail Message

Proofread the e-mail message below for eight misspelled words. Then rewrite the message. Write the spelling words correctly and make the corrections shown by the proofreading marks.

Proofreading Marks

≡	Capital Letter
/	Small Letter
∧	Add
℮	Delete
⊙	Add a Period
⌗	Indent

Send   Save as a Draft   Cancel   Attach Files

To: SteinJ@mail.net.com

From: Joshboy27@kids.net

Subject: My Baseball Team

Dear Uncle Jake∧

I had anuther great year in baseball. The regular Season is ovr. My team is in the playoffs agin in a cupple of weeks. My Team nevur, evur gives up. See you at Lum Field uround noon. after the game, I will tell you abowt our season⊙

Your nephew,

josh

EXPOSITORY Writing Prompt
Write an E-Mail Message

Invite a couple of friends to come over to your house. Include the day and time. Use as many spelling words as you can.

- Use the writing process: prewrite, draft, revise, edit, and publish.
- Be sure to describe what you would like to play.
- Use complete sentences with correct capitalization, punctuation, grammar, and spelling.
- Read your work. Circle three words you are unsure about, and check their spellings in a dictionary.

Transfer

Think of three new words with the **schwa** sound spelled **a** as in **about, u** as in **upon,** or **e** as in **over**. Check the phonetic spelling in a dictionary to make sure the spelling includes the **schwa** symbol, ə. Then write the words in your Spelling Journal and circle the letter that makes the **schwa** sound.

 TEKS 3.24A Use knowledge of letter sounds, word parts, word segmentation, and syllabication to spell. **3.24Bvi** Spell words with more advanced orthographic patterns and rules: abstract vowels. **3.24C** Spell high-frequency and compound words from a commonly used list. **3.24G** Use print and electronic resources to find and check correct spellings.

model	open	afraid	above	banana
planted	animal	upon	agree	gorilla
seven	about	ever	alarm	odor
wagon	again	couple	tractor	several
around	another	awake	water	
never	over	asleep	award	

Pattern Power

Use words from the list to complete these exercises.

1–4. Write **ee** or **ai** to complete these words.

ag __ __ n   afr __ __ d

asl __ __ p   agr __ __

5–6. Write two words with the spelling pattern __ p __ n. Circle the vowel that makes the **schwa** sound.

7–8. Write two words with the spelling pattern __ v __ r. Circle the vowel that makes the **schwa** sound.

9–10. Write two words that end with the spelling pattern **vowel-consonant-e**. Circle the vowel that makes the **schwa** sound.

Syllables

11–15. Write the three-syllable words, and circle the letter or letters that spell the **schwa** sound in each word.

TEKS 3.24A Use knowledge of letter sounds, word parts, word segmentation, and syllabication to spell. **3.24Bvi** Spell words with more advanced orthographic patterns and rules: abstract vowels. **3.24C** Spell high-frequency and compound words from a commonly used list. **3.24D** Spell words with common syllable constructions.

Fine Arts

Word Hunt

Read the paragraphs below. Look for words with the **schwa** sound spelled with **a** as in **about, u** as in **upon**, and **e** as in **never**.

Think of a fairy tale, such as "Little Red Riding Hood." Do you know it well enough to tell it to someone else? If you do, you can put on a puppet show!

Puppet shows are fun if you like to write, make craft projects, or perform. To start, find a fairy tale in a book. Make a list of the main characters and then write a script. A script shows the speaking lines for all of the characters. Start a new line for each new speaker.

Next, make your puppets. Get a supply of paper bags. You can decorate them with buttons, crayons, yarn, and things from around the house. Make a stage. Find a quiet place to practice your lines. Say them over and over and be sure to speak clearly. You are ready to perform your show in front of an audience!

Follow the directions. Write each word only once.

1. Write the word with the **schwa** sound spelled **u**.
2. Write the word with two **schwa** sounds, one spelled **a** and one spelled **e**.
3. Write the word with the **schwa** sound spelled **a**.
4–8. Write the words with the **schwa** sound spelled **e**.

TEKS 3.24A Use knowledge of letter sounds, word parts, word segmentation, and syllabication to spell.
3.24Bvi Spell words with more advanced orthographic patterns and rules: abstract vowels.
3.24C Spell high-frequency and compound words from a commonly used list.

113

Connections to THINKING

Read the spelling words and sentences.

1. friend	*friend*	I play with my **friend,** Jonathan.
2. very	*very*	That is a **very** tall building.
3. people	*people*	Many **people** wait in line for tickets.
4. your	*your*	I will give you **your** present.
5. after	*after*	We have gym **after** lunch.
6. busy	*busy*	The **busy** woman worked two jobs.
7. other	*other*	What **other** books have you read?
8. were	*were*	We **were** sleeping when Abe visited.
9. should	*should*	You **should** take off your hat in school.
10. once	*once*	I will ask you this just **once.**
11. would	*would*	She asked if I **would** sing to her.
12. sure	*sure*	Are you **sure** you forgot the key?
13. little	*little*	The **little** boy cried for his mom.
14. every	*every*	Ted ate **every** bite of his dinner.
15. could	*could*	We **could** ride our bikes to the park.

Think & Sort the spelling words.

1–8. Write the words with one syllable.

9–15. Write the words with two syllables.

Remember

It is important to correctly spell words that you use often in your writing.

 TEKS 3.24A Use knowledge of letter sounds, word parts, word segmentation, and syllabication to spell.
3.24C Spell high-frequency and compound words from a commonly used list.

Connections to PHONICS

Use Sound and Letter Patterns

Write the spelling word for each clue.

1. This word is inside **another**.
2. It has the /**sh**/ sound and ends with a vowel.
3. In this word, the letters **ie** spell the **short e** sound.
4. It begins with **sh** and rhymes with **could**.
5. It has the /**k**/ sound but no letter **k**.
6. It sounds the same as the word **wood**.
7. It has two syllables. Both begin with the same consonant.

Word Building

Write the spelling word for each clue.

8. Add **e** to **very** to make this word.
9. Change the vowel in **vary** to make this word.
10. Change the last two letters in **litter** to make this word.
11. Add a consonant to **one** to make this word.
12. Take a letter away from **yours** to make this word.
13. Take a letter away from **where** to make this word.

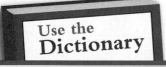

Use the
Dictionary

Write the spelling word that would be on the same page as these guide words.

14. about • alive   15. bunny • caterpillar

Dictionary Check Be sure to check your answers in your **Spelling Dictionary**.

TEKS 3.24A Use knowledge of letter sounds, word parts, word segmentation, and syllabication to spell. **3.24Bv** Spell words with more advanced orthographic patterns and rules: complex consonants. **3.24Bvi** Spell words with more advanced orthographic patterns and rules: abstract vowels. **3.24C** Spell high-frequency and compound words from a commonly used list.

friend	very	people	your	after
busy	other	were	should	once
would	sure	little	every	could

Use Synonyms

Replace the underlined part of each sentence with a synonym that is a spelling word.

1. Heather was <u>certain</u> that she had won.

2. Rico is <u>quite</u> proud of his garden.

3. I only had to give the speech <u>one time</u>.

4. John is a <u>pal</u> of mine.

5. He knocked on <u>each</u> door.

6. That <u>small</u> dog has a big bark!

7. We will eat dessert <u>following</u> dinner.

Use Context Clues

Write the spelling words that complete the paragraph so that it makes sense.

You **8.** read about Clara Barton in **9.** history books. During her lifetime, Clara Barton was a **10.** woman. She was a teacher, a nurse, and the founder of the American Red Cross. During the Civil War, she **11.** go out on the battlefield while soldiers **12.** still shooting at each **13.**. Even after the war ended, she knew she **14.** do more to help **15.**. That is when she started the American Red Cross.

 TEKS 3.24C Spell high-frequency and compound words from a commonly used list.

Proofread a Personal Narrative

Proofread the personal narrative below for eight misspelled words. Then rewrite the narrative. Write the spelling words correctly and make the corrections shown by the proofreading marks.

¶ I went to my frend Adi's house affter school to play with his model cars. He has about 100 litle cars. Most ware given to him by his Parents. There is one for evry kind of car, from ~~from~~ race cars to jeeps. We were so bizy playing I was surprised when it was 5:00. I wuld like adi to come to my house next time. We shure have fun together.

Proofreading Marks

≡	Capital Letter
/	Small Letter
∧	Add
ℓ	Delete
⊙	Add a Period
¶	Indent

NARRATIVE Writing Prompt
Write a Personal Narrative

Think of something fun you did with a friend. Write a paragraph telling what you did together. Use as many spelling words as you can.

- Use the writing process: prewrite, draft, revise, edit, and publish.
- Explain what made the event fun.
- What made your experience important or memorable?
- Use complete sentences with correct capitalization, punctuation, grammar, and spelling.
- Key your narrative in a word-processing program. Use the spell-check feature to check your spelling.

Transfer

Think of four more words that have four or more letters that writers use often. Write the words in your Spelling Journal. Then write a sentence using each word.

TEKS 3.24C Spell high-frequency and compound words from a commonly used list. **3.24G** Use print and electronic resources to find and check correct spellings.

Word Study

any	other	very	every	poor
does	were	your	between	secret
myself	once	after	either	sugar
said	would	busy	however	yourself
friend	little	should	though	
people	could	sure	o'clock	

Meaning Mastery

Write the spelling word that is part of each contraction.

1. should've: _____ + have
3. could've: _____ + have
2. wouldn't: _____ + not
4. doesn't: _____ + not

Pattern Power

5. Write a word from the list with double consonants in the middle of the word.

6–8. Write the compound words from the list.

9–10. Add **e** to a spelling word to make a new spelling word. Write both words.

Word Building

Add vowels to complete the spelling words. One of the missing vowels will always be an **o**.

11. p __ __ pl __
14. __ nc __
12. y __ __ r
15. p __ __ r
13. __ th __ r

 **TEKS 3.24A** Use knowledge of letter sounds, word parts, word segmentation, and syllabication to spell.
3.24Biv Spell words with more advanced orthographic patterns and rules: double consonants in middle of words. **3.24Bvi** Spell words with more advanced orthographic patterns and rules: abstract vowels.
3.24C Spell high-frequency and compound words from a commonly used list.

Technology

WordHunt

Read the paragraphs below. Look for spelling words from the list on page 118.

Think about how you use a search engine to do research. Do you type in every key word? You may find some helpful websites that way. However, there are other ways to make your Internet search more exact.

Imagine you are interested in getting a rescue dog. You want one that is part border collie. You are not sure what other breed the dog should be.

You decide to research dogs that are part border collie and part Labrador retriever. To search for these, you should use a plus sign between key words. You would type: "rescue dogs border collie mix + lab."

What if you do not want a border collie mix that is part lab? Put a minus sign directly before the word, like this: "border collie mix -lab." You can find the perfect dog by making your Internet search more exact!

Use the list on page 118 to complete the following exercises. Write each word only once.

1–4. Write words used in the story that have one syllable.

5–8. Write words used in the story that have two or more syllables.

 TEKS 3.24A Use knowledge of letter sounds, word parts, word segmentation, and syllabication to spell.
3.24C Spell high-frequency and compound words from a commonly used list.

Units 13–17

Assessment

Write each assessment word under the unit number it fits.

Unit 13

1–5. Two or more consonants can spell a single sound: **wr** as in **wrap** and **ck** as in **thick**. Other examples of complex consonants are **ch** as in **chase, sh** as in **shape, th** as in **thick,** and **tch** as in **watch**.

Unit 14

6–9. The /j/ in **age** is spelled **g**. The /s/ in **ice** and **city** is spelled **c**.

Unit 15

10–12. Consonant digraphs are two or more consonants that work together to make one new sound: **sh** as in **shook**. **Consonant blends** are two or more consonants that make more than one sound when they are used together: **br** as in **brook**.

Unit 16

13–15. The **schwa** sound can be spelled **a** as in **about, u** as in **upon,** and **e** as in **over**.

Unit 17

It is important to correctly spell words that you use often in your writing.

Words for Assessment

blush

charm

cage

wren

await

gem

stung

siren

pitch

brace

stack

flood

aside

patch

rage

Unit 13: ch, sh, tch, th, wr, ck

father	finish	mother	write
shall	watch	check	

Remove two- or three-letter consonant blends from each word below and replace with one of the patterns from the unit to make a spelling word.

1. faster
2. trite
3. speck
4. stall

Unscramble the letters to make a spelling word. Make sure each word includes one of the unit patterns. Circle the pattern you used.

5. ehmort
6. fishin
7. chawt

Unit 14: Complex Consonants: Soft g, Soft c

change	place	large	since
dance	age	city	

8–11. Write the words that have the **soft c** sound.
12–14. Write the words that have the **soft g** sound.

Review

Unit 15: Digraphs, Blends

splash	strong	stretch	think
	speech	cloth	shook

Write the spelling word that rhymes with the underlined word and completes the sentence.

1. After a <u>dash</u>, I made a _____.
2. This stick is <u>long</u> and very _____.
3. I _____ I will throw this in the <u>sink</u>.
4. He <u>took</u> the jar and _____ out the beans.
5. The speaker's _____ sounded like a <u>screech</u>!
6. She got up to _____ after she finished her <u>sketch</u>.
7. Oh, no! There's a <u>moth</u> in the _____.

Unit 16: The Schwa Sound

again	another	animal	around
	about	open	never

Each spelling word is missing one or more letters. Write each spelling word.

8. __gain
9. an__m__l
10. __round
11. __bout

Write a spelling word for each of these clues.

12. It has two syllables. The first syllable is the **long o** sound.
13. The letter **e** is found in both syllables.
14. The words **not, the,** and **her** can be found in this word.

Unit 17: Words Writers Use

friend	people	once	would
other	were	could	

Write the spelling word that completes each sentence.

1. The girls _____ like to go.
2. Many _____ waited for the bus.
3. That person is my good _____.
4. She was sure that she _____ do it.
5. Bring me the _____ book, not that one.
6. Where _____ you going yesterday?
7. Many stories begin with "_____ upon a time."

Spelling Study Strategy

Spelling Tic-Tac-Toe

Practicing spelling words can be fun if you make it into a game.

1. Write your spelling words in a list. Ask your friend to do the same. Trade spelling lists.

2. Draw a tic-tac-toe board on a scrap of paper. Decide who will use **X** and who will use **O**.

3. Ask your partner to read the first word on your spelling list to you. Spell it out loud. If you spell it correctly, make an **X** or an **O** on the tic-tac-toe board. If you misspell it, you miss your turn. Ask your partner to spell the word for you.

4. Now call a word from your partner's list. Play until one of you makes three in a row.

Standardized Test Practice

Directions: Read the introduction and the passage that follows. Then read each question and fill in the space in front of the correct answer on your answer sheet.

Nina wrote this story about giving her first speech. She chose Eleanor Roosevelt as her topic and found a new hero. She wants you to review her paper. As you read, think about ways that Nina can improve her story.

Thank You, Mrs. Roosevelt

(1) Last week I had to give a speetch in class. (2) I felt very ufraid. (3) I wrote my speech about Eleanor Roosevelt. (4) Before she became First Lady in 1933, she also was afraid to speak to larje groups. (5) She became good at it, though. (6) She talked to peeple all around the country about her ideas to solve problems.

(7) After I finished writing my talk, I practiced it in front of my father. (8) I asked him to watch me closely and chek that my words were clear. (9) He said I should chanje some words and give a few other details about Mrs. Roosevelt. (10) I made some changes and practiced the speech again for my muther. (11) She said I did well.

(12) I thought I was in good shape, but my hands schook as I got up to speak. (13) As I gave my speech about Mrs. Roosevelt, though, I began to feel strong. (14) I talked about how many people were poor then, and how Mrs. Roosevelt would work so hard to help them.

(15) I guess my speech was good. (16) No one fell asleep! (17) If I cood, I would say, "Thank you, Mrs. Roosevelt, for helping me, too."

GO ON

1 What change, if any, should be made in sentence 1?

- ⬭ Change *week* to **weak**
- ⬭ Change *speetch* to **speech**
- ⬭ Change *class* to **clas**
- ⬭ Make no change

2 What change, if any, should be made in sentence 2?

- ⬭ Change *felt* to **fell**
- ⬭ Change *very* to **verry**
- ⬭ Change *ufraid* to **afraid**
- ⬭ Make no change

3 What change, if any, should be made in sentence 4?

- ⬭ Change *Before* to **Befor**
- ⬭ Change *larje* to **large**
- ⬭ Change *groups* to **groops**
- ⬭ Make no change

4 What change, if any, should be made in sentence 6?

- ⬭ Change *peeple* to **people**
- ⬭ Change *around* to **arond**
- ⬭ Change *about* to **abowt**
- ⬭ Make no change

5 What change, if any, should be made in sentence 8?

- ⬭ Change *watch* to **wach**
- ⬭ Change *chek* to **check**
- ⬭ Change *clear* to **cleer**
- ⬭ Make no change

6 What change, if any, should be made in sentence 9?

- ⬭ Change *should* to **shuld**
- ⬭ Change *chanje* to **change**
- ⬭ Change *other* to **uther**
- ⬭ Make no change

7 What change, if any, should be made in sentence 10?

- ⬭ Change *changes* to **changs**
- ⬭ Change *again* to **agin**
- ⬭ Change *muther* to **mother**
- ⬭ Make no change

8 What change, if any, should be made in sentence 12?

- ⬭ Change *shape* to **schape**
- ⬭ Change *schook* to **shook**
- ⬭ Change *speak* to **speek**
- ⬭ Make no change

9 What change, if any, should be made in sentence 14?

- ⬭ Change *people* to **peeple**
- ⬭ Change *poor* to **por**
- ⬭ Change *would* to **wuld**
- ⬭ Make no change

10 What change, if any, should be made in sentence 17?

- ⬭ Change *cood* to **could**
- ⬭ Change *would* to **wood**
- ⬭ Change *Thank* to **Tank**
- ⬭ Make no change

Grammar, Usage, and Mechanics
Action Verbs

An **action verb** tells what the subject of a sentence does or did.

> They **drill** for oil here.
> The dog **barked** at the men.
> The whistle **blows** at noon.

Practice Activity

A. Write the action verb in these sentences.

1. He will finish the book today.
2. Rani shook salt over her chicken.
3. Please watch the show with me.
4. The ducks splash in the water.
5. The girls dance in their class.

B. Write an action verb from the box to complete each sentence.

check	write	think	open	change

6. I will _____ Aunt Molly a letter.
7. Please _____ that the water is turned off.
8. It is time to _____ the sheets on the bed.
9. Ben and I can _____ the door for you.
10. The children _____ the play is funny.

TEKS 3.24C Spell high-frequency and compound words from a commonly used list.

The Writing Process: Descriptive
Writing a Descriptive Paragraph

PREWRITING

Choose a country you would like to visit. Write down words and phrases that describe things you could see, hear, taste, touch, or smell in this place. You can find facts about new places in books at the library. An adult can help you learn about other countries on the Internet.

DRAFTING

Use your list to write a descriptive paragraph. Describe the place using the five senses. Use as many spelling words as you can.

REVISING

When you have finished your first draft, read your paragraph from beginning to end. Check to make sure that you included many describing words. Now write your final draft.

EDITING

Use the **Editing Checklist** to proofread your paragraph. Be sure to use proofreading marks when you make corrections. Circle at least two words that may be misspelled. Use a dictionary or electronic resource to check the spelling.

PUBLISHING

Write or print a final copy of your descriptive paragraph. Include a drawing or map of the place you wrote about and share it with your classmates.

EDITING CHECKLIST

Spelling

- ✓ Circle words that contain the spelling patterns and rules learned in Units 13–17.
- ✓ Check the circled words in your **Spelling Dictionary**.
- ✓ Check for other spelling errors.

Capital Letters

- ✓ Capitalize important words in the title.
- ✓ Capitalize the first word in each sentence.
- ✓ Capitalize proper nouns.

Punctuation

- ✓ End each sentence with the correct punctuation.
- ✓ Use commas, apostrophes, and quotation marks correctly.

Grammar, Usage, and Mechanics

- ✓ Make sure each action verb tells what the subject of a sentence does or did.

TEKS 3.24A Use knowledge of letter sounds, word parts, word segmentation, and syllabication to spell.
3.24G Use print and electronic resources to find and check correct spellings.

127

Connections to THINKING

Read the spelling words and sentences.

1. draw	*draw*	I **draw** pictures of my dog.
2. cost	*cost*	The **cost** of that hat is five dollars.
3. dawn	*dawn*	It is dark and chilly at **dawn**.
4. across	*across*	Aaron lives **across** the street.
5. belong	*belong*	Do you **belong** to that club?
6. cross	*cross*	Be careful when you **cross** the street.
7. soft	*soft*	This pillow is very **soft**.
8. crawl	*crawl*	The baby is learning to **crawl**.
9. song	*song*	We will sing a **song** together.
10. boss	*boss*	The **boss** hired her for the new job.
11. straw	*straw*	Sip your drink through this **straw**.
12. lawn	*lawn*	That **lawn** is thick and green.
13. raw	*raw*	Never eat **raw** meat or eggs.
14. lost	*lost*	We **lost** the ball in the woods.
15. law	*law*	Everyone must obey the **law**.

Think & Sort the spelling words.

Write the words that have:

   1–7. /ô/ spelled **aw**.

   8–15. /ô/ spelled **o**.

Remember

The vowel sound in **song** and **lawn** can be spelled in different ways: **o** as in **song** and **aw** as in **lawn**. The pattern **aw** is sometimes called an abstract vowel.

 TEKS 3.24A Use knowledge of letter sounds, word parts, word segmentation, and syllabication to spell. **3.24Bvi** Spell words with more advanced orthographic patterns and rules: abstract vowels. **3.24C** Spell high-frequency and compound words from a commonly used list.

Identify Word Structure

Change the vowel sound in each word below and write a spelling word. You may need to change more than one letter.

1. sang
2. ray
3. base
4-5. Write the two spelling words that have two syllables. Underline the syllable that has the /ô/ sound.

Analyze Vowel Sounds

Look at each pair of words. Write the word that has /ô/ as in **wrong** or **fawn**. Check pronunciations and spellings in a dictionary if you are unsure.

6. crows   cross
7. crawl   cruel
8. straw   stroll

9. low   law
10. lawn   loan
11. lost   look

Use the **Thesaurus**

Write a spelling word that is a synonym for each of these words. Check your answers in the **Writing Thesaurus**.

12. sunrise
13. gentle
14. sketch
15. amount

TEKS 3.24A Use knowledge of letter sounds, word parts, word segmentation, and syllabication to spell. **3.24Bvi** Spell words with more advanced orthographic patterns and rules: abstract vowels. **3.24C** Spell high-frequency and compound words from a commonly used list.

129

draw	cost	dawn	across	belong
cross	soft	crawl	song	boss
straw	lawn	raw	lost	law

Use Analogies

Write the spelling word that completes each analogy.

1. **Read** is to **story** as **sing** is to _____.
2. **Student** is to **teacher** as **worker** is to _____.
3. **Dot** is to **i** as _____ is to **t**.
4. **Follow** is to **rule** as **obey** is to _____.

Use Antonyms

Replace the underlined word in each sentence with an antonym that is a spelling word.

5. The pillow was not <u>hard</u> enough.
6. Jacob didn't use a map and <u>found</u> his way.
7. I get up at <u>sunset</u> to jog on the beach.

Use Context Clues

Write the spelling word that completes each sentence.

8. It is not easy to _____ a map.
9. My horse likes to eat _____ carrots.
10. I saw a scarecrow made of _____.
11. A smile spread _____ his face.
12. Does that scarf _____ to you?
13. Caterpillars _____ very slowly.
14. How much did that flashlight _____?
15. It is Dana's job to mow the _____.

 TEKS 3.24C Spell high-frequency and compound words from a commonly used list.

Connections to WRITING

Proofread a Book Report

Proofread the book report below for eight misspelled words. Then rewrite the book report. Write the spelling words correctly and make the corrections shown by the proofreading marks.

¶ You should read <u>Arthur's Pet Business</u>. It is by Marc Brown. I wish I could drow like Mr. Brown. In this book, Arthur wants to get a job⊙Instead of mowing someone's lon or babysitting, Arthur becomes his own bos. He watches pets that blong to other people. He tells them what it will cawst and they pay him. One pet gets lawst. arthur has to croll around looking for it. He finds the Pet. He also finds something new and sof! This book is fun to read.

Proofreading Marks

≡	Capital Letter
/	Small Letter
∧	Add
ℒ	Delete
⊙	Add a Period
¶	Indent

PERSUASIVE Writing Prompt
Write a Book Report

Think of a book you enjoyed. Write a book report explaining why other people would like it, too. Use as many spelling words as you can.

- Use the writing process: prewrite, draft, revise, edit, and publish.
- Be sure to include the title and underline it. Tell the author's name and one or more reasons to read the book.
- Use complete sentences with correct capitalization, punctuation, grammar, and spelling.
- Read your work. Circle three words you are unsure about and check their spellings in a dictionary.

Transfer

Think of three more words with the vowel sound /ô/ spelled **o** or **aw** that you might use in a book report. Then write the words in your Spelling Journal and circle the letters that spell /ô/.

TEKS 3.24A Use knowledge of letter sounds, word parts, word segmentation, and syllabication to spell. **3.24Bvi** Spell words with more advanced orthographic patterns and rules: abstract vowels. **3.24C** Spell high-frequency and compound words from a commonly used list. **3.24G** Use print and electronic resources to find and check correct spellings.

dog	belong	cost	raw	drawer
jaw	soft	dawn	because	jigsaw
moth	song	cross	bought	mossy
saw	straw	crawl	caught	yawning
draw	lost	boss	haul	
across	law	lawn	defrost	

Pattern Power

Write the one-syllable words that:

1–6. end with a vowel sound.

7–8. end with /ôn/ as in **drawn**.

9. end with /ông/ as in **long**.

10–11. end with /ôs/ as in **floss**.

Open and Closed Syllables

Remember that an open syllable ends with a vowel sound. A closed syllable ends with a consonant sound. Write each word below and draw a slash between the syllables. Is the first syllable open or closed? Write O for open or C for closed next to each word. Check your answers in your **Spelling Dictionary**.

12. across

13. drawer

14. mossy

15. jigsaw

TEKS 3.24A Use knowledge of letter sounds, word parts, word segmentation, and syllabication to spell. **3.24Bvi** Spell words with more advanced orthographic patterns and rules: abstract vowels. **3.24C** Spell high-frequency and compound words from a commonly used list. **3.24D** Spell words with common syllable constructions.

Science

Word Hunt

Read the paragraphs below. Look for words that have /ô/ spelled **aw** and **o**.

Do you know anyone who ever saw a pink moth? Biologist Bruce Walsh has seen one! Walsh teaches at a university in Arizona. But he doesn't collect moths in an office or a classroom. He collects them in the mountains.

One night, Walsh was collecting moths in Arizona. He lit up a cloth with a bright light, and a pink-winged moth landed on it. Walsh had often seen moths with a bit of pink color. But this moth seemed to belong to a different moth family. When Walsh studied it, his jaw dropped. It was a brand-new kind of moth!

Some moths hibernate when there is frost on the ground. Walsh thought this moth had been hibernating. He named the new moth "Leeae," after his wife, Lee, who likes the color pink.

WORD SORT

Follow the directions. Write each word only once. Check pronunciations in a dictionary.

1–2. Write words that have /ô/ spelled **aw**.

3–8. Write words that have /ô/ spelled **o**.

 TEKS 3.24A Use knowledge of letter sounds, word parts, word segmentation, and syllabication to spell. **3.24Bvi** Spell words with more advanced orthographic patterns and rules: abstract vowels. **3.24C** Spell high-frequency and compound words from a commonly used list.

Connections to THINKING

Read the spelling words and sentences.

1. story   *story*   Please read me that **story**.
2. wore   *wore*   Jen **wore** a red dress to the party.
3. north   *north*   We will head **north** to Canada.
4. board   *board*   That **board** in the floor is loose.
5. form   *form*   You can **form** the clay into any shape.
6. corner   *corner*   Turn left at the next **corner**.
7. warm   *warm*   You can **warm** up by the fire.
8. score   *score*   What was the final **score**?
9. morning   *morning*   Dad gets up early each **morning**.
10. forget   *forget*   I will not **forget** to drink my milk.
11. before   *before*   We brush our teeth **before** bed.
12. storm   *storm*   The noise of the **storm** scared Spot.
13. tore   *tore*   Matt **tore** his new pants in the game.
14. order   *order*   My **order** was for a hamburger.
15. war   *war*   We fight the **war** against pollution.

Think & Sort the spelling words.

Write the words that have:

1–4. /ôr/ spelled **ore**.   13–14. /ôr/ spelled **ar**.

5–12. /ôr/ spelled **or**.   15. /ôr/ spelled **oar**.

Remember

The vowel sound in **form** can be spelled in different ways: **or** as in **form**, **ore** as in **tore**, **oar** as in **board**, and **ar** in **warm**.

 TEKS 3.24A Use knowledge of letter sounds, word parts, word segmentation, and syllabication to spell.
3.24C Spell high-frequency and compound words from a commonly used list.

Use Sound and Letter Patterns

Identify the missing letters that spell /ôr/. Write the spelling word.

1. b __ __ __ d
2. m __ __ ning
3. bef __ __ __
4. w __ __
5. __ __ der

6. f __ __ m
7. w __ __ m
8. st __ __ y
9. f __ __ get
10. c __ __ ner

Segment Words

Write a spelling word for each set of letter sounds.

11. It begins like **wax** and ends like **sore**.
12. It begins like **stare** and ends like **form**.
13. It begins like **new** and ends like **forth**.
14. It begins like **top** and ends like **core**.
15. It begins like **scare** and ends like **bore**.

Use the Dictionary

The dictionary lists the part of speech after the respelling for each entry word.

cor • ner /**kôr'**nər/ *n.*

Find the part of speech for each spelling word in your **Spelling Dictionary**. Write its abbreviation next to each word on the list you made for the activity above. If a word has more than one entry, write all parts of speech for that word.

TEKS 3.24A Use knowledge of letter sounds, word parts, word segmentation, and syllabication to spell.
3.24C Spell high-frequency and compound words from a commonly used list.

135

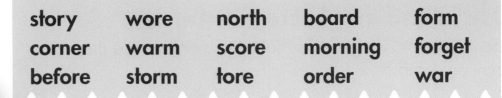

story	wore	north	board	form
corner	warm	score	morning	forget
before	storm	tore	order	war

Categorize Words

Use the clues below and information you already know to figure out the missing spelling word.

1. game, points, win: _____

2. dawn, wake up, breakfast: _____

3. book, fairy tale, read: _____

4. square, intersection, bus stop: _____

Use Context Clues

Write the spelling word that completes each sentence.

5. Kevin _____ a blue sweater to school today.

6. Julie _____ her jacket on the fence at recess.

7. May we have this _____ to finish building our tree house?

8. The boat was damaged during the _____.

9. Icicles will _____ when dripping water freezes in the cold weather.

10. Ed did not _____ to put a stamp on the letter.

11. I will give you the book _____ you go.

12. Ryan plays tennis in _____ weather.

13. The train tracks are _____ of our house.

14. Orange juice and eggs is my _____ for breakfast at Joe's Restaurant.

15. My grandfather fought in that _____.

 TEKS 3.24C Spell high-frequency and compound words from a commonly used list.

Connections to WRITING

Proofread a Story Beginning

Proofread the paragraph below for eight misspelled words. Then rewrite the paragraph. Write the spelling words correctly and make the corrections shown by the proofreading marks.

The Case of the Missing Cat

It was late morening when Marisol and Pedro began to search for the missing cat. they woar warm clothes because dark storme clouds were beginning to foarm. They headed noarth. As they they turned the corener onto Main Street, they saw a woman running down the street. She tripped and tor her sleeve, and a cat's jeweled collar fell out of her pocket. Befur Marisol and pedro could say anything, the woman was gone.

NARRATIVE Writing Prompt
Write a Story

Finish the story about the missing cat that begins at the top of this page. Will Marisol and Pedro find the missing cat? What happens? Use as many spelling words as you can.

- Use the writing process: prewrite, draft, revise, edit, and publish.
- Build the story to a high point, or climax, that shows how the mystery is solved. Think about the characters and the setting and add details about them.
- Use complete sentences with correct capitalization, punctuation, grammar, and spelling.
- Key your story in a word-processing program. Use the spell-check feature to check your spelling.

Transfer

Think of four more words with /ôr/ spelled **ore, or, ar,** or **oar** that a writer might use in a mystery. Then write the words in your Spelling Journal and circle the letters that spell the /ôr/ sound.

TEKS 3.24A Use knowledge of letter sounds, word parts, word segmentation, and syllabication to spell. **3.24C** Spell high-frequency and compound words from a commonly used list. **3.24G** Use print and electronic resources to find and check correct spellings.

137

corn	form	wore	war	glory
horse	warm	north	forest	hoarse
more	morning	corner	forty	warn
short	forget	score	report	warp
story	before	storm	sport	
board	order	tore	boredom	

Homophones

Remember that homophones are words that sound the same but have different spellings and meanings.

1–4. Write the two sets of homophones from the list.

5–6. Write the homophones for **bored** and **worn**.

Use Syllables

7–10. Match two syllables from the box below to write a spelling word. Put a slash between syllables.

der	for	bore	port
est	or	dom	re

Adding Endings to Base Words

Write the spelling words that become new words when the endings are added.

11. _____ – y + ies = stories

12. _____ – y + ies = glories

13. _____ + ing = warming

14. _____ – e + ing = scoring

15. _____ + t + ing = forgetting

TEKS 3.24Bi Spell words with more advanced orthographic patterns and rules: consonant doubling when adding an ending. **3.244Bii** Spell words with more advanced orthographic patterns and rules: dropping final "e" when endings are added. **3.24Biii** Spell words with more advanced orthographic patterns and rules: changing y to i before adding an ending. **3.24C** Spell high-frequency and compound words from a commonly used list. **3.24D** Spell words with common syllable constructions. **3.24E** Spell single syllable homophones.

Social Studies

Word Hunt

Read the paragraphs below. Look for words that have /ôr/ spelled **ore, or, ar,** or **oar**.

In 1847, John Singer and his family were sailing off the Texas coast. A sudden storm blew up. Singer tried to get to shore. Before he could do that, the boat reached a deserted island. It was called Padre Island.

The family loved the island. They decided to live there. They used boards from their boat to build a house. One day, the Singer children found some coins on the beach. Centuries earlier, Spanish ships had sunk near the island. The tide washed the gold and silver ashore. The Singers found more and more coins! John Singer buried a fortune in treasure.

The Civil War came in 1861, and the family moved to the Texas mainland. They returned after the war ended. But Singer could not find the treasure. Today, about 150 years later, people are still looking for his fortune.

 **WORD SORT**

Follow the directions. Write each word only once.

1–4. Write words that have /ôr/ spelled **ore**.
5–6. Write words that have /ôr/ spelled **or**.
7. Write a word that has /ôr/ spelled **ar**.
8. Write a word that has /ôr/ spelled **oar**.

 TEKS 3.24A Use knowledge of letter sounds, word parts, word segmentation, and syllabication to spell.
3.24C Spell high-frequency and compound words from a commonly used list.

139

Connections to THINKING

Read the spelling words and sentences.

1. word	*word*	Be very quiet and do not say a **word**.
2. fur	*fur*	Maria brushed her puppy's soft **fur**.
3. early	*early*	We get up **early** to go to school.
4. circus	*circus*	Keiko saw clowns at the **circus**.
5. turn	*turn*	We took a left **turn** at the stop sign.
6. skirt	*skirt*	I wore my new **skirt** and sweater.
7. earth	*earth*	The **earth** was too wet for planting.
8. work	*work*	They **work** hard caring for the crops.
9. curl	*curl*	How do I **curl** my hair?
10. learn	*learn*	Dad will **learn** to use my computer.
11. hurt	*hurt*	The boy **hurt** his knee when he fell.
12. dirt	*dirt*	Bill digs in the **dirt** for worms.
13. earn	*earn*	The class will **earn** money.
14. shirt	*shirt*	Juan lost a button on his **shirt**.
15. heard	*heard*	Tyler **heard** his mother calling him.

Think & Sort the spelling words.

Write the words that have:

1–2. /ûr/ spelled **or**.   **7–11.** /ûr/ spelled **ear**.

3–6. /ûr/ spelled **ur**.   **12–15.** /ûr/ spelled **ir**.

Remember

The vowel sound in **fur** can be spelled in different ways:
ur as in **fur, ear** as in **earn, or** as in **word,** and **ir** as in **dirt.**

 TEKS 3.24A Use knowledge of letter sounds, word parts, word segmentation, and syllabication to spell. **3.24C** Spell high-frequency and compound words from a commonly used list.

Analyze Sound Spellings

Write the spelling words for these clues.

1–2. These two words rhyme with **fern** but have /ûr/ spelled **ear**.

3. This word rhymes with **pearl** but has /ûr/ spelled **ur**.

4. This word rhymes with **jerk** but has /ûr/ spelled **or**.

5. This word begins with /ûr/ and ends with **th**.

6. This word has two syllables. The first syllable begins with the /s/ sound spelled **c**.

Use Sound and Letter Patterns

Identify the missing letters that spell /ûr/ and write the spelling word.

7. __ __ __ ly   **9.** d __ __ t   **11.** t __ __ n

8. h __ __ t   **10.** h __ __ __ d

Use the Dictionary

The r-controlled vowel sound you hear in **turn** has the dictionary respelling /ûr/. Write the spelling word for each dictionary respelling.

12. /fûr/   **14.** /shûrt/

13. /skûrt/   **15.** /wûrd/

Dictionary Check Be sure to check your answers in your **Spelling Dictionary**.

TEKS 3.24A Use knowledge of letter sounds, word parts, word segmentation, and syllabication to spell. **3.24C** Spell high-frequency and compound words from a commonly used list. **3.24G** Use print and electronic resources to find and check correct spellings.

Connections to READING

word	fur	early	circus	turn
skirt	earth	work	curl	learn
hurt	dirt	earn	shirt	heard

Identify the Categories

The words below are smaller parts of something bigger.
Write the spelling word that names that bigger something.

1. consonants, vowels

2. buttons, collar, cuffs

3. zipper, hem, button

4. hills, plains, mountains, oceans

5. clowns, jugglers, elephants

Understand Meaning

Write the spelling word that fits each clue.

6. It means "harm."

7. It is something you can do to hair.

8. This is what you do in school.

Use Context Clues

Write spelling words to complete the story.

Do you know what I __9.__? The circus is coming to town!
I need to __10.__ some money to buy a ticket. Where can I
__11.__? Mr. Ozawa needs help with his garden. Maybe I
could help him __12.__ over the soil for planting. I could put
the extra __13.__ into flower pots. I would have to start __14.__
in the morning. It will be so cold, I will wish I had my
dog's __15.__ coat!

 TEKS 3.24C Spell high-frequency and compound words from a commonly used list.

Connections to WRITING

Proofread a Poster

Proofread the poster below for eight misspelled words. Then rewrite the poster. Write the spelling words correctly and make the corrections shown by the proofreading marks.

The Best Show on Erth

Have you hurd? The werd is out!

A circous will be held at Jefferson School on

saturday, March 2, at Noon.

You can lern more about it and buy your Tickets online.

Don't be sorry. Get your tickets urly. You can also urn

money if you werk at the show.

Proofreading Marks

≡	Capital Letter
/	Small Letter
∧	Add
ℓ	Delete
⊙	Add a Period
⌗	Indent

EXPOSITORY Writing Prompt
Write a Poster

Think of an event in your school or your town. Make a poster telling about the event. Include when and where it will happen. Use as many spelling words as you can.

- Use the writing process: prewrite, draft, revise, edit, and publish.
- Be sure to tell about what is going to happen at the event. Include a drawing.
- Use complete sentences with correct capitalization, punctuation, grammar, and spelling.
- Read your work. Circle three words you are unsure about and check their spellings in a print or online dictionary.

Transfer

Think of four more words with /ûr/ spelled **or, ur, ear,** or **ir** that a writer might use to describe an event. Then write the words in your Spelling Journal and circle the letters that spell the /ûr/ sound.

TEKS 3.24A Use knowledge of letter sounds, word parts, word segmentation, and syllabication to spell. **3.24C** Spell high-frequency and compound words from a commonly used list. **3.24G** Use print and electronic resources to find and check correct spellings.

143

birds	circus	fur	shirt	pearl
chirp	turn	skirt	firm	twirl
girls	work	earth	return	whirl
nurse	hurt	curl	thirst	worm
word	dirt	learn	turkey	
early	heard	earn	curve	

Use Homophones

Homophones are words that sound the same but have different spellings and meanings. Write a spelling word that is a homophone for each word below.

1. fir   **2.** urn   **3.** herd

Adding Endings to Base Words

Write the spelling words that become new words when the endings are added.

4. _____ – y + i + er = earlier
5. _____ + y = curly
6. _____ + ed = turned
7. _____ + s = turkeys

Word Building

Write **ur** or **ir** to complete the spelling word.

8. h __ __ t   **12.** sh __ __ t
9. d __ __ t   **13.** ret __ __ n
10. sk __ __ t   **14.** g __ __ ls
11. c __ __ ve   **15.** n __ __ se

TEKS 3.24A Use knowledge of letter sounds, word parts, word segmentation, and syllabication to spell. **3.24Biii** Spell words with more advanced orthographic patterns and rules: changing y to i before adding an ending. **3.24C** Spell high-frequency and compound words from a commonly used list. **3.24E** Spell single syllable homophones.

Math
Word Hunt

Read the paragraphs below. Look for words that have /ûr/ spelled **or**, **ur**, **ear**, or **ir**.

> The Tanaka family was having a garage sale. They woke up early in the day to put the items out on tables. It was hard work. Lily Tanaka and her big brother Jay spent the morning getting ready.
>
> Lily held up a box of toy cars priced at a quarter each. "There are ten cars in here," she said. "What if someone buys the whole box?"
>
> "You learned multiplication, didn't you?" Jay asked. "We would earn $2.50, which is ten times twenty-five cents."
>
> Soon they had their first customer. "My purpose is to complete a collection of toy cars for my son," he explained. The children pointed out the box of cars. "We've searched for these toy cars everywhere!" the man said. "Will it disturb you if I buy the whole box?"
>
> "Not at all," Lily said. With a wink at Jay, she added, "That will be $2.50, please."

WORD SORT

Follow the directions. Write each word only once.

1. Write a word that has /ûr/ spelled **or**.
2–3. Write words that have /ûr/ spelled **ur**.
4–7. Write words that have /ûr/ spelled **ear**.
8. Write a word that has /ûr/ spelled **ir**.

 TEKS 3.24A Use knowledge of letter sounds, word parts, word segmentation, and syllabication to spell. **3.24C** Spell high-frequency and compound words from a commonly used list.

Connections to THINKING

Read the spelling words and sentences.

1.	pear	*pear*	Eat the **pear** that is soft and ripe.
2.	pair	*pair*	I got a new **pair** of shoes.
3.	hare	*hare*	The fox chased the **hare** in the woods.
4.	barefoot	*barefoot*	I love to walk **barefoot** in the grass.
5.	fare	*fare*	Do you have change for your bus **fare**?
6.	their	*their*	They put the food in **their** packs.
7.	hair	*hair*	You should brush your **hair**.
8.	bare	*bare*	The wind felt cold on Ed's **bare** neck.
9.	nowhere	*nowhere*	My keys are **nowhere** in sight.
10.	there	*there*	Please place your marker **there**.
11.	software	*software*	The computer **software** was easy to learn.
12.	wear	*wear*	Which hat should I **wear** to the party?
13.	fair	*fair*	I played a **fair** game and did not cheat.
14.	where	*where*	I know **where** to find the lost dog.
15.	hardware	*hardware*	Get some nails at the **hardware** store.

Think & Sort the spelling words.

Write the words that have:

1–3. /âr/ spelled **air**. **12–14.** /âr/ spelled **ere**.

4–5. /âr/ spelled **ear**. **15.** /âr/ spelled **eir**.

6–11. /âr/ spelled **are**.

Remember

The vowel sound in **fair** can be spelled in different ways: **air** as in **fair, ear** as in **bear, are** as in **care, ere** as in **where,** and **eir** as in **their**.

TEKS 3.24A Use knowledge of letter sounds, word parts, word segmentation, and syllabication to spell.
3.24C Spell high-frequency and compound words from a commonly used list.

Understand Complex Consonants

1–3. Remember that **consonant digraphs** are two or more letters that make a single sound, such as **ch** in **chair**. Write the other spelling words that begin with a consonant digraph.

Identify Sounds and Spellings

Say each word below. For each word, write one or two spelling words that have the same sounds at the beginning and end. Circle the letters that spell /âr/.

4–5. hire

6–7. poor

8–9. far

10. bore

Use the
Dictionary

Write the spelling words that have the following words in their definitions. Look up each word in your **Spelling Dictionary** to check.

11. body

12. feet

13. tools

14. programs

15. anywhere

 TEKS 3.24A Use knowledge of letter sounds, word parts, word segmentation, and syllabication to spell. **3.24Bv** Spell words with more advanced orthographic patterns and rules: complex consonants. **3.24C** Spell high-frequency and compound words from a commonly used list.

pear	pair	hare	barefoot	fare
their	hair	bare	nowhere	there
software	wear	fair	where	hardware

Categorize Words

Fill in each blank with a word that either names a category or shares a similarity with the other words.

1. _____: nails, hammer, saw, tools
2. _____: word processing, database, computer games
3. socks and shoes, slippers, sandals, _____
4. somewhere, everywhere, anywhere, _____

Homophones

Decide which homophone fits in each blank in the sentence. One sentence has only one missing word.

(pair, pear)

I packed a water bottle, a juicy **5.**, a GPS, and an extra **6.** of socks for the hike.

(where, wear)

7. is my lucky hat I always **8.** during the football game?

(hare, hair)

The **9.** on a **10.** is called fur.

(fair, fare)

How much is the bus **11.** to the county **12.**?

(there, their)

They're putting on **13.** uniforms over **14.**.

(bear, bare)

Usually my desk is covered with papers, but today it is **15.**.

 TEKS 3.24C Spell high-frequency and compound words from a commonly used list. **3.24E** Spell single syllable homophones.

Connections to WRITING

Proofread a Poem

Proofread the poem below for eight misspelled words. Then rewrite the poem. Write the spelling words correctly and make the corrections shown by the proofreading marks.

The Hoppers

Mr. Hoppers is a rabbit.

He is a little har.

Mrs. hoppers is his wife.

They are a fuzzy pare.

When they have an outing,

Silly hats they like to wair.

Were are the Hoppers' children?

They are nowere to be found.

Mr. Hoppers looks for Them

In thier burrow underground.

Ther Mr. Hoppers finds

Harrison, Sarah, and Claire,

Putting on on some silly hats

For a trip to the state faire!

DESCRIPTIVE Writing Prompt
Write a Poem

Think of something funny that happened to you, or make something up. Write a poem about it. You can decide whether or not the lines in the poem should rhyme. Use as many spelling words as you can.

- Use the writing process: prewrite, draft, revise, edit, and publish.
- Use words that will help readers see, hear, feel, taste, and touch the details you are describing.
- Use complete sentences with correct capitalization, punctuation, grammar, and spelling.
- Read your work. Circle three words you are unsure about and check their spellings in a dictionary.

Transfer

Think of four more words with /âr/ spelled **air, ear, are, ere,** or **eir** that a writer might use to describe a situation. Then write the words in your Spelling Journal and circle the letters that spell the /âr/ sound.

TEKS 3.24A Use knowledge of letter sounds, word parts, word segmentation, and syllabication to spell. **3.24C** Spell high-frequency and compound words from a commonly used list. **3.24G** Use print and electronic resources to find and check correct spellings.

Extend & Transfer Word Study

air	their	hair	rare
chair	there	bare	stare
care	wear	hardware	armchair
bear	fair	software	wheelchair
pear	where	hare	farewell
pair	barefoot	beware	fairy tale
fare	nowhere	compare	somewhere

Compound Words

Remember that a compound word is a word made up of two smaller words.

1–10. Write each compound word from the list. Draw a slash between the two smaller words in the compound.

Meaning Mastery

One word is used incorrectly in each sentence. Write the correct word.

11. When you want to go somewhere in the city, there is usually a cheap bus fair.

12. If you compare the taste of an orange and a pare, which is sweeter?

13. Beware of the cord when you are using a hare dryer.

14. The chilly air probably feels cold on their bear arms.

15. Do you care if they stair at you?

 TEKS 3.24A Use knowledge of letter sounds, word parts, word segmentation, and syllabication to spell. **3.24C** Spell high-frequency and compound words from a commonly used list. **3.24E** Spell single syllable homophones.

Fine Arts

Word Hunt

Read the paragraphs below. Look for words that have /âr/ spelled **ere, eir, air,** and **are.**

Did you know that elephants can paint? Some elephants have a flair for painting pictures. Once there was an elephant named Ruby that loved to paint. Two artists heard about Ruby after she died. They knew that there are a lot of elephants in Thailand. They declared that they would start an elephant art school in Thailand. The artists weren't scared of the huge animals.

Trainers taught the elephants to hold a brush in the tip of their trunk. They also helped by dipping the brush in paint. They carefully guided the animals by tugging on their ears.

Now there arc more art schools for elephants. If you compare the art, you see that some elephants paint flowers. Others paint trees. Some use short brushstrokes. Some have broad or curvy strokes. Would you buy an elephant painting? A share of the money made from these paintings goes to help the elephants.

WORD SORT

Follow the directions. Write each word only once.

1. Write a word that has /âr/ spelled **ere**.
2. Write a word that has /âr/ spelled **eir**.
3. Write a word that has /âr/ spelled **air**.
4–8. Write words that have /âr/ spelled **are**.

TEKS 3.24A Use knowledge of letter sounds, word parts, word segmentation, and syllabication to spell.
3.24C Spell high-frequency and compound words from a commonly used list.

Connections to THINKING

Read the spelling words and sentences.

1.	way	*way*	I don't know which **way** to turn.
2.	its	*its*	The dog put **its** head on my lap.
3.	owe	*owe*	I **owe** Jay three dollars for the hat.
4.	sell	*sell*	If you will **sell** that, I will buy it.
5.	great	*great*	What a **great** day we had at the park.
6.	sail	*sail*	We **sail** our boat on the bay.
7.	cell	*cell*	A **cell** is part of all living things.
8.	scent	*scent*	The **scent** of that perfume is strong.
9.	oh	*oh*	It was, **oh**, such a beautiful day.
10.	cent	*cent*	One **cent** does not buy much!
11.	it's	*it's*	I lost my sock, but I know **it's** here.
12.	grate	*grate*	Use this tool to **grate** the cheese.
13.	weigh	*weigh*	Do you **weigh** the baby on that scale?
14.	sale	*sale*	I buy jeans cheap at the **sale**.
15.	sent	*sent*	Meg **sent** me a letter from camp.

Think & Sort the spelling words.

1–15. Write each pair of homophones. There will be one set of homophones that has three words. Think about how spelling affects meaning.

Remember

Homophones are words that sound the same but have different spellings and meanings.

 TEKS 3.24C Spell high-frequency and compound words from a commonly used list. **3.24E** Spell single syllable homophones.

Analyze Words

1–3. Write the word that has /s/ spelled **sc**. Then write its homophones. Circle the letters that make the /s/ sound in each word.

4–5. Write two words that rhyme with **bits**.

6–7. Write the three-letter word that has the **vowel-consonant-e** pattern. Then write its homophone.

Identify Sound Spellings

Write **ea, ai,** or the missing letters in **a-consonant-e** to spell the **long a** sound.

8. s __ __ l

9. gr __ __ t

10. s __ l __

11. gr __ t __

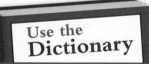

Use the Dictionary

Write two spelling words for these dictionary respellings:

12–13. /sĕl/   **14–15.** /wā/

Dictionary Check Be sure to check the respellings in your **Spelling Dictionary**.

TEKS 3.24A Use knowledge of letter sounds, word parts, word segmentation, and syllabication to spell.
3.24Bv Spell words with more advanced orthographic patterns and rules: complex consonants. **3.24C** Spell high-frequency and compound words from a commonly used list. **3.24E** Spell single syllable homophones.
3.24G Use print and electronic resources to find and check correct spellings.

way	its	owe	sell	great
sail	cell	scent	oh	cent
it's	grate	weigh	sale	sent

Categorize Words

Write the spelling word that belongs in each group.

1. dime, nickel, _____

2. fly, drive, _____

3. bargain, deal, _____

Use Context Clues

Look at each pair of homophones. Write them in the correct order to complete the sentences.

(weigh, way)

Is there a **4.** we can **5.** these bananas?

(scent, sent)

We **6.** Grandma a bottle of perfume with a delicious **7.** .

(its, it's)

The lost dog was wearing **8.** collar, so **9.** going to be returned to the owner.

(grate, great)

Mom says it is **10.** that you want to **11.** the carrots for the muffins.

(cell, sell)

I hope you will **12.** that fancy **13.** phone to me.

(oh, owe)

Dad said, " **14.** , I think I **15.** you an apology."

 TEKS 3.24C Spell high-frequency and compound words from a commonly used list. **3.24E** Spell single syllable homophones.

Proofread a Paragraph

Proofread the paragraph below for eight homophones that are misspelled or are not used correctly. Then rewrite the paragraph. Write the spelling words correctly and make the corrections shown by the proofreading marks.

¶When a person is missing, sometimes a Dog can find the person. It uses it's sense of smell to do this. Someone gives the dog something with the person's sent. Then the dog is cent out to find the person. for many people, its fun to watch a dog pick up the trail. The wae a dog follows its nose is something to See. How grate it is when the dog can find the person. That is when a dog is worth every cint you paid for it. In fact, you could even say you oh the dog.

Proofreading Marks

≡	Capital Letter
/	Small Letter
∧	Add
℮	Delete
⊙	Add a Period
¶	Indent

EXPOSITORY Writing Prompt
Write a Paragraph

Choose an animal and write about it. Be sure to write a sentence that gives a main idea about the animal. Use as many spelling words as you can.

- Use the writing process: prewrite, draft, revise, edit, and publish.
- Include facts and other details that support your main idea and end with a summary sentence.
- Use complete sentences with correct capitalization, punctuation, grammar, and spelling.
- Read your work. Circle three words you are unsure about and check their spellings in a dictionary.

Transfer

Think of two more pairs of homophones. Write the words in your Spelling Journal and then write a sentence using each word.

TEKS 3.24C Spell high-frequency and compound words from a commonly used list. **3.24E** Spell single syllable homophones. **3.24G** Use print and electronic resources to find and check correct spellings.

for	oh	sell	heal
four	it's	scent	heel
meat	weigh	cent	foul
meet	sent	grate	fowl
way	great	sale	yoke
its	sail	roll	yolk
owe	cell	role	

Meaning Mastery

Write the word that matches each meaning.

1. **(owe, oh)** a sound that expresses surprise
2. **(weigh, way)** to determine weight by using a scale
3. **(heel, heal)** part of a foot
4. **(foul, fowl)** birds raised for food, such as turkeys and chickens
5. **(sail, sale)** to move swiftly on water
6. **(yolk, yoke)** the yellow part of an egg
7. **(for, four)** a number following three
8. **(role, roll)** to move by turning over

Pattern Power

Use words from the list to answer these questions.

9–10. Which two homophones rhyme with **tell**?
11–15. Which five words have the **vowel-consonant-e** pattern?

TEKS 3.24A Use knowledge of letter sounds, word parts, word segmentation, and syllabication to spell.
3.24C Spell high-frequency and compound words from a commonly used list. **3.24E** Spell single syllable homophones.

Technology

Word Hunt

Read the paragraphs below. Look for pairs of words that are homophones.

Spell checkers are good at finding spelling errors in words that are spelled incorrectly. However, they are not as smart as humans! Spell checkers don't catch homophones that are used incorrectly. Let's say you wrote, "I am on the weigh to way myself." Both *weigh* and *way* are spelled correctly, but they should be switched. A spell checker would not catch this error.

This problem can lead to some silly sentences. Find the four words that are in the wrong place in the next sentence. *I past the our riding passed hour new house.* Did you find them? Try using the homophones in this unit to write your own sentences. Use some homophones correctly. Here's an example: "The cut on my heel was starting to heal." Slip in some silly sentences by mixing up homophones. Then trade with a friend. See if he or she can spot the errors!

Follow the directions. Write each word only once.

1–2. Write a pair of homophones that rhyme with **say**.

3–4. Write a pair of homophones that rhyme with **last**.

5–6. Write a pair of homophones that rhyme with **sour**.

7–8. Write a pair of homophones that rhyme with **meal**.

 TEKS 3.24A Use knowledge of letter sounds, word parts, word segmentation, and syllabication to spell. **3.24C** Spell high-frequency and compound words from a commonly used list. **3.24E** Spell single syllable homophones.

Unit 24

Units 19–23

Assessment

Each assessment word in the box fits one of the spelling patterns and rules you have studied over the past five weeks. Read the unit descriptions. Then write each assessment word under the unit number it fits.

Unit 19

1–3. The vowel sound /ô/ can be spelled **o** as in **song** and **aw** as in **lawn**.

Unit 20

4–6. The r-controlled vowel sound /ôr/ can be spelled **or** as in **form, ore** as in **tore, oar** as in **board,** and **ar** as in **warm**.

Unit 21

7–9. The r-controlled vowel sound /ûr/ can be spelled **ur** as in **fur, ear** as in **earn, or** as in **word,** and **ir** as in **dirt**.

Unit 22

10–12. The r-controlled vowel sound /âr/ can be spelled **air** as in **fair, ear** as in **bear, are** as in **care, ere** as in **where,** and **eir** as in **their**.

Unit 23

13–15. Homophones are words that sound the same but have different spellings and meanings.

Words for Assessment

sir
bog
waste
dare
horses
purse
paw
steel
stair
claw
snore
blur
aware
steal

Review

Unit 19: /ô/: aw, o

| across | draw | belong | straw |
| soft | lost | song | |

1–2. Write the spelling words that end with a consonant blend.

3–4. Write the spelling words that end with a consonant digraph.

5–6. Write the spelling words that end with a vowel sound.

7. Write the spelling word that ends with a double consonant.

Unit 20: r-Controlled Vowel /ôr/: or, ore, oar, ar

| before | forget | warm | morning |
| story | board | form | |

Write the spelling word or words for each clue.

8–9. Each of these words has two syllables. The accent is on the first syllable. The first syllable is closed.

10. This word has two syllables. The first syllable is open.

11. This word has two syllables. The accent is on the second syllable. The first syllable is closed.

12–14. These words have one syllable.

159

Review

Unit 21: r-Controlled Vowel /ûr/: or, ur, ear, ir

circus	heard	early	work
turn	dirt	word	

Write the spelling word that completes the sentence.

1. That is a _____ that I have never heard before.

2. Elephants performed in the _____ tent.

3. How _____ should we be ready to leave?

4. I have too much _____ to do to leave tomorrow.

Write a spelling word for each clue.

5. This word rhymes with **burn** and sometimes comes before the word **around**.

6. This word is the past tense of **hear**.

7. Change the first and last letter of **girl** to make this word.

Unit 22: r-Controlled Vowel /âr/: air, ear, are, ere, eir

their	wear	there	where
fair	pear	pair	

Write the review words that are homophones for each word below.

8–9. ware

10. fare

11–12. they're

13–14. pare

Unit 23: Single-Syllable Homophones

great	sent	it's	weigh
cent	oh	its	

1–2. These words have the **long a** vowel sound.

3–4. These words have the **short e** vowel sound.

5–6. These words have the **short i** vowel sound.

7. This word has the **long o** vowel sound.

Spelling Study Strategy

Sorting by Vowel Sounds

Here is one way to practice spelling words.

1. Write your spelling words on 3" × 5" cards.

2. Make a stack of words that have the vowel sound you hear in **song** and the **r-controlled vowel** sounds you hear in **warm, fur,** and **fair**.

3. With a partner, take turns reading each other's word cards aloud. Put words with the same vowel sound in the same pile.

4. Read the words in each pile again. Then sort them according to the spelling patterns that spell the vowel sound.

Directions: Read the introduction and the passage that follows. Then read each question and fill in the space in front of the correct answer on your answer sheet.

Evan wrote this story about a boy who misses a circus because he has to work. A special visitor raises his spirits. He wants you to review his paper. As you read, think about ways that Evan can improve his story.

The Visitor

(1) As Earl drove the shovel into the erth, he tried not to think about what he was missing. (2) Today the circus would pass through their town on its weigh north to Dallas. (3) Many people would see it, but he had work to do.

(4) His mom wanted to plant seeds early so they could grow there own food. (5) It was 1944, Earl's father was off fighting in the wore, and every cent counted.

(6) Earl heard a noise and raised his head to see a dark form creeping acros the land. (7) He lifted his hand to shade his eyes. (8) The hair on his arms stood on end.

(9) The bear scratched his fir and sniffed the air. (10) Maybe it caught Earl's sent, because suddenly it turned to look right at him. (11) They stared at each other, and then the bear made a slow tern and disappeared into the woods.

(12) Earl would forget about the circus, but he would never forget that bear.

GO ON

1 What change, if any, should be made in sentence 1?

- ⊂⊃ Change *drove* to **drov**
- ⊂⊃ Change *erth* to **earth**
- ⊂⊃ Change *think* to **thing**
- ⊂⊃ Make no change

2 What change, if any, should be made in sentence 2?

- ⊂⊃ Change *would* to **wood**
- ⊂⊃ Change *their* to **there**
- ⊂⊃ Change *weigh* to **way**
- ⊂⊃ Make no change

3 What change, if any, should be made in sentence 3?

- ⊂⊃ Change *people* to **peeple**
- ⊂⊃ Change *would* to **wood**
- ⊂⊃ Change *work* to **werk**
- ⊂⊃ Make no change

4 What change, if any, should be made in sentence 4?

- ⊂⊃ Change *early* to **earley**
- ⊂⊃ Change *could* to **cood**
- ⊂⊃ Change *there* to **their**
- ⊂⊃ Make no change

5 What change, if any, should be made in sentence 5?

- ⊂⊃ Change *father* to **fother**
- ⊂⊃ Change *wore* to **war**
- ⊂⊃ Change *cent* to **sent**
- ⊂⊃ Make no change

6 What change, if any, should be made in sentence 6?

- ⊂⊃ Change *heard* to **herd**
- ⊂⊃ Change *form* to **from**
- ⊂⊃ Change *acros* to **across**
- ⊂⊃ Make no change

7 What change, if any, should be made in sentence 9?

- ⊂⊃ Change *bear* to **bair**
- ⊂⊃ Change *fir* to **fur**
- ⊂⊃ Change *air* to **are**
- ⊂⊃ Make no change

8 What change, if any, should be made in sentence 10?

- ⊂⊃ Change *Maybe* to **Mabye**
- ⊂⊃ Change *sent* to **scent**
- ⊂⊃ Change *turned* to **terned**
- ⊂⊃ Make no change

9 What change, if any, should be made in sentence 11?

- ⊂⊃ Change *stared* to **staired**
- ⊂⊃ Change *tern* to **turn**
- ⊂⊃ Change *woods* to **woulds**
- ⊂⊃ Make no change

10 What change, if any, should be made in sentence 12?

- ⊂⊃ Change *would* to **wood**
- ⊂⊃ Change *about* to **ubout**
- ⊂⊃ Change *forgot* to **fergot**
- ⊂⊃ Make no change

STOP

163

Grammar, Usage, and Mechanics
Verbs That Tell About the Past

Past tense verbs show that the action happened in the past. Many past tense verbs end in **-ed**.

> Yesterday we **worked** in the yard.
> The children **played** in the sand.

The past tense of some verbs is formed in other ways.

> We **give** presents on birthdays.
> Last year, I **gave** her a book.

Practice Activity

A. Write the past tense verb in each sentence.

1. Uncle Rick sent me a package.
2. Emma's team lost the game by two points.
3. I never heard that joke before.

B. Write the present tense verb for each underlined word. Make sure the sentence makes sense with the new word.

4. Anna and Ian <u>earned</u> money from their dog-walking job.
5. Shawn and Amy <u>belonged</u> to that club.
6. They <u>turned</u> around in the driveway.
7. The players <u>wore</u> the same uniform for each game.
8. Dad and Mom <u>worked</u> on Saturday.
9. We <u>drew</u> pictures to illustrate our posters.
10. You <u>forgot</u> your permission slip for every field trip.

 TEKS 3.24C Spell high-frequency and compound words from a commonly used list.

The Writing Process: Expository
Writing a Biographical Sketch

PREWRITING
Who is your hero? What makes this person special? As you think about this person, write down why he or she is your hero. You can find books at the library about special people. An adult can help you look for heroes on the Internet.

DRAFTING
Use your ideas to write a biographical sketch about your hero. Include several describing words to tell about him or her. Use as many spelling words as possible. If you don't know how to spell a word, make your best guess.

REVISING
When you have finished your first draft, read your sketch from beginning to end. Have you used words that will help readers understand why your hero is special? Now revise your draft.

EDITING
Use the **Editing Checklist** to proofread your biographical sketch. Be sure to use proofreading marks when you make corrections. Circle at least two words that may be misspelled. Use a dictionary or electronic resource to check the spelling. Write a final draft.

PUBLISHING
Make a copy of your biographical sketch. Draw a portrait of your hero to share with your readers.

EDITING CHECKLIST

Spelling
✓ Circle words that contain the spelling patterns and rules learned in Units 19–23.

✓ Check the circled words in your **Spelling Dictionary**.

✓ Check for other spelling errors.

Capital Letters
✓ Capitalize important words in the title.

✓ Capitalize the first word in each sentence.

✓ Capitalize proper nouns.

Punctuation
✓ End each sentence with the correct punctuation.

✓ Use commas, apostrophes, and quotation marks correctly.

Grammar, Usage, and Mechanics
✓ Each past tense verb tells about actions that already happened.

 TEKS 3.24A Use knowledge of letter sounds, word parts, word segmentation, and syllabication to spell.
3.24G Use print and electronic resources to find and check correct spellings.

165

Connections to THINKING

Read the spelling words and sentences.

1. supper *supper* — We often have soup for **supper**.
2. happen *happen* — What will **happen** at the game?
3. pepper *pepper* — I put **pepper** on my potatoes.
4. kitten *kitten* — The **kitten** stayed near its mother.
5. sudden *sudden* — We heard a **sudden** clap of thunder.
6. letter *letter* — Mail the **letter** at the post office.
7. dinner *dinner* — We ate rice and beans for **dinner**.
8. cotton *cotton* — These pants are made from **cotton**.
9. lesson *lesson* — My piano **lesson** lasts one hour.
10. mitten *mitten* — I lost one **mitten** in the snow.
11. bottom *bottom* — The **bottom** of a glass is flat.
12. summer *summer* — We go to the beach in the **summer**.
13. better *better* — Colin will feel **better** after a rest.
14. ladder *ladder* — Climb the **ladder** to reach the window.
15. ribbon *ribbon* — The bow is made from red **ribbon**.

Think & Sort the spelling words.

Write the spelling words that have the targeted vowel sound in the first syllable:

1–2. short a	**11–12. short o**
3–6. short e	**13–15. short u**
7–10. short i	

Remember

Two-syllable words with a short vowel sound in the first syllable are often spelled with double consonants: **dinner, better**.

TEKS 3.24A Use knowledge of letter sounds, word parts, word segmentation, and syllabication to spell. **3.24Biv** Spell words with more advanced orthographic patterns and rules: double consonants in middle of words. **3.24C** Spell high-frequency and compound words from a commonly used list. **3.24D** Spell words with common syllable constructions.

Connections to PHONICS

Identify Sound and Letter Patterns

Write the spelling word that matches each clue. Then underline the letter that makes the short vowel sound in the first syllable.

1. It has the /**k**/ sound spelled **c**.
2. It has three of the same consonants.
3. The consonant **b** is doubled.
4. It has the /**k**/ sound spelled **k**.

For each word below, replace one letter with a double consonant. If the vowel sound changes, circle the word.

5–6. super   9. later
  7. lemon   10. lever
  8. diver   11. haven

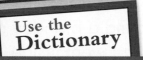
Use the **Dictionary**

Write the spelling words that have the following words in their dictionary definition. Look up each word to check. Draw a slash mark to show where the word has been divided in the dictionary entry word.

12. expected   14. thumb
13. higher   15. lowest

Dictionary Check Be sure to check your answers in your **Spelling Dictionary**.

 TEKS 3.24A Use knowledge of letter sounds, word parts, word segmentation, and syllabication to spell. **3.24Biv** Spell words with more advanced orthographic patterns and rules: double consonants in middle of words. **3.24C** Spell high-frequency and compound words from a commonly used list. **3.24D** Spell words with common syllable constructions.

167

supper	happen	pepper	kitten	sudden
letter	dinner	cotton	lesson	mitten
bottom	summer	better	ladder	ribbon

Complete the Groups

Write the spelling word that belongs in each group.

1. silk, wool, _____
2. chili powder, salt, _____
3. scarf, hat, _____
4. occur, take place, _____
5. escalator, steps, _____
6. dinner, evening meal, _____

Use Context Clues

Write the spelling words to complete the story.

I'll never forget my eighth birthday. It was a very hot **7.** day. After my swimming **8.**, my mother took me home. I looked in our mailbox and found a birthday card and a **9.** from my grandparents. Then I went inside. All of a **10.**, my friends yelled, "Happy birthday!" I was so surprised!

We all played games on the **11.** table. Finally, it was time to open the presents. Mom said I should open the box with holes that was tied with yellow **12.**. Inside was a soft, furry **13.**. It looked so tiny sitting in the **14.** of that box. I've never gotten a **15.** present in my whole life!

TEKS 3.24C Spell high-frequency and compound words from a commonly used list.

Connections to WRITING

Proofread a Letter

Proofread the letter below for eight misspelled words. Then rewrite the letter. Write the spelling words correctly and make the corrections shown by the proofreading marks.

Dear kenesha,

   My mom just said I could have a sleepover on friday. I hoped this would happin. It is kind of suden, but can you come? You can have diner here. My mom will make the peper steak that you like! After super, we can play with my kiten. please answer this leter soon! It might be our last chance this summur.

                              Your pal,

                              Alison

Proofreading Marks

≡	Capital Letter
/	Small Letter
∧	Add
℘	Delete
⊙	Add a Period
¶	Indent

PERSUASIVE Writing Prompt
Write a Letter

Write a letter inviting a friend to do something with you. Be sure to use as many spelling words as you can.

- Use the writing process: prewrite, draft, revise, edit, and publish.
- Persuade your friend with interesting ideas and details.
- Use commas after your opening and closing.
- Indent your paragraphs, your closing, and your signature.
- Use complete sentences with correct capitalization, punctuation, grammar, and spelling.
- Read your work. Circle three words you are unsure about and check their spelling in a dictionary.

Transfer

Think of three more words that have two syllables and double consonants in the middle of the word. Write the words in your Spelling Journal and put a slash where you would divide each word.

TEKS 3.24A Use knowledge of letter sounds, word parts, word segmentation, and syllabication to spell. **3.24Biv** Spell words with more advanced orthographic patterns and rules: double consonants in middle of words. **3.24C** Spell high-frequency and compound words from a commonly used list. **3.24D** Spell words with common syllable constructions. **3.24G** Use print and electronic resources to find and check correct spellings.

Word Study

apple	letter	supper	ribbon	carrot
cannot	dinner	pepper	bubble	hiccup
puzzle	cotton	kitten	collar	platter
yellow	lesson	mitten	rattle	shutter
happen	summer	bottom	zipper	
sudden	better	ladder	barrel	

Word Building

Add double consonants to make a spelling word.

1. le __ __ on

2. mi __ __ en

3. ri __ __ on

4. la __ __ er

5. co __ __ on

6. be __ __ er

7. bo __ __ om

Syllable Scramble

Add a syllable from the box to each syllable below to write a spelling word.

per	low	cup	pen	ble	ple	zle	ter

8. bub

9. puz

10. zip

11. yel

12. hap

13. hic

14. ap

15. shut

 TEKS 3.24A Use knowledge of letter sounds, word parts, word segmentation, and syllabication to spell. **3.24Biv** Spell words with more advanced orthographic patterns and rules: double consonants in middle of words. **3.24C** Spell high-frequency and compound words from a commonly used list. **3.24D** Spell words with common syllable constructions.

Science

 Word Hunt

Read the paragraphs below. Look for words with double consonants in the middle of the word.

What are the properties of matter? Matter is anything that takes up space and has weight, from a little ant to a tall ladder to a giant space shuttle. Think of water. It might not have a color, but it still takes up space, just like an apple or a mitten does.

Matter has mass. Some scientists say that mass is the amount of "stuff" an object contains. Picture yourself standing in the middle of a crater on the Moon. You are holding a stick of butter. The butter weighs less on the Moon than it does on Earth. That's because the Moon's force of gravity is less than Earth's. The Moon is not as big as Earth, so it pulls less on objects on its surface. The butter has the same amount of matter, or "stuff," on the Moon that it has on Earth. And you can still put it on your toast for breakfast!

WORD SORT

Follow the directions. Write each word only once.

1–3. Write words with double consonants in the middle and **short a** in the first syllable.

4–6. Write words with double consonants in the middle and **short i** in the first syllable.

7–8. Write words with double consonants in the middle and **short u** in the first syllable.

 TEKS 3.24A Use knowledge of letter sounds, word parts, word segmentation, and syllabication to spell. **3.24Biv** Spell words with more advanced orthographic patterns and rules: double consonants in middle of words. **3.24C** Spell high-frequency and compound words from a commonly used list. **3.24D** Spell words with common syllable constructions.

Connections to THINKING

Read the spelling words and sentences.

1. carry — *carry* — Please help me **carry** this box.
2. bunny — *bunny* — The **bunny** has big ears.
3. happy — *happy* — The clown made the children **happy**.
4. muddy — *muddy* — I will take off my **muddy** shoes.
5. berry — *berry* — What kind of **berry** is on that bush?
6. furry — *furry* — A hamster is a small **furry** animal.
7. puppy — *puppy* — The **puppy** is just six weeks old.
8. sorry — *sorry* — She felt **sorry** for the hurt bird.
9. merry — *merry* — Everyone at the party was **merry**.
10. jelly — *jelly* — I eat peanut butter with **jelly**.
11. hurry — *hurry* — We **hurry** to catch the bus.
12. pretty — *pretty* — Erica looks **pretty** in that dress.
13. cherry — *cherry* — This **cherry** is big, red, and ripe.
14. worry — *worry* — Did Pam **worry** about her lost dog?
15. funny — *funny* — The joke Matt told was **funny**.

Think & Sort the spelling words.

1–8. Write the words with double **r**.

9–10. Write the words with double **n**.

11–12. Write the words with double **p**.

13–15. Write the words with double **d, l,** or **t**.

Remember

The final **long e** sound in words like **happy** is spelled **y** and often follows a double consonant.

TEKS 3.24A Use knowledge of letter sounds, word parts, word segmentation, and syllabication to spell.
3.24Biv Spell words with more advanced orthographic patterns and rules: double consonants in middle of words. **3.24C** Spell high-frequency and compound words from a commonly used list.

Apply Common Sounds and Spellings

Complete the exercises. Check your answers in your **Spelling Dictionary**.

1–3. Write spelling words that rhyme with **ferry**.

4–6. Write the spelling words that rhyme with **flurry**. Underline the word that has a different spelling.

Identify Vowel Sounds

Write the spelling words that have the following vowel sounds. If you are unsure, check the respellings in the **Spelling Dictionary**.

7–8. short a   **11.** short o

9. short e   **12–15.** short u

10. short i

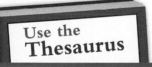

The **Writing Thesaurus** gives synonyms for your spelling words. Remember that synonyms are words that have the same or similar meanings. The **Writing Thesaurus** also provides antonyms for some words. Antonyms have opposite meanings.

Look up each spelling word in the **Writing Thesaurus**. If your **Writing Thesaurus** has an entry for a spelling word, circle the word on the answer lists for the activities above.

TEKS 3.24A Use knowledge of letter sounds, word parts, word segmentation, and syllabication to spell. **3.24Biv** Spell words with more advanced orthographic patterns and rules: double consonants in middle of words. **3.24C** Spell high-frequency and compound words from a commonly used list. **3.24G** Use print and electronic resources to find and check correct spellings.

carry	bunny	happy	muddy	berry
furry	puppy	sorry	merry	jelly
hurry	pretty	cherry	worry	funny

Use Synonyms

Write the spelling word that is a synonym
for the underlined word or words.
Sometimes the words will rhyme, too.

1–2. The <u>silly</u> <u>young rabbit</u> made me
laugh. He was a _____ _____.

3–4. That <u>baby dog</u> was so <u>dirty</u> from
rolling in the puddle. She was a _____ _____.

5–6. Don't <u>be concerned</u>. If we <u>go fast</u>, we can make
our flight.

7–8. The <u>happy</u> <u>red fruit</u> has a pit and a long stem.
It is a _____ _____.

Use Context Clues

Write the spelling word to complete each sentence.

9. I like grape _____ on my toast.

10. I feel so _____ when I hear my baby sister giggle.

11. Look at the _____ flowers.

12. A kitten is soft and _____.

13. I am _____ that I bumped your leg.

14. Please help me _____ this heavy package.

15. That _____ is blue and juicy.

 TEKS 3.24C Spell high-frequency and compound words from a commonly used list.

Connections to WRITING

Proofread a Poem

Proofread the poem below for eight misspelled words. Then rewrite the poem. Write the spelling words correctly and make the corrections shown by the proofreading marks.

Some kids like a bunney that hops all around.

Some kids like a pupy they've chosen from the pound⊙

For some kids, a ℄at that is pritty and furrey

Is the best kind of pet—and it's also so purry!

my favorite pet is one that's a bit funy,

But it it makes me happy (and mery and sunny).

I can carrie its cage∧though mom says not to pet it.

My tarantula's the best pet—and don't you forget it!

Proofreading Marks

≡ Capital Letter

/ Small Letter

∧ Add

ℒ Delete

⊙ Add a Period

⫪ Indent

DESCRIPTIVE Writing Prompt
Write a Poem

Write a poem that describes your favorite kind of pet. You can choose whether or not to make the poem rhyme. Be sure to explain why this pet is your favorite. Use as many spelling words as you can.

- Use the writing process: prewrite, draft, revise, edit, and publish.
- Include vivid images and sensory details that show what is special about your favorite kind of pet.
- Use complete sentences with correct capitalization, punctuation, grammar, and spelling.
- Read your work. Circle three words you are unsure about and check their spelling in a dictionary.

Transfer

Think of three more words that have double consonants in the middle of the word and end with **y**. Write the words in your Spelling Journal and circle the double consonants.

3.24Biv Spell words with more advanced orthographic patterns and rules: double consonants in middle of words. **3.24C** Spell high-frequency and compound words from a commonly used list. **3.24G** Use print and electronic resources to find and check correct spellings.

fluffy	puppy	bunny	cherry	holly
glossy	sorry	muddy	ferry	lobby
messy	hurry	berry	silly	shaggy
penny	pretty	furry	unhappy	woolly
carry	worry	merry	witty	
happy	funny	jelly	fuzzy	

Adding Endings to Base Words

Before adding an ending to a base word that ends with **y,** you must first change the **y** to an **i**. Write the base word for each word below.

1. sorrier
2. fuzziest
3. cherries
4. berries
5. jellies

6. unhappiest
7. hurried
8. worrier
9. fluffier

Consonant Doubling

Write the spelling word that is made by doubling the last consonant and adding **y** to each word below.

10. mud
11. fur
12. wool

13. fun
14. shag
15. wit

TEKS 3.24Bi Spell words with more advanced orthographic patterns and rules: consonant doubling when adding an ending. **3.24Biii** Spell words with more advanced orthographic patterns and rules: changing y to i before adding an ending. **3.24Biv** Spell words with more advanced orthographic patterns and rules: double consonants in middle of words. **3.24C** Spell high-frequency and compound words from a commonly used list.

Social Studies

WordHunt

Read the paragraphs below. Look for words with double consonants followed by **y**.

How is an animal shelter like an art museum? They might not seem to have much in common. At a shelter, you can find a lost puppy or adopt a fluffy bunny. There is not a painting or a mummy in sight! However, both an art museum and a shelter are nonprofit organizations, or NPOs. All the money that an NPO takes in goes to meeting its goals.

Think of an animal shelter. It has many expenses. A cute, fuzzy kitty needs to eat. It needs shots to keep it healthy. It must be handled often so it will be a happy pet. As an NPO, a shelter tries to stretch every penny it takes in. So shelters use many volunteers. The volunteers feed, walk, and pet the animals. They don't do it for money. Purrs and wagging tails are their reward!

Find the words that have double consonants followed by **y**. Write the words that have:

1. the **short a** sound.
2. the **short e** sound.
3. the **short i** sound.
4–8. the **short u** sound.

TEKS 3.24A Use knowledge of letter sounds, word parts, word segmentation, and syllabication to spell.
3.24Biv Spell words with more advanced orthographic patterns and rules: double consonants in middle of words.
3.24C Spell high-frequency and compound words from a commonly used list.

Connections to THINKING

Read the spelling words and sentences.

1. coming — *coming* — Is Zach **coming** to your party?
2. skating — *skating* — We went ice **skating** at the rink.
3. taking — *taking* — Ron is **taking** Spot for a walk.
4. giving — *giving* — Mr. Kay is **giving** me a ride home.
5. choosing — *choosing* — We are **choosing** a team leader.
6. smiling — *smiling* — The boys are **smiling** at the clown.
7. baking — *baking* — I like the smell of bread **baking**.
8. sliding — *sliding* — Mud is **sliding** onto the road.
9. changing — *changing* — Is the car **changing** lanes?
10. waving — *waving* — The flag is **waving** in the breeze.
11. leaving — *leaving* — Is Ned **leaving** your house?
12. making — *making* — I am **making** a salad for dinner.
13. hoping — *hoping* — We are **hoping** you feel better soon.
14. trading — *trading* — Are you **trading** those cards?
15. having — *having* — I am **having** a sleepover tonight.

Think & Sort the spelling words.

Write the word that goes with each base word.

1–5.	6–10.	11–15.
come	make	change
smile	take	trade
leave	slide	choose
skate	hope	wave
bake	give	have

Remember

When adding **-ing** to a word that ends in **silent e,** drop the **e** and add the ending: **take, taking**.

TEKS 3.24A Use knowledge of letter sounds, word parts, word segmentation, and syllabication to spell.
3.24Bii Spell words with more advanced orthographic patterns and rules: dropping final "e" when endings are added. **3.24C** Spell high-frequency and compound words from a commonly used list.

Connections to PHONICS

Analyze Words

Write the spelling word that fits each clue.

1. It has the **long e** sound spelled **ea**.
2. It has the **short u** sound spelled **o**.
3. It has a **short a** sound in the first syllable.
4. Change one letter in **living**.

Identify Spelling Rules

Complete the verb chart.

5. skate   skated   _____
6. take   took   _____
7. bake   baked   _____
8. wave   waved   _____
9. slide   slid   _____
10. make   made   _____
11. choose   chose   _____
12. hope   hoped   _____

Use the Dictionary

An entry word in a dictionary is usually the base form of a word. Write the spelling word that might be found in the entry for each of these base words. Circle the word if there is more than one entry for its base word.

13. change   14. trade   15. smile

Dictionary Check Be sure to check your answers and spellings in your **Spelling Dictionary**.

 TEKS 3.24A Use knowledge of letter sounds, word parts, word segmentation, and syllabication to spell. **3.24Bii** Spell words with more advanced orthographic patterns and rules: dropping final "e" when endings are added. **3.24C** Spell high-frequency and compound words from a commonly used list. **3.24G** Use print and electronic resources to find and check correct spellings.

coming	skating	taking	giving	choosing
smiling	baking	sliding	changing	waving
leaving	making	hoping	trading	having

Solve the Analogies

Write a spelling word to complete each analogy.

1. **Foot** is to **kicking** as **hand** is to _____.
2. **Coming** is to **going** as **arriving** is to _____.
3. **Brushing** is to **teeth** as _____ is to **clothes**.
4. **Give** is to **giving** as **have** is to _____.
5. **Sad** is to **frowning** as **happy** is to _____.
6. **Ball** is to **rolling** as **sled** is to _____.

Use Context Clues

Write the spelling word that rhymes with the underlined word and completes each sentence.

7. The judges are <u>rating</u> each skater's _____.
8. The man who is <u>humming</u> is _____ this way.
9. I am <u>raking</u> leaves, and Jan is _____ them away.
10. Fred is <u>making</u> soup, and Jill is _____ bread.
11. The babies keep _____ noise and <u>waking</u> us up.
12. Many people are _____ to leave because their team is <u>losing</u>.
13. Leah was <u>wading</u> in the pool, and Theo was _____ baseball cards with Dylan.
14. Teri makes a <u>living</u> by _____ advice about money.
15. Everyone is _____ that Andy isn't <u>moping</u> around all day.

TEKS 3.24A Use knowledge of letter sounds, word parts, word segmentation, and syllabication to spell.
3.24C Spell high-frequency and compound words from a commonly used list.

Connections to WRITING

Proofread a Character Description

Proofread the character description below for eight misspelled words. Then rewrite the description. Write the spelling words correctly and make the corrections shown by the proofreading marks.

¶ Mrs. Hawthorne has curly brown hair and twinkly dark eyes, and she is always smileing. If you see her takking a walk, you will see her waveing at the neighbors and tradeng hellos with them. Mrs. hawthorne is only 28 years old, but she is good at many things, including inline skating and bakking bread. she is never happier than when she is slidding a loaf of fresh-baked bread onto a plate to give to a friend. She is hopeing to enter a Baking contest soon.

DESCRIPTIVE Writing Prompt
Write a Character Description

Write a description of a character you have made up. First decide what makes this character special. How old is he or she? What does the character look like? What are his or her hobbies? Use as many spelling words as you can.

- Use the writing process: prewrite, draft, revise, edit, and publish.
- Include details that show a reader exactly how you picture your character.
- Use complete sentences with correct capitalization, punctuation, grammar, and spelling.
- Key your work in a word-processing program. Use the spell-check feature to check your spelling.

Transfer

Think of four or more examples of words that follow the unit spelling rule: drop the final **e** before adding **-ing**. Write each base word in your Spelling Journal. Then add **-ing** to each base word to write a new word.

TEKS 3.24A Use knowledge of letter sounds, word parts, word segmentation, and syllabication to spell. **3.24Bii** Spell words with more advanced orthographic patterns and rules: dropping final "e" when endings are added. **3.24C** Spell high-frequency and compound words from a commonly used list. **3.24G** Use print and electronic resources to find and check correct spellings.

grading	baking	smiling	dancing
driving	changing	sliding	weaving
living	leaving	waving	becoming
saving	making	hoping	curving
coming	having	trading	facing
taking	skating	rising	loving
giving	choosing	handwriting	bouncing

Adding Endings

When adding an ending to a base word that ends with **silent e,** you must drop the **e** before adding the ending. Write the spelling words that have these base words.

1. have
2. leave
3. change
4. give
5. make

6. come
7. curve
8. weave
9. love

Categorizing Words

Write the spelling word that belongs to each group.

10. print, cursive, _____
11. selecting, taking, _____
12. wishing, dreaming, _____
13. cooking, boiling, _____
14. slipping, gliding, _____
15. climbing, growing, _____

TEKS 3.24A Use knowledge of letter sounds, word parts, word segmentation, and syllabication to spell. **3.24Bii** Spell words with more advanced orthographic patterns and rules: dropping final "e" when endings are added. **3.24C** Spell high-frequency and compound words from a commonly used list.

Math

Word Hunt

Read the paragraphs below. Look for words that follow the unit spelling rule: drop the final **e** before adding **-ing**.

"Julia," asked her little brother Mike, "what's a fraction?"

Julia stopped writing in her journal and said, "A fraction is a small part of something."

"What does that mean?" Mike asked.

"It's snacktime; come into the kitchen and I'll show you," Julia said, hoping to satisfy Mike's curiosity.

She broke a blueberry muffin in half. Choosing one piece, she gave it to Mike and explained, "That's one-half. There are two halves in one whole muffin."

"What are some other fractions?" Mike asked, mumbling with his mouth full.

Julia found a cracker and broke it into four sections, sliding one piece toward Mike. "That's one-quarter. There are four quarters in the whole cracker."

Mike popped the section in his mouth. "You're good at proving stuff in math," he said, "but don't you want some snacks, too?"

"Yes," Julia said, smiling. "I'm good at math, but you're good at sharing!"

1–8. Find and write the words that follow the unit spelling rule: drop the final **e** before adding **-ing**.

 TEKS 3.24A Use knowledge of letter sounds, word parts, word segmentation, and syllabication to spell. **3.24Bii** Spell words with more advanced orthographic patterns and rules: dropping final "e" when endings are added. **3.24C** Spell high-frequency and compound words from a commonly used list.

183

Connections to THINKING

Read the spelling words and sentences.

1. stopped — *stopped* — The car **stopped** at the stop sign.
2. digging — *digging* — The dog is **digging** a hole.
3. rubbed — *rubbed* — I **rubbed** the cat's back.
4. sitting — *sitting* — Who was **sitting** in my chair?
5. planned — *planned* — We **planned** Mom's birthday party.
6. wrapping — *wrapping* — We are **wrapping** the gift.
7. sledding — *sledding* — Brett went **sledding** on that hill.
8. dropped — *dropped* — Pat **dropped** the bat on my toe.
9. scrubbing — *scrubbing* — Pete is **scrubbing** the pot clean.
10. hopped — *hopped* — The rabbit **hopped** away.
11. putting — *putting* — I am **putting** on my shoes now.
12. tripped — *tripped* — Ari **tripped** over the dog's bone.
13. swimming — *swimming* — We went **swimming** in the pool.
14. spotted — *spotted* — Ty **spotted** an eagle on the cliff.
15. running — *running* — Who is **running** in today's race?

Think & Sort the spelling words.

Write the spelling words that were formed by:

1–7. doubling the final consonant of the base word and adding **-ed**.

8–15. doubling the final consonant of the base word and adding **-ing**.

Remember

When you add **-ed** or **-ing** to a word that ends with one vowel and one consonant, double the consonant and add the ending: **stop, stopped, stopping**.

TEKS 3.24A Use knowledge of letter sounds, word parts, word segmentation, and syllabication to spell.
3.24Bi Spell words with more advanced orthographic patterns and rules: consonant doubling when adding an ending. **3.24C** Spell high-frequency and compound words from a commonly used list.

Connections to PHONICS

Understand Complex Consonants

Remember that in a consonant blend, two or more consonants are used together and each consonant sound can be heard. In a consonant digraph, two or more consonants work together to make a single sound.

1–4. Write the two-syllable spelling words that begin with a consonant blend.

5. Write the two-syllable spelling word that begins with a consonant digraph.

Identify Ending Sounds

The **-ed** ending can make the **/t/** sound as in **tapped,** the **/d/** sound as in **scanned,** or the **/əd/** sound as in **spotted**.

6–9. Write the one-syllable spelling words that end with the **/t/** sound.

10–11. Write the one-syllable spelling words that end with the **/d/** sound.

Use your **Spelling Dictionary**. Write the spelling word that you find under each of these dictionary entry words. Draw a slash mark to show how the spelling word is divided in the **Spelling Dictionary** entry.

12. run

13. dig

14. put

15. sit

 TEKS 3.24A Use knowledge of letter sounds, word parts, word segmentation, and syllabication to spell.
3.24Bi Spell words with more advanced orthographic patterns and rules: consonant doubling when adding an ending. **3.24Bv** Spell words with more advanced orthographic patterns and rules: complex consonants.
3.24C Spell high-frequency and compound words from a commonly used list.

stopped	digging	rubbed	sitting	planned
wrapping	sledding	dropped	scrubbing	hopped
putting	tripped	swimming	spotted	running

Edit the Categories

Write the spelling word that does not belong in each group.

1. walking, jogging, running, sitting
2. swimming, putting, setting, placing
3. sledding, scrubbing, skating, swimming
4. hopped, jumped, tripped, bounced
5. planned, hoped, stopped, dreamed
6. skated, walked, dropped, jogged
7. hopping, putting, jumping, bouncing

Use Context Clues

Write the spelling word that completes each sentence.

8. Carol _____ her hands together near the campfire to warm them.
9. The dog was _____ a hole in the ground to bury its bone.
10. Roberto was _____ on these steep hills after a snowstorm.
11. A frog _____ in the mud by the pond.
12. Angela _____ to build a doghouse.
13. Some of the kittens were striped, and some of the puppies were _____.
14. Kaitlin is _____ after her dog again.
15. We have finished _____ the gifts and making the cookies for the party.

 TEKS 3.24C Spell high-frequency and compound words from a commonly used list.

Connections to WRITING

Proofread a Paragraph

Proofread the paragraph below for eight misspelled words. Then rewrite the paragraph. Write the spelling words correctly and make the corrections shown by the proofreading marks.

¶ We had a great time at the zoo⊙ We saw sea /ions swiming in their tank. We heard the monkeys screaming as they ~~they~~ jumped and droped from trees. We saw a spoted snake wrappin itself around a tree trunk. A prairie /Dog hoped around in the prairie dog town. Then a chipmunk went runing by. That stoped us in our tracks! We couldn't have plannd a better trip to the zoo.

Proofreading Marks

☰	Capital Letter
/	Small Letter
∧	Add
℘	Delete
⊙	Add a Period
¶	Indent

NARRATIVE Writing Prompt
Write a Paragraph

Write a paragraph about a trip to a special place. Tell about the events in the order they happened and include details about why the trip was important to you. Use as many spelling words as you can.

- Use the writing process: prewrite, draft, revise, edit, and publish.
- Make a timeline to order the events of the trip.
- Take a few minutes to list details about the place before you begin writing.
- Use complete sentences with correct capitalization, punctuation, grammar, and spelling.
- Read your work. Circle three words you are unsure about and check their spelling in a dictionary.

Transfer

Think of four more examples of words that follow the unit spelling rule: double the final consonant before adding **-ed** or **-ing**. Write each base word in your Spelling Journal. Then add **-ed** or **-ing** to each base word to write a new word.

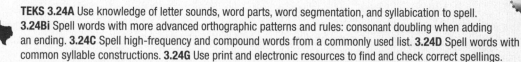

TEKS 3.24A Use knowledge of letter sounds, word parts, word segmentation, and syllabication to spell. **3.24Bi** Spell words with more advanced orthographic patterns and rules: consonant doubling when adding an ending. **3.24C** Spell high-frequency and compound words from a commonly used list. **3.24D** Spell words with common syllable constructions. **3.24G** Use print and electronic resources to find and check correct spellings.

187

batting	dropped	wrapping	knitting
chopping	putting	sledding	skipped
nodding	tripped	scrubbing	hugged
stopping	swimming	hopped	planning
stopped	running	spotted	shopping
sitting	digging	grabbed	spinning
planned	rubbed	jogging	wrapped

Pattern Power

Complete the verb chart with spelling words. If the word has more than one syllable, look in your **Spelling Dictionary** to find out where the word should be divided. Draw a slash mark to show the division.

1. sled	sledded	_____	
2. trip	_____	tripping	
3. put	put	_____	
4. dig	dug	_____	
5. spot	_____	spotting	
6. spin	spun	_____	

Double the Consonants

Double the final consonant and add **-ed** or **-ing** to write a word from the list.

7. rub	**10.** sit	**13.** chop
8. grab	**11.** jog	**14.** knit
9. run	**12.** scrub	**15.** shop

TEKS 3.24A Use knowledge of letter sounds, word parts, word segmentation, and syllabication to spell. **3.24Bi** Spell words with more advanced orthographic patterns and rules: consonant doubling when adding an ending. **3.24C** Spell high-frequency and compound words from a commonly used list. **3.24D** Spell words with common syllable constructions.

Fine Arts

Word Hunt

Read the paragraphs below. Look for words that follow the unit spelling rule: double the final consonant when adding **-ed** or **-ing**.

Drumming is a very important part of Caddo (CAD-oh) culture. The Caddos were the first people to live in the southern plains of the U.S. They play a very large drum by hitting it with drumsticks. The drum is so big that a group of people plays it.

A Caddo dance is always planned to start in the afternoon. The first dance is the Turkey Dance. Men sing and beat on the drum. Then the women get up from where they were sitting to dance. The songs and steps for this dance are very old.

In another dance, couples walk around a circle. The woman puts her foot on top of the man's foot. Then they begin hopping around the circle. In the Drum Dance, the drummers carry the drum. The people walk behind them. The group starts in the west and keeps stopping at points around the compass. They sing songs of how the Caddo people began.

WORD SORT

Find words that follow the unit spelling rule: double the final consonant when adding **-ed** or **-ing**. Write each word once.

1. Write the word that follows the unit spelling rule and ends with **-ed**.

2–6. Write the words that follow the unit spelling rule and end with **-ing**.

 TEKS 3.24A Use knowledge of letter sounds, word parts, word segmentation, and syllabication to spell. **3.24Bi** Spell words with more advanced orthographic patterns and rules: consonant doubling when adding an ending. **3.24C** Spell high-frequency and compound words from a commonly used list.

Connections to THINKING

Read the spelling words and sentences.

1.	must've	*must've*	We **must've** misplaced the toy.
2.	I've	*I've*	**I've** finally learned how to swim.
3.	we'll	*we'll*	At noon **we'll** stop to have lunch.
4.	you'll	*you'll*	When do you think **you'll** arrive?
5.	they'll	*they'll*	The boys said **they'll** wash the car.
6.	she'll	*she'll*	My aunt says **she'll** take me shopping.
7.	we've	*we've*	Look at how much **we've** done today.
8.	I'll	*I'll*	On my next birthday **I'll** be ten.
9.	he'll	*he'll*	Tran is sure **he'll** win the spelling bee.
10.	should've	*should've*	We **should've** brought our umbrellas.
11.	won't	*won't*	My cat **won't** go near the vacuum.
12.	who'll	*who'll*	Do you know **who'll** win the game?
13.	might've	*might've*	Fareida **might've** seen the new student.
14.	you've	*you've*	Let me know when **you've** finished.
15.	that'll	*that'll*	I hope **that'll** fix the broken bike.

Think & Sort the spelling words.

Write the spelling words in which:

    1. two words have been shortened.

  2–7. **have** has been shortened.

8–15. **will** has been shortened.

Remember

A contraction is a shortened form of two words: **I have** becomes **I've, we will** becomes **we'll,** and **will not** becomes **won't.** An apostrophe (') shows where letters have been left out.

 TEKS 3.24A Use knowledge of letter sounds, word parts, word segmentation, and syllabication to spell.
3.24C Spell high-frequency and compound words from a commonly used list. **3.24F** Spell complex contractions.

Connections to PHONICS

Identify Rhyming Words

Write the spelling words that match the clues.

1–3. Write the spelling words that rhyme with **peel**.

4–5. Write two spelling words that rhyme with **jewel**.

6. Write a spelling word that rhymes with **would've**.

Use Word Structure

Follow the directions to write a spelling word.
Be sure to add an apostrophe in the correct place.

7. they + will – wi = _____

8. might + have – ha = _____

9. we + have – ha = _____

10. that + will – wi = _____

11. must + have – ha = _____

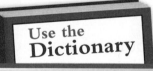

Use the Dictionary

Write the spelling word for each dictionary respelling.

12. /wōnt/   **14.** /īl/

13. /īv/   **15.** /yo͞ov/

Dictionary Check Be sure to check each spelling and respelling in your **Spelling Dictionary**.

 TEKS 3.24A Use knowledge of letter sounds, word parts, word segmentation, and syllabication to spell.
3.24C Spell high-frequency and compound words from a commonly used list. **3.24F** Spell complex contractions.
3.24G Use print and electronic resources to find and check correct spellings.

Connections to READING

must've	I've	we'll	you'll	they'll
she'll	we've	I'll	he'll	should've
won't	who'll	might've	you've	that'll

Understand Idioms

Write the spelling word that best completes each sentence. Each sentence contains an idiom—a phrase whose meaning is different than the dictionary definition of each word.

1. _____ have a bee in her bonnet when she finds out you won.

2. My dog just _____ go outside when it's raining cats and dogs!

3. _____ give you a penny for your thoughts—tell me what you are thinking.

4. The painters _____ worked around the clock to have finished so soon.

5. When my sister gets up early for school, _____ be the day that pigs fly!

6. I wonder _____ have a bone to pick with me over the colors I chose.

Use Contractions

7–15. In the paragraphs below, nine pairs of words can be made into a contraction. Write each contraction.

Today I have promised to finish unpacking. We have got a lot of work to do. The job might have been easier if we unpacked right after we moved. I know that we will be busy all morning. Dad said that he will help me. We really should have labeled the boxes before we moved.

Mom said, "I hope you will find some of my books. They will be in a box with a red sticker. Let me know when you have found them."

 TEKS 3.24A Use knowledge of letter sounds, word parts, word segmentation, and syllabication to spell. **3.24C** Spell high-frequency and compound words from a commonly used list. **3.24F** Spell complex contractions.

Connections to WRITING

Proofread a Postcard

Proofread the postcard for eight misspelled words. Then rewrite it. Write the spelling words correctly and make the corrections shown by the proofreading marks.

d̲ear Mark,

¶ I'm having so much fun visiting my cousins! Weve already gone to the beach. You'l never believe what I saw. There was ~~was~~ a gigantic horseshoe crab crawling slowly through the sand in the shallow water. Ive never seen one so big. It mus've been twenty inches long. Tomorrow we'l go to the zoo. Thatill be so much fun! We wont see the S̶hark tank, though, because it is being repaired. Ill write you again after that.

your friend,

J̲ames

Proofreading Marks

≡	Capital Letter
/	Small Letter
∧	Add
ℒ	Delete
⊙	Add a Period
¶	Indent

DESCRIPTIVE Writing Prompt
Write a Postcard

Write a postcard to an out-of-town friend. Describe the town where you live. Use vivid language to describe what you can see, hear, smell, taste, and touch. Use as many spelling words as you can.

- Use the writing process: prewrite, draft, revise, edit, and publish.
- Before you draft, make a list of details to include.
- Use complete sentences with correct capitalization, punctuation, grammar, and spelling.
- Read your work. Circle three words you are unsure about and check their spelling in a dictionary.

Transfer

Think of four more contractions. Write the words in your Spelling Journal along with the words that each contraction stands for.

TEKS 3.24A Use knowledge of letter sounds, word parts, word segmentation, and syllabication to spell.
3.24C Spell high-frequency and compound words from a commonly used list. **3.24F** Spell complex contractions.
3.24G Use print and electronic resources to find and check correct spellings.

they've	we'll	he'll	that'll	it'd
you'd	you'll	should've	they'd	it'll
she'd	they'll	won't	could've	who've
he'd	she'll	who'll	would've	we'd
must've	we've	might've	how'd	
I've	I'll	you've	who'd	

Spell Check

The sentences below do not make sense. Why? Find the word that is causing the problem and write it correctly.

1. Wed have the cookout at our house.
2. She said that shed be going to town with us.
3. I wonder if shell be at the beach tomorrow.
4. The coach said ill be starting in tomorrow's game.

Write Contractions

Write the contraction that is a shortened form of each pair of words.

5. you have
6. who will
7. should have
8. they have
9. might have
10. they will

Homophones

Homophones are words that sound the same but have different spellings and meanings. Write a spelling word that is a homophone for each word below.

11. heal
12. heed
13. yule
14. weave
15. wheel

TEKS 3.24A Use knowledge of letter sounds, word parts, word segmentation, and syllabication to spell. **3.24C** Spell high-frequency and compound words from a commonly used list. **3.24E** Spell single syllable homophones. **3.24F** Spell complex contractions.

Technology

Word Hunt

Read the paragraphs below. Look for contractions for **have, not, would, will,** and **is**.

How would you save a document on the computer? It's easy! You'd use a shortcut to save the file, such as "Command+S" or "Control+S." Or you'd click on File in your top menu and select Save. Your program will let you choose a name for the file. It'll also let you decide where you want to save it, such as your Documents folder or your desktop.

What'll you do if you forget what you named the file? Don't panic! You've got several ways to find it. Open the folder where you stored the file. You'll see an alphabetical list of file names. You can search by the date when the file was last modified, too. You can also put key words in the search box to find every file that contains those words. Don't worry: the file won't disappear!

WORD SORT

Follow the directions. Write each word only once.

1. Write the contraction for **will** and **not**.
2–4. Write contractions for **will**.
5. Write the contraction for **not**.
6. Write the contraction for **would**.
7. Write the contraction for **have**.
8. Write the contraction for **is**.

 TEKS 3.24A Use knowledge of letter sounds, word parts, word segmentation, and syllabication to spell.
3.24C Spell high-frequency and compound words from a commonly used list. **3.24F** Spell complex contractions.

195

Unit 30

Assess for Transfer

Assessment

Each assessment word in the box fits one of the spelling patterns or rules you have studied over the past five weeks. Read the unit descriptions. Then write each assessment word under the unit number it fits.

Unit 25

1–3. Two-syllable words with a short vowel sound in the first syllable are often spelled with double consonants: **dinner, better**.

Unit 26

4–6. The final **long e** sound in words like **happy** is spelled **y** and often follows a double consonant.

Unit 27

7–9. When adding **-ing** to a word that ends in **silent e**, drop the **e** and add the ending: **take, taking**.

Unit 28

10–12. When you add **-ed** or **-ing** to a word that ends with one vowel and one consonant, double the consonant and add the ending: **stop, stopped**.

Unit 29

13–15. A contraction shortens two words: **we will** becomes **we'll**.

Words for Assessment

getting

where'd

storing

mommy

butter

puppet

daddy

what'll

chasing

hopping

gallop

dizzy

using

stepped

what've

Unit 25: Double Consonants in Middle of Words

| happen | sudden | letter | summer |
| cotton | lesson | better | |

Write the spelling word that completes the sentence.

1. The brakes squealed as the car came to a _____ stop.

2. I studied my science _____ carefully.

3. My teacher says I am doing _____.

4. How could that accident _____?

5. It gets very hot in the _____.

6. My new shirt is made of _____.

7. There was a long _____ from my grandmother in today's mail.

Unit 26: Double Consonants + y

| funny | pretty | happy | sorry |
| hurry | carry | puppy | |

Write the spelling word that means the opposite of each word or words.

8. ugly   **10.** grown dog

9. sad   **11.** glad

Write the spelling word that rhymes with each word.

12. scurry   **14.** honey

13. marry

Review

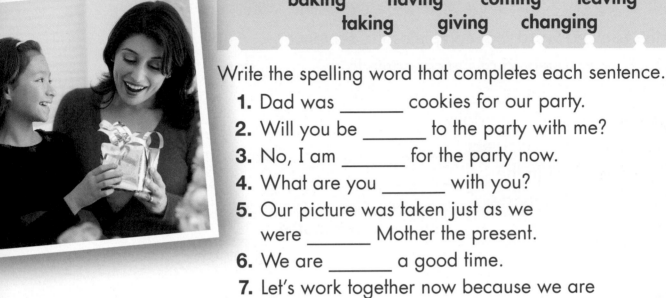

Unit 27: Drop Final e, Add -ing

| baking | having | coming | leaving |
| taking | giving | changing |

Write the spelling word that completes each sentence.

1. Dad was _____ cookies for our party.
2. Will you be _____ to the party with me?
3. No, I am _____ for the party now.
4. What are you _____ with you?
5. Our picture was taken just as we were _____ Mother the present.
6. We are _____ a good time.
7. Let's work together now because we are supposed to start _____ partners soon.

Unit 28: Consonant Doubling: Add -ed, -ing

| dropped | stopped | running | swimming |
| planned | putting | sitting |

Find the misspelled word in each sentence. Write it correctly.

8. He droped the ball.
9. It was stoppped in time.
10. No runing is allowed at the pool.
11. He was sittin on the porch.
12. Meg planed to go with me.
13. My favorite sport is swiming.
14. He was puttng away the art supplies.

Unit 29: Contractions

she'll	we've	I'll	must've
we'll	I've	you'll	

Write the spelling word that is a contraction for each pair of words below.

1. we will

2. you will

3. must have

4. I have

5. she will

6. we have

7. I will

Spelling Study Strategy

Word Swap

Practicing spelling words can be fun if you make it into a game.

1. Swap spelling lists with a partner.

2. Ask your partner to read the first word on your list. Write the word on a piece of scrap paper.

3. Ask your partner to check your spelling. If you spelled the word correctly, your partner should say the next word on your list. If you did not spell the word correctly, ask your partner to spell the word aloud for you. Write the correct spelling.

4. Keep going until you have practiced five words. Then trade jobs. Continue until you and your partner have practiced all words on your lists.

Directions: Read the introduction and the passage that follows. Then read each question and fill in the space in front of the correct answer on your answer sheet.

Rachel wrote this story about some surprising things that happened during her first job. She wants you to review her paper. As you read, think about ways that Rachel can improve her story.

A Hard Lesson

(1) To earn money for swiming lessons, I agreed to care for a neighbor's puppy while she was away. (2) I planned to feed and walk Banjo before diner every night. (3) It was my first job!

(4) At first, things went well. (5) But on the fourth day, Fred, the man next door, spotted Banjo digging up his flowers. (6) I mustv'e left the gate unlocked and the puppy escaped! (7) "I'm sory, but you'll have to pay for those pretty flowers," said Mom.

(8) One day, I brought Banjo home to my house to play. (9) When I wasn't looking, he ate my brother Tim's favorite cotton shirt. (10) "That'l be five dollars," declared Tim.

(11) Another time, I took a chance and let Banjo off his leash. (12) Soon he was slideing through muddy puddles and splattering Fred's clean car. (13) The car wash cost me four dollars. (14) I was losing more money than I was making! (15) It's time to do a beter job!

GO ON

1 What change, if any, should be made in sentence 1?

- ⬭ Change *swiming* to **swimming**
- ⬭ Change *lessons* to **lesons**
- ⬭ Change *puppy* to **puppey**
- ⬭ Make no change

2 What change, if any, should be made in sentence 2?

- ⬭ Change *planned* to **planed**
- ⬭ Change *diner* to **dinner**
- ⬭ Change *every* to **evry**
- ⬭ Make no change

3 What change, if any, should be made in sentence 5?

- ⬭ Change *spotted* to **spoted**
- ⬭ Change *digging* to **diging**
- ⬭ Change *flowers* to **flouers**
- ⬭ Make no change

4 What change, if any, should be made in sentence 6?

- ⬭ Change *mustv'e* to **must've**
- ⬭ Change *puppy* to **puppey**
- ⬭ Change *escaped* to **escapped**
- ⬭ Make no change

5 What change, if any, should be made in sentence 7?

- ⬭ Change *sory* to **sorry**
- ⬭ Change *you'll* to **you'l**
- ⬭ Change *pretty* to **pritty**
- ⬭ Make no change

6 What change, if any, should be made in sentence 9?

- ⬭ Change *wasn't* to **was'nt**
- ⬭ Change *cotton* to **coton**
- ⬭ Change *shirt* to **shert**
- ⬭ Make no change

7 What change, if any, should be made in sentence 10?

- ⬭ Change *That'l* to **That'll**
- ⬭ Change *dollars* to **dollers**
- ⬭ Change *declared* to **declaired**
- ⬭ Make no change

8 What change, if any, should be made in sentence 12?

- ⬭ Change *slideing* to **sliding**
- ⬭ Change *muddy* to **mudy**
- ⬭ Change *puddles* to **puddels**
- ⬭ Make no change

9 What change, if any, should be made in sentence 14?

- ⬭ Change *losing* to **loosing**
- ⬭ Change *money* to **mony**
- ⬭ Change *making* to **makeing**
- ⬭ Make no change

10 What change, if any, should be made in sentence 15?

- ⬭ Change *It's* to **Its**
- ⬭ Change *beter* to **better**
- ⬭ Change *job* to **jab**
- ⬭ Make no change

STOP

Grammar, Usage, and Mechanics
Adjectives

An **adjective** describes, or tells about, a noun. Adjectives make sentences more interesting.

A **huge** lizard hid behind the **open** door.

The **hungry** girls quickly ate the **delicious** pizza.

happy	funny	sudden	pretty

A. Write an adjective from the box that best completes each sentence.

1. The _____ rain caught us all by surprise.
2. Everyone laughed at Chad's _____ joke.
3. Those flowers are very _____.
4. A _____ baby giggles and smiles.

must've	we'll	you'll	we've

B. Write a contraction from the box to complete the sentence. Then write the adjective in the sentence.

5–6. My family decided that _____ buy a better rug.

7–8. Do you think _____ wash your muddy dog?

9–10. His joke _____ caused the merry laughter.

TEKS 3.24C Spell high-frequency and compound words from a commonly used list.

The Writing Process: Persuasive
Writing a Persuasive Paragraph

PREWRITING

There are so many careers in the world! Which do you think is the best? There are books about different careers at the library. You can also have an adult help you find information on the Internet. As you think about a career, take notes. Choose one career and list the reasons you think that career is the best to have.

DRAFTING

Use your reasons to write a persuasive paragraph. Begin with a topic sentence. Follow your ideas as you write supporting sentences. Use as many spelling words as possible.

REVISING

When you have finished your first draft, read your paragraph from beginning to end. Check to see if you have included all of your reasons. Write your final draft.

EDITING

Use the **Editing Checklist** to proofread your paragraph. Be sure to use proofreading marks when you make corrections. Circle at least two words that might be misspelled. Use a dictionary or electronic resource to check the spelling.

PUBLISHING

Write or print a final copy of your persuasive paragraph. Add a picture of a person who has the best career and share it with your readers.

EDITING CHECKLIST

Spelling

✓ Circle words that contain the spelling patterns and rules learned in Units 25–29.

✓ Check the circled words in your **Spelling Dictionary**.

✓ Check for other spelling errors.

Capital Letters

✓ Capitalize important words in the title.

✓ Capitalize the first word in each sentence.

✓ Capitalize proper nouns.

Punctuation

✓ End each sentence with the correct punctuation.

✓ Use commas, apostrophes, and quotation marks correctly.

Grammar, Usage, and Mechanics

✓ Use adjectives correctly to make sentences more interesting.

 TEKS 3.24A Use knowledge of letter sounds, word parts, word segmentation, and syllabication to spell.
3.24G Use print and electronic resources to find and check correct spellings.

203

Connections to THINKING

Read the spelling words and sentences.

1. flags — *flags* — That ship is flying two **flags**.
2. inches — *inches* — There are twelve **inches** in a foot.
3. dresses — *dresses* — Pam's **dresses** are all too short.
4. pies — *pies* — Two **pies** are baking in the oven.
5. bushes — *bushes* — The ball is lost in the **bushes**.
6. classes — *classes* — My dad takes **classes** in French.
7. apples — *apples* — Some **apples** fell from the tree.
8. colors — *colors* — What **colors** are in the painting?
9. drums — *drums* — Marge plays the **drums** in the band.
10. branches — *branches* — Some tree **branches** need cutting.
11. things — *things* — I put my **things** in my pack.
12. buses — *buses* — The school **buses** take us home.
13. benches — *benches* — People sit on **benches** in the park.
14. tracks — *tracks* — We followed the deer's **tracks**.
15. brushes — *brushes* — Those **brushes** are for oil painting.

Think & Sort the spelling words.

1–7. Write the plural spelling words that are formed by adding **-s**.

8–15. Write the plural spelling words that are formed by adding **-es**.

Remember

You can add the endings **-s** or **-es** to many words to make them plural. When a word ends in **s, ch,** or **sh,** add **-es** and make a new syllable.

 TEKS 3.24A Use knowledge of letter sounds, word parts, word segmentation, and syllabication to spell.
3.24C Spell high-frequency and compound words from a commonly used list.

Identify Ending Sounds

The inflectional endings **-s** and **-es** can make the /s/ sound as in **tricks,** the /z/ sound as in **wings,** or the /əz/ sound as in **glasses**.

1–4. Write the one-syllable spelling words that end with the /z/ sound.

5. Write the one-syllable spelling word that ends with the /s/ sound.

Understand Complex Consonants

Remember that in a consonant digraph, two or more consonants work together to make a single sound, such as **th** in **things**.

6–7. Write the two-syllable spelling words that have the /sh/ sound spelled **sh**. Circle the plural endings.

8–10. Write the two-syllable spelling words that have the /ch/ sound spelled **ch**. Circle the plural endings.

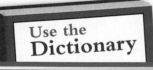

Use the **Dictionary**

Look at the pronunciations below. Write each word, and add **-s** or **-es** to make a spelling word.

11. /ăp′ əl/   **14.** /kŭl′ ər/

12. /bŭs/   **15.** /drĕs/

13. /klăs/

Dictionary Check Be sure to check your answers in your **Spelling Dictionary**.

TEKS 3.24A Use knowledge of letter sounds, word parts, word segmentation, and syllabication to spell.
3.24Bv Spell words with more advanced orthographic patterns and rules: complex consonants.
3.24C Spell high-frequency and compound words from a commonly used list.

205

Connections to READING

flags	inches	dresses	pies	bushes
classes	apples	colors	drums	branches
things	buses	benches	tracks	brushes

Complete the Groups

Write the spelling word that belongs
in each group.

1. flutes, pianos, _____
2. miles, yards, feet, _____
3. bananas, peaches, pears, _____
4. cookies, cakes, _____
5. cars, trucks, _____
6. skirts, pants, _____
7. banners, symbols, _____

Use Context Clues

Write the spelling word that completes each sentence.

8. We will need several different sizes of _____ to paint this wall.
9. Orange and red are warm _____.
10. There are many _____ happening after school this week.
11. A train is coming down the _____.
12. Two _____ from nearby trees fell on the roof during the storm.
13. Those rose _____ have grown a lot since we planted them last year.
14. There are new _____ on the field for each team's players to sit on.
15. Nell is taking karate _____.

 TEKS 3.24C Spell high-frequency and compound words from a commonly used list.

Connections to WRITING

Proofread an E-Mail Message

Proofread the e-mail message for eight misspelled words. Then rewrite it. Write the spelling words correctly and make the corrections shown by the proofreading marks.

Send   Save as a Draft   Cancel   Attach Files

From: Rferrara@fastserve.com

To: LaurenCat@edirect.com

Subject: Picking Apples

Dear lauren,

After my brother finishes his clases, he will take us to pick appels. Can you come?He wants to see the fall colores of the Leaves on the branchs. I want to follow the rabbit trackes through the bushs. There are are many thinges we can make with the apples. You can eat pis with us later.

Ava

Proofreading Marks

≡   Capital Letter

/   Small Letter

∧   Add

℘   Delete

⊙   Add a Period

⁋   Indent

PERSUASIVE Writing Prompt
Write an E-Mail Message

Write an e-mail message inviting someone to go somewhere with you. Tell where you will go and what you will do. Use as many spelling words as you can.

- Use the writing process: prewrite, draft, revise, edit, and publish.
- Be persuasive. Whom will you invite? Include details that will make him or her want to come with you.
- Use complete sentences with correct capitalization, punctuation, grammar, and spelling.
- Read your work. Circle three words you are unsure about, and check their spellings in a dictionary.

Transfer
Think of six more plural words that are formed by adding **-s** or **-es**. Write the words in your Spelling Journal and circle the plural endings.

TEKS 3.24A Use knowledge of letter sounds, word parts, word segmentation, and syllabication to spell. **3.24C** Spell high-frequency and compound words from a commonly used list. **3.24G** Use print and electronic resources to find and check correct spellings.

207

boats	classes	flags	brushes	roofs
foxes	colors	pies	friends	scarfs
snacks	branches	bushes	patches	switches
wishes	things	apples	sandwiches	walruses
inches	buses	drums	slippers	
dresses	tracks	benches	gulfs	

Word Building

When a base word ends in **ch, sh, s, x,** or **z,** add **-es** to form the plural: **branch, branches**. Write the plural form of each word below.

1. brush
2. drum
3. bench

4. sandwich
5. inch
6. flag

Use Syllables

If a plural word ends in **-es,** divide the word into syllables between the end of the base word and the **es: class/es.** Write the plural of each word below and include a slash mark to show where the words are divided. Check your answers in the **Spelling Dictionary**.

7. fox
8. patch
9. bus
10. dress
11. bush

12. class
13. wish
14. branch
15. switch

TEKS 3.24A Use knowledge of letter sounds, word parts, word segmentation, and syllabication to spell. **3.24C** Spell high-frequency and compound words from a commonly used list. **3.24D** Spell words with common syllable constructions.

Word Hunt

Read the paragraphs below. Look for plural words that are formed by adding **-s** or **-es**.

Did you know that birds have several kinds of feathers? Contour feathers are the bright feathers we think of when we picture a bird in a tree. The colors and shapes of these feathers help us tell the kinds of birds apart. A bird is usually the same color as its parents.

Birds have other kinds of feathers. Some birds have stiff bristle feathers that help it catch food. Other birds have eyelashes that are actually bristle feathers. Down feathers are soft and fluffy. Found close to the bird's body, these feathers help keep the bird warm. Down feathers can be used to stuff clothing and quilts. Then they keep people warm, too.

WORD SORT

Follow the directions. Write each word only once.

1. Write the plural word that is formed by adding **-es**.

2–8. Write the plural words that are formed by adding **-s**.

 TEKS 3.24A Use knowledge of letter sounds, word parts, word segmentation, and syllabication to spell.
3.24C Spell high-frequency and compound words from a commonly used list.

209

Connections to THINKING

Read the spelling words and sentences.

1.	party	*party*	I will bring juice for the class **party**.
2.	baby	*baby*	There is a new **baby** at Laila's house.
3.	fairy	*fairy*	My favorite story is a **fairy** tale.
4.	parties	*parties*	Our class had two **parties** last month.
5.	spy	*spy*	A **spy** finds out secret information.
6.	babies	*babies*	This is a daycare center for **babies**.
7.	spies	*spies*	The exciting movie was about **spies**.
8.	fairies	*fairies*	In the story, **fairies** granted wishes.
9.	mystery	*mystery*	The location of the ring is a **mystery**.
10.	factories	*factories*	Many people work in **factories**.
11.	mysteries	*mysteries*	I have read that series of **mysteries**.
12.	hobby	*hobby*	What is your favorite **hobby**?
13.	factory	*factory*	My aunt works in a toy **factory**.
14.	ruby	*ruby*	The beautiful jewel was a red **ruby**.
15.	hobbies	*hobbies*	Reading and skating are my **hobbies**.

Think & Sort the spelling words.

1–14. Write each singular and plural pair. Think about how the spelling changes when you write the plural word.

15. Write the word that does not have a plural partner on the list. Can you spell that plural?

Remember

Plural nouns name more than one person, place, or thing. If a word ends with a consonant followed by **y,** change the final **y** to **i** and add **-es** to form the plural.

 TEKS 3.24A Use knowledge of letter sounds, word parts, word segmentation, and syllabication to spell.
3.24Biii Spell words with more advanced orthographic patterns and rules: changing y to i before adding an ending. **3.24C** Spell high-frequency and compound words from a commonly used list.

Identify Open and Closed Syllables

An open syllable ends with a vowel sound. A closed syllable ends with a consonant sound. Read and say each singular spelling word. Is the first syllable open or closed? Check the pronunciations in your **Spelling Dictionary** if you are unsure.

1–3. Write the singular spelling words that have an open first syllable.

4–8. Write the singular spelling words that have a closed first syllable.

Apply the Spelling Rule

Write the plural form of each word below by changing the **y** to **i** before adding **-es**.

9. spy
10. baby
11. fairy
12. hobby
13. factory
14. mystery
15. party

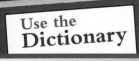

Use the **Dictionary**

Look up each singular spelling word in your **Spelling Dictionary**. For each singular word you wrote for the activities above, draw a slash mark to indicate where each word is divided into syllables.

 TEKS 3.24A Use knowledge of letter sounds, word parts, word segmentation, and syllabication to spell. **3.24Biii** Spell words with more advanced orthographic patterns and rules: changing y to i before adding an ending. **3.24C** Spell high-frequency and compound words from a commonly used list. **3.24D** Spell words with common syllable constructions.

party	baby	fairy	parties	spy
babies	spies	fairies	mystery	factories
mysteries	hobby	factory	ruby	hobbies

Complete the Groups

Write the spelling word that belongs in each group.

1. thriller, suspense, _____

2. diamond, emerald, _____

3. gnomes, sprites, _____

4. toddler, newborn, _____

5. event, festival, _____

6. detective, secret agent, _____

7. sports, pastimes, _____

8. plants, buildings, _____

Use Synonyms

Write spelling words that are synonyms for these words.

9. celebrations

10. pixie

11. infants

12. undercover agents

13. workplace

14. favorite activity

15. unsolved puzzles

 TEKS 3.24C Spell high-frequency and compound words from a commonly used list.

Connections to WRITING

Proofread a Setting Description

Proofread the setting description below for eight misspelled words. Then rewrite it. Write the spelling words correctly and make the corrections shown by the proofreading marks.

¶ It is one of those old factorys that looks like the
setting for a mysterie. it has broken, boarded-up
windows, and the wind whistles through holes in the
roof. There are so many dark hiding places₀It is the
perfect Place for me to be a spey with my buddy, Eli.
We can pretend to be spys at a fancy partey. Solving
mysterys, our favorite hobbie, will be fun in the factry.

Proofreading Marks

≡	Capital Letter
/	Small Letter
∧	Add
ℓ	Delete
⊙	Add a Period
¶	Indent

DESCRIPTIVE Writing Prompt
Write a Setting Description

Write a description of a setting. It can be a place you know well or a place you make up. Bring your setting to life by carefully choosing words that appeal to readers' senses. Use as many spelling words as you can.

- Use the writing process: prewrite, draft, revise, edit, and publish.
- After you draft your description, look it over again. Did you use words that will help your readers picture the setting in their minds?
- Use complete sentences with correct capitalization, punctuation, grammar, and spelling.
- Read your work. Circle three words you are unsure about. Check spellings in a print or online resource.

Transfer
Think of three more nouns that end in **consonant** + **y**. Write the words in your Spelling Journal, and then write their plurals by changing **y** to **i** and adding **-es**.

TEKS 3.24A Use knowledge of letter sounds, word parts, word segmentation, and syllabication to spell.
3.24Biii Spell words with more advanced orthographic patterns and rules: changing y to i before adding an ending. **3.24C** Spell high-frequency and compound words from a commonly used list. **3.24G** Use print and electronic resources to find and check correct spellings.

213

Word Study

butterfly	fairy	mystery	hobbies	strawberry
sky	parties	factories	ladies	buddies
skies	spy	mysteries	lady	cavities
butterflies	babies	hobby	rubies	strawberries
party	spies	factory	buddy	
baby	fairies	ruby	cavity	

Base Words

Write a **consonant + y** to complete the spelling words. Then write the plural form of each word.

1–2. fai __ __   **7–8.** par __ __

3–4. ru __ __   **9–10.** cavi __ __

5–6. ba __ __

Meaning Mastery

Write the word that matches each meaning. Check your answers in your **Spelling Dictionary**. Circle the compound words.

11. activities or interests that people do for pleasure

12. insect with a slender body and four colorful wings

13. red fruit that is sweet and juicy

14. women

15. good friends

TEKS 3.24A Use knowledge of letter sounds, word parts, word segmentation, and syllabication to spell.
3.24Biii Spell words with more advanced orthographic patterns and rules: changing y to i before adding an ending. **3.24C** Spell high-frequency and compound words from a commonly used list.

Social Studies

Word Hunt

Read the paragraphs below. Look for nouns that end with **consonant + y** and plural words that are formed by changing **y** to **i** and adding **-es**.

History has many mysteries. The story of the first English colony in America is one of them.

In 1587, a group of English people landed on Roanoke Island. They were led by John White. There were 117 men, ladies, and children. They hoped to farm the rich soil of the Americas.

Soon the first child was born on the island. John White sailed to England to get supplies for the colony. He had a lot of delays, from weather to war. He finally returned in 1590.

White could find no trace of the people he had left behind. The only clues were words carved into a tree. They told the name of a nearby island. Had the settlers moved there? Did they go to live with friendly Native Americans? A huge storm blew up. White had to leave the island. Later studies could not discover what became of the lost colony.

 **WORD SORT**

Follow the directions. Write each word only once.

1–3. Write the singular nouns ending with **consonant + y** that can be made plural by changing **y** to **i** and adding **-es**.

4–7. Write the plural nouns that were formed by changing **y** to **i** and adding **-es**.

 TEKS 3.24A Use knowledge of letter sounds, word parts, word segmentation, and syllabication to spell.
3.24Biii Spell words with more advanced orthographic patterns and rules: changing y to i before adding an ending.
3.24C Spell high-frequency and compound words from a commonly used list.

Connections to THINKING

Read the spelling words and sentences.

1.	larger	*larger*	This shoe is **larger** than that one.
2.	sadder	*sadder*	Ed is **sadder** than I am.
3.	widest	*widest*	I have more room on the **widest** track.
4.	sharper	*sharper*	I need to make this pencil **sharper**.
5.	closest	*closest*	Leah sits **closest** to the door.
6.	hotter	*hotter*	Upstairs is **hotter** than downstairs.
7.	saddest	*saddest*	The **saddest** child cried and cried.
8.	redder	*redder*	The more he ran, the **redder** he got.
9.	reddest	*reddest*	Tara has the **reddest** cheeks of all.
10.	wider	*wider*	Trucks can drive on this **wider** road.
11.	later	*later*	I will get there **later** than Sue will.
12.	largest	*largest*	The whale is the **largest** animal.
13.	closer	*closer*	Can you ride **closer** to the fence?
14.	hottest	*hottest*	Which frying pan is the **hottest**?
15.	latest	*latest*	We listen to the **latest** news on TV.

Think & Sort the spelling words.

Write the spelling words that follow these spelling rules:

1–8. Drop final **e** before adding **-er** or **-est**.

9–14. Double the final consonant and add **-er** or **-est**.

15. Make no change before adding **-er** or **-est**.

Remember

When adding **-er** or **-est** to a base word, follow these rules:
If a word ends with final **e,** drop the **e** before adding **-er**
or **-est**. If a word ends with a single consonant, double the
consonant and add the ending. If a word ends with two
consonants, add the ending.

TEKS 3.24A Use knowledge of letter sounds, word parts, word segmentation, and syllabication to spell.
3.24Bi Spell words with more advanced orthographic patterns and rules: consonant doubling before adding
an ending. **3.24Bii** Spell words with more advanced orthographic patterns and rules: dropping final "e"
when endings are added. **3.24C** Spell high-frequency and compound words from a commonly used list.

Connections to PHONICS

Match Beginning and Ending Sounds

Write the spelling word that fits each clue.

1. It begins like **shop**.
2. It begins like **clap** and ends like **best**.
3. It begins like **hop** and ends like **after**.
4. It begins like **won** and ends like **test**.
5. It begins like **rock** and ends like **best**.

Understand Word Structure

Add **-er** to the following words to write a spelling word.

6. sad
7. late
8. red

9. close
10. large

Add **-est** to the following words to write a spelling word.

11. large
12. hot

13. late

Use the
Thesaurus

Write a spelling word that is a synonym for each of these words. Check your answers by looking up the base word for the spelling word in your **Writing Thesaurus**.

14. most unhappy

15. broader

 TEKS 3.24A Use knowledge of letter sounds, word parts, word segmentation, and syllabication to spell.
3.24Bi Spell words with more advanced orthographic patterns and rules: consonant doubling before adding an ending. **3.24Bii** Spell words with more advanced orthographic patterns and rules: dropping final "e" when endings are added. **3.24C** Spell high-frequency and compound words from a commonly used list.

larger	sadder	widest	sharper	closest
hotter	saddest	redder	reddest	wider
later	largest	closer	hottest	latest

Complete the Sentences

Write the **-er** or **-est** form of the underlined word to complete each sentence.

1. His <u>red</u> shirt is _____ than mine.

2. That <u>sad</u> clown has the _____ face I have ever seen.

3. Miguel's <u>hot</u> chili is the _____ chili in town.

4. I am <u>late</u> because the bus was _____ than usual.

5. The _____ pig of all is that <u>large</u> one over there.

6. This <u>wide</u> path is _____ than the one behind my house.

Complete the Groups

Write the spelling word that completes each group.

7. sad, _____, saddest

8. wide, wider, _____

9. sharp, _____, sharpest

10. red, redder, _____

Use Context Clues

Write spelling words from the box to complete the paragraph.

We went to the mall on a hot day. In fact, we couldn't have picked a **11.** day. It was also a busy day. The **12.** we got to the mall, the more traffic we saw. The **13.** we could park our car was in the **14.** of the two lots. By the time we walked to the stores, it was 5:00. The **15.** the stores are open is 6:00.

TEKS 3.24A Use knowledge of letter sounds, word parts, word segmentation, and syllabication to spell. **3.24Bi** Spell words with more advanced orthographic patterns and rules: consonant doubling before adding an ending. **3.24Bii** Spell words with more advanced orthographic patterns and rules: dropping final "e" when endings are added. **3.24C** Spell high-frequency and compound words from a commonly used list.

Connections to WRITING

Proofread an Ad

Proofread the ad below for eight misspelled words. Then rewrite the ad. Write the spelling words correctly and make the corrections shown by the proofreading marks.

Cool clothes for Kids

We have the lattest and hotest styles. We have a largger selection than other Stores. You won't find a wyder choice anywhere. We have all sizes, from largesst to smallest. You will will look sharpper, and you will pay less Latur in the year, our prices might go even lower. If you are paying high prices, take a closser look at Cool Clothes for kids.

PERSUASIVE Writing Prompt
Write an Ad

Write an ad for something you want to sell. Persuade your reader to buy what you are selling by using interesting details. Use as many spelling words as you can.

- Use the writing process: prewrite, draft, revise, edit, and publish.
- Be persuasive. Include details that will make a person want to buy the item you are selling.
- Use complete sentences with correct capitalization, punctuation, grammar, and spelling.
- Read your work. Circle three words you are unsure about and check their spelling in a dictionary.

Transfer

Think of more words that follow the unit spelling rules. Write two words for each rule in your Spelling Journal and circle the suffixes.

TEKS 3.24A Use knowledge of letter sounds, word parts, word segmentation, and syllabication to spell.
3.24Bi Spell words with more advanced orthographic patterns and rules: consonant doubling before adding an ending. **3.24Bii** Spell words with more advanced orthographic patterns and rules: dropping final "e" when endings are added. **3.24C** Spell high-frequency and compound words from a commonly used list.
3.24G Use print and electronic resources to find and check correct spellings.

longer	sharper	larger	latest	bravest
longest	reddest	closest	safer	flatter
whiter	later	hotter	safest	flattest
whitest	largest	saddest	thinner	smoothest
sadder	closer	redder	thinnest	smoother
widest	hottest	wider	braver	

Meaning Mastery

Write the spelling word that means the same as each phrase below. Circle the word if you dropped an **e** before adding the ending. Draw a box around the word if you doubled a final consonant.

1. more safe
2. most wide
3. most long
4. more red
5. more sharp
6. most close
7. most brave
8. most smooth

Identify Syllables

If the last consonant in a word is doubled before **-er** or **-est** is added, then the new word is divided into syllables between the double consonants: **hot/test**. Write each word below and use a slash mark to show where the word is divided. Check your answers in your **Spelling Dictionary**.

9. sadder
10. flatter
11. hotter
12. saddest
13. reddest
14. thinnest
15. flattest

TEKS 3.24A Use knowledge of letter sounds, word parts, word segmentation, and syllabication to spell. **3.24Bi** Spell words with more advanced orthographic patterns and rules: consonant doubling before adding an ending. **3.24Bii** Spell words with more advanced orthographic patterns and rules: dropping final "e" when endings are added. **3.24C** Spell high-frequency and compound words from a commonly used list. **3.24D** Spell words with common syllable constructions.

Math

Word Hunt

Read the paragraphs below. Look for words that end with **-er** and **-est**.

"This math worksheet is the hardest one yet," Doug complained from the backseat of the car.

His mom asked, "What is the latest subject you're studying?"

"Symmetry," he said. "I still need examples of figures with one, two, and three lines of symmetry."

His mother asked, "Both sides of a figure must match along the fold line for it to have symmetry, right?"

"Right. One side can't be bigger or smaller." They drove closer to a field where children were flying kites. "Hey, a kite has one line of symmetry," Doug said.

Then his mother pointed to a sign with the largest and reddest triangle Doug had ever seen. "How about that triangle?" Doug counted three lines of symmetry.

They passed Hix Street. Doug drew an H and an X. "Hey, Mom," he said. "Capital H and capital X *both* have two lines of symmetry. Maybe I'll get extra credit!"

WORD SORT

Follow the directions.

1–3. Write the words for which the final **e** was dropped from the base word before **-er** or **-est** was added.

4–5. Write the words for which the final consonant of the base word was doubled before **-er** or **-est** was added.

6–7. Write the words whose base word was not changed.

 TEKS 3.24A Use knowledge of letter sounds, word parts, word segmentation, and syllabication to spell. **3.24Bi** Spell words with more advanced orthographic patterns and rules: consonant doubling before adding an ending. **3.24Bii** Spell words with more advanced orthographic patterns and rules: dropping final "e" when endings are added. **3.24C** Spell high-frequency and compound words from a commonly used list.

Connections to THINKING

Read the spelling words and sentences.

1.	slowly	*slowly*	Cars move **slowly** in a traffic jam.
2.	mainly	*mainly*	Often we walk, but **mainly** we run.
3.	badly	*badly*	I **badly** need new sneakers.
4.	hourly	*hourly*	The clock chimes **hourly**.
5.	suddenly	*suddenly*	Rain fell **suddenly,** without warning.
6.	lately	*lately*	Our team has been winning **lately**.
7.	partly	*partly*	The **partly** open door let in air.
8.	closely	*closely*	We listened **closely** to his speech.
9.	really	*really*	Will I be a bit late or **really** late?
10.	lastly	*lastly*	We ate stew and **lastly** had dessert.
11.	plainly	*plainly*	I could see the boat **plainly**.
12.	loudly	*loudly*	Cows moo **loudly** at milking time.
13.	shortly	*shortly*	Mom will help us **shortly**.
14.	monthly	*monthly*	Many people are paid **monthly**.
15.	softly	*softly*	I talk **softly** so the baby can sleep.

Think & Sort the spelling words.

Write a word that goes with each base word.

1. slow
2. late
3. plain
4. main
5. part
6. loud
7. bad
8. close
9. short
10. hour
11. real
12. month
13. sudden
14. last
15. soft

Remember

You can add the suffix **-ly** to some words to make new words. If the base word ends with a consonant other than **y**, there is usually no spelling change before **-ly** is added.

 TEKS 3.24A Use knowledge of letter sounds, word parts, word segmentation, and syllabication to spell.
3.24C Spell high-frequency and compound words from a commonly used list.

Identify Complex Consonants

Remember that in a consonant blend, two or more consonants are used together and each consonant sound can be heard. In a consonant digraph, two or more consonants work together to make a single sound. A blend or digraph may come at the beginning or end of a syllable.

1. Write the spelling word that has both a consonant digraph and a consonant blend in its base word.

2–7. Write the other spelling words that have a consonant blend in the base word.

8. Write the spelling word that has a consonant digraph in its base word.

Identify Rhyme

Write the spelling word that rhymes with each word below.

9. sadly
10. plainly
11. proudly
12. stately

Use the Dictionary

Write the spelling word that matches each dictionary definition.

13. once each hour

14. in fact; actually

15. quickly and without warning

Dictionary Check Be sure to check the answers in your **Spelling Dictionary**.

TEKS 3.24A Use knowledge of letter sounds, word parts, word segmentation, and syllabication to spell.
3.24Bv Spell words with more advanced orthographic patterns and rules: complex consonants.
3.24C Spell high-frequency and compound words from a commonly used list.

slowly	mainly	badly	hourly	suddenly
lately	partly	closely	really	lastly
plainly	loudly	shortly	monthly	softly

Identify Synonyms

Write the spelling word that is a synonym for the underlined word or words.

1. Most cats swim <u>poorly</u>.
2. Have you been to the movies <u>recently</u>?
3. Aesop <u>mostly</u> wrote stories about animals to teach a lesson.
4. I clean my room <u>once a month</u>.
5. Tomatoes are <u>actually</u> fruits, not vegetables.
6. We turned off the lights, closed our eyes, and <u>finally</u> went to sleep.
7. We could <u>clearly</u> see the stars and the full moon in the dark sky.
8. The thunderstorm hit the area <u>without warning</u>.
9. The train will arrive <u>soon</u>.

Understand Meaning

Answer the clues by writing spelling words.

10. A snail crawls this way.
11. A noisy rooster crows this way.
12. A gentle breeze blows this way.
13. This is how often sixty minutes pass.
14. This is how a half-built house has been constructed.
15. This is how you view something under a magnifying glass.

TEKS 3.24C Spell high-frequency and compound words from a commonly used list.

Connections to WRITING

Proofread a Book Report

Proofread the book report below for eight misspelled words. Then rewrite the report. Write the spelling words correctly and make the corrections shown by the proofreading marks.

¶ The best book I have read lateley is <u>The Magic School</u> <u>bus Inside a Hurricane</u> by Joanna cole. The magic school bus changes sudenly into a hot-air balloon. It rises slowley but surely into a storm⊙The children look closly at how a hurricane forms. Then the bus becomes an airplane, and the children realy have an exciting⌃Time. This book is planely fiction, but it is fun to read. I liked the book, parrtly because of the pictures. I mainley enjoyed it because I learned about hurricanes.

Proofreading Marks

≡	Capital Letter
/	Small Letter
⌃	Add
ℓ	Delete
⊙	Add a Period
¶	Indent

EXPOSITORY Writing Prompt
Write a Book Report

Write a book report about a book you liked. Be sure to give the title and author. Tell why you liked the book and include details about it. Use as many spelling words as you can.

- Use the writing process: prewrite, draft, revise, edit, and publish.
- Tell what the book is about and explain why other readers will like it.
- Use complete sentences with correct capitalization, punctuation, grammar, and spelling.
- Read your work. Circle three words you are unsure about and check their spellings in a dictionary.

Transfer
Think of three more words that end with the suffix **-ly**. Write them in your Spelling Journal and circle the suffixes.

TEKS 3.24A Use knowledge of letter sounds, word parts, word segmentation, and syllabication to spell.
3.24C Spell high-frequency and compound words from a commonly used list. **3.24G** Use print and electronic resources to find and check correct spellings.

deeply	suddenly	mainly	softly	easily
gladly	partly	badly	carelessly	greatly
neatly	really	lately	carefully	happily
timely	lastly	closely	keenly	secretly
slowly	shortly	plainly	unfriendly	
hourly	monthly	loudly	brightly	

Meaning Mastery

Write a word from the list that matches each definition.

1. poorly or in a bad manner
2. at the end or finally
3. in a way that is not fast or quick
4. happening every 30 days
5. in a way that is clear or easy to see
6. happening at a good time

Use Syllables

If a word ends with the suffix **-ly,** the word is divided into syllables between the base word and **-ly: slow/ly, sud/den/ly**. Add the suffix **-ly** to each word below. Include a slash mark to show where the word is divided into syllables. Then circle the words in which the final **y** was changed to **i** before **-ly** was added. Check your answers in the **Spelling Dictionary**.

7. loud
8. soft
9. happy
10. short
11. hour
12. secret
13. careful
14. easy
15. bright

TEKS 3.24A Use knowledge of letter sounds, word parts, word segmentation, and syllabication to spell. **3.24Biii** Spell words with more advanced orthographic patterns and rules: changing y to i before adding an ending. **3.24C** Spell high-frequency and compound words from a commonly used list. **3.24D** Spell words with common syllable constructions.

Fine Arts

Word Hunt

Read the paragraphs below. Look for words that end with **-ly**.

Have you ever heard music written by John Williams? Chances are, you have. Williams has written the scores for more than seventy-five movies. They include *Star Wars, Jaws,* and *E.T.*

At first, his career developed slowly. In 1974 he met the director Steven Spielberg, and his career suddenly took off. They have worked closely for more than thirty-five years. They are clearly a great team. Did you ever hum a scary, two-note song to mean that a shark is coming? This is the theme from the team's film, *Jaws.* Williams also wrote the music to six *Star Wars* films. To play all that music would take an orchestra many hours!

In his film music, Williams usually uses a *motif.* This is a piece of music that repeats over and over. It can be played softly or loudly. Think of the famous *Star Wars* theme. It will play endlessly in your head!

 **WORD SORT**

Follow the directions. Write the words that have:

1–7. base words ending with a consonant sound.
8. a base word ending with a vowel sound.

 TEKS 3.24A Use knowledge of letter sounds, word parts, word segmentation, and syllabication to spell.
3.24C Spell high-frequency and compound words from a commonly used list.

227

Connections to THINKING

Read the spelling words and sentences.

1. herself	*herself*	Li made a cake by **herself**.
2. nobody	*nobody*	There's **nobody** home now.
3. airplane	*airplane*	The **airplane** flies overhead.
4. grandfather	*grandfather*	Our **grandfather** visited us.
5. someone	*someone*	Did you see **someone** run by?
6. rainbow	*rainbow*	We saw a colorful **rainbow**.
7. anything	*anything*	Is there **anything** in the box?
8. grandmother	*grandmother*	My **grandmother** lives here.
9. everything	*everything*	I put **everything** away.
10. afternoon	*afternoon*	I eat lunch in the **afternoon**.
11. sunshine	*sunshine*	The **sunshine** feels warm.
12. himself	*himself*	He drew that by **himself**.
13. anybody	*anybody*	Has **anybody** seen my cat?
14. something	*something*	Tell me **something** about him.
15. without	*without*	Don't go out **without** a hat.

Think & Sort the spelling words.

Write a compound word that is built from each word below.

1. her	6. him	11. grand
2. bow	7. plane	12. every
3. sun	8. mother	13. one
4. no	9. body	14. noon
5. any	10. with	15. thing

Remember

A **compound word** is formed from two or more words: **rainbow, sunshine**.

 TEKS 3.24A Use knowledge of letter sounds, word parts, word segmentation, and syllabication to spell.
3.24C Spell high-frequency and compound words from a commonly used list.

Match Beginning and Ending Sounds

Write spelling words that match the clues. Write each word only once. Circle the smaller words in each compound.

1–2. The first syllable rhymes with **come**.

3–4. The first syllable rhymes with **many**.

5. The last syllable rhymes with **shout**.

6. The first syllable rhymes with **fair**.

7. The last syllable rhymes with **soon**.

Segment Words

Write the spelling words that begin with:

8. a short vowel followed by /**v**/.

9–10. the blend /**gr**/.

11–12. the /**h**/ sound.

13. the /**n**/ sound.

Use the Dictionary

Write the spelling words that you would find between each pair of guide words.

14. rabbit • resource   **15.** strong • switches

Dictionary Check Be sure to check your answers in your **Spelling Dictionary**.

TEKS 3.24A Use knowledge of letter sounds, word parts, word segmentation, and syllabication to spell.
3.24C Spell high-frequency and compound words from a commonly used list.

229

herself	nobody	airplane
grandfather	someone	rainbow
anything	grandmother	everything
afternoon	sunshine	himself
anybody	something	without

Solve the Analogies

Answer the clues by writing spelling words.

1. **All** is to **everybody** as **none** is to _____.
2. **Every** is to **everyone** as **some** is to _____.
3. **Everyone** is to **everybody** as **anyone** is to _____.
4. **Present** is to **absent** as **with** is to _____.
5. **Whole** is to **part** as **everything** is to _____.

Use Context Clues

Part of a spelling word is missing from one word in each sentence. Add the missing part and write the spelling word.

6. I would give any_____ to visit England.
7. The _____plane was an hour late.
8. My _____father will be sixty-five years old tomorrow.
9. Judy's grand_____ was the first woman doctor in our town.
10. Pam decided to make the dress by _____self.
11. Jack looks at _____self in the mirror.
12. The sun_____ always follows the rain.
13. Can you work this _____noon?
14. A rain_____ hung in the clouds for several minutes.
15. Some people lost _____thing in the fire.

 TEKS 3.24C Spell high-frequency and compound words from a commonly used list.

Connections to WRITING

Proofread a Letter

Proofread the letter for eight misspelled words. Then rewrite it. Write the spelling words correctly and make the corrections shown by the proofreading marks.

Dear Luella,

¶ If anebody had told me evrything I would do at the fair, i would not have believed it. First my granfather and I took an airplain ride. I have never done anythinng so fun before! In the afternon, we saw prize-winning pies and animals. We couldn't leave withowt playing a few games. Grandpa enjoyed hisself, too! You can come with ~~with~~ us next year!

love,
Jess

NARRATIVE Writing Prompt
Write a Letter

Write a letter to a friend telling about somewhere you went and what you did there. Be sure to include details about some different events or parts of what happened. Use as many spelling words as you can.

- Use the writing process: prewrite, draft, revise, edit, and publish.
- Make a list of the events in the order in which they happened. Tell about the events in that order.
- Use complete sentences with correct capitalization, punctuation, grammar, and spelling.
- Read your work. Circle three words you are unsure about and check their spellings in a dictionary.

Transfer
Think of four more compound words you might use in a letter. Write them in your Spelling Journal and circle each shorter word that makes up the compound word.

TEKS 3.24A Use knowledge of letter sounds, word parts, word segmentation, and syllabication to spell. **3.24C** Spell high-frequency and compound words from a commonly used list. **3.24G** Use print and electronic resources to find and check correct spellings.

baseball	someone	grandmother	newspaper
downtown	anything	sunshine	seat belt
notebook	everything	himself	anyone
shoelace	afternoon	anybody	bathroom
herself	without	something	everywhere
nobody	airplane	basketball	paintbrush
grandfather	rainbow	everyday	washcloth

Base Words

Write the words from the list that have one of the same word parts as the given word.

1–4. somebody

5–6. myself

7–8. everyday

9–10. grandson

Word Categories

Write words that fit in each word family.

11. clouds, rain, sun, _____

12. helicopter, jet, _____

13. magazine, television, _____

14. baseball, volleyball, _____

15. sunbeams, sunlight, _____

 TEKS 3.24A Use knowledge of letter sounds, word parts, word segmentation, and syllabication to spell.
3.24C Spell high-frequency and compound words from a commonly used list.

Technology

Word Hunt

Read the paragraphs below. Look for compound words.

It's a weekend afternoon. You are making your family tree. You start to e-mail some questions to your grandmother. You think Uncle Pete might be able to help you, too. However, where should you put his e-mail address? You could add it in the "To" list, or you could add it in the "cc" list. Did you ever wonder what those letters really mean?

The letters *cc* stand for "carbon copy." Years ago, people used typewriters. Carbon paper made the copies. It had ink on one side. People put a sheet of carbon paper between blank pieces of paper. They put the stack into the typewriter. Then they started typing. Each keystroke made a key hit the stack of paper. Ink from the carbon paper pressed onto the paper beneath. Stroke by stroke, a copy was made.

Today, carbon paper is hard to find. Computers and copiers are easier to use. Only the handy letters *cc* remain.

Write each word only once.

1–8. Find the compound words.

TEKS 3.24A Use knowledge of letter sounds, word parts, word segmentation, and syllabication to spell.
3.24C Spell high-frequency and compound words from a commonly used list.

233

Units 31–34

Assessment

Each assessment word in the box fits one of the spelling patterns or rules you have studied over the past five weeks. Read the unit descriptions. Then write each assessment word under the unit number it fits.

Unit 31

1–3. You can add the endings **-s** or **-es** to many words to make them plural.

Unit 32

4–6. If a word ends with a consonant followed by **y**, change the final **y** to **i** and add **-es** to form the plural.

Unit 33

7–9. If a word ends with final **e**, drop the **e** before adding **-er** or **-est**. If a word ends with a single consonant, double the consonant and add the ending. If a word ends with two consonants, add the ending.

Unit 34

10–12. You can add the suffix **-ly** to some words to make new words.

Unit 35

13–15. A **compound word** is formed from two or more words: **rainbow, sunshine**.

Words for Assessment

animals

bigger

safely

families

sunlight

states

older

mostly

counties

rowboat

sunglasses

friendly

speeches

nicest

nineties

Unit 31: Inflectional Endings: -s, -es

branches	colors	classes	things
	tracks	dresses	buses

Write the spelling word that completes each group of words.

1. a small branch; several _____ on the tree
2. one thing; three _____
3. one dress; many _____
4. this bus; those big yellow _____
5. my class; all the _____ in the school
6. that broken track; those railroad _____
7. the color red; all the _____ of the rainbow

Unit 32: Plurals: Change y to i

party	baby	fairies	parties
	spies	fairy	babies

Write the spelling word that completes the sentence.

8. I am going to a _____ at my cousin's house.
9. I read a story about a tiny _____ that lived in a tree.
10. Will the _____ like his new rattle?
11. In movies, _____ often drive fast cars.
12. Many cultures have stories about imaginary beings called _____.
13. It is naptime for the twin _____.
14. My teacher brings a piñata to all our class _____.

Review

Unit 33: Suffixes: -er, -est

hotter	latest	hottest	sadder
saddest	sharper	later	

Write the spelling words that belong in each group.

1. sharp, _____, sharpest

2. late, _____, _____

3. sad, _____, _____

4. hot, _____, _____

Unit 34: Suffix: -ly

hourly	really	monthly	shortly
slowly	suddenly	lastly	

Write the spelling word that can replace each underlined word.

Once a month our class goes to the zoo. I count the days very carefully. It seems that time goes by **5.** real **6.** slow. Monday is the day for our class's **7.** month zoo visit. We will do a lot on Monday. At ten o'clock we will begin by watching the **8.** hour feedings of the animals. **9.** Short after each feeding, we will watch the animals play in their cages. Before we know it, the day will be over. **10.** Last, we will ride the zoo train back to the gate. Then **11.** sudden we will find ourselves back at school. I always look forward to our trips to the zoo.

Unit 35: Compound Words

afternoon   nobody   everything   without
herself   grandfather   anything

1–7. Match a word in Column A with a word in Column B
and write a spelling word.

Column A	Column B
any	out
after	body
her	father
every	self
grand	thing
with	noon
no	thing

Spelling Study Strategy

Sorting by Endings

A good way to practice spelling is to place words
into groups according to a spelling pattern.

1. Make five columns on a large piece of
   paper or on the board.
2. Write one of the following words at
   the top of each column: **things**, **classes**,
   rubies, **closer**, **closest**, **slowly**. Include the
   underlines.
3. Have a partner choose a spelling word
   from Units 31 through 34 and say it aloud.
4. Write the spelling word under the word
   with the same ending.

Standardized Test Practice

Directions: Read the introduction and the passage that follows. Then read each question and fill in the space in front of the correct answer on your answer sheet.

Hana wrote this story about a girl who must quickly change her plans when her grandparents come to visit. She wants you to review her story. As you read, think about ways that Hana can improve it.

Remember the Alamo

(1) Jin's gramother and grandfather had visited many times before. (2) This time, Jin realy wanted to take them to see the Alamo. (3) She loved learning about the famous fort in school.

(4) Shortly after Jin entered the airport, her grandparents arrived on an airplane. (5) Jin watched as they slowley walked toward her. (6) Grandfather looked very tired and leaned on a cane. (7) Jin suddenly thought, "How will he be able to do enything?" (8) It was the saddest she'd ever felt.

(9) "There's more than one way to see the Alamo!" said Grandfather latter. (10) That week, Jin checked out books about the Alamo from the closist library. (11) She and her grandfather looked at pictures of its famous flags in bright colores. (12) They read about spys and other things, too. (13) Jin also told them what she'd learned about the Alamo in her classes.

(14) On their last day, Jin's grandparents thanked her. (15) "I'll always remember the Alamo!" said Grandfather. (16) "With out you, we never would have seen it," he said.

1 What change, if any, should be made in sentence 1?

- ◯ Change *gramother* to **grandmother**
- ◯ Change *grandfather* to **gramfather**
- ◯ Change *before* to **befour**
- ◯ Make no change

2 What change, if any, should be made in sentence 2?

- ◯ Change *realy* to **really**
- ◯ Change *wanted* to **wantid**
- ◯ Change *them* to **theme**
- ◯ Make no change

3 What change, if any, should be made in sentence 4?

- ◯ Change *Shortly* to **Shortley**
- ◯ Change *entered* to **enterred**
- ◯ Change *airplane* to **airplain**
- ◯ Make no change

4 What change, if any, should be made in sentence 5?

- ◯ Change *watched* to **watcht**
- ◯ Change *slowley* to **slowly**
- ◯ Change *walked* to **walkt**
- ◯ Make no change

5 What change, if any, should be made in sentence 7?

- ◯ Change *suddenly* to **suddnly**
- ◯ Change *able* to **abel**
- ◯ Change *enything* to **anything**
- ◯ Make no change

6 What change, if any, should be made in sentence 9?

- ◯ Change *There's* to **Theres**
- ◯ Change *Grandfather* to **Gramfather**
- ◯ Change *latter* to **later**
- ◯ Make no change

7 What change, if any, should be made in sentence 10?

- ◯ Change *checked* to **cheked**
- ◯ Change *about* to **ubout**
- ◯ Change *closist* to **closest**
- ◯ Make no change

8 What change, if any, should be made in sentence 11?

- ◯ Change *its* to **it's**
- ◯ Change *flags* to **flaggs**
- ◯ Change *colores* to **colors**
- ◯ Make no change

9 What change, if any, should be made in sentence 12?

- ◯ Change *read* to **red**
- ◯ Change *spys* to **spies**
- ◯ Change *things* to **thangs**
- ◯ Make no change

10 What change, if any, should be made in sentence 16?

- ◯ Change *With out* to **Without**
- ◯ Change *never* to **nevur**
- ◯ Change *would* to **wood**
- ◯ Make no change

STOP

Grammar, Usage, and Mechanics
Pronouns

A **pronoun** takes the place of one or more nouns.
A pronoun can be singular or plural.

> My friends met Rosa. **They** liked **her**.
> Roberto saw Tom and **me**. **He** saw **us**.

These pronouns are singular: **I, me, you, he, she, him, her, it**.
These pronouns are plural: **we, us, you, they, them**.

Practice Activity

A. Write the word that agrees with the underlined pronoun.
1. The (branch, branches) were pretty because <u>they</u> were covered in ice.
2. Give the (baby, babies) a bottle when <u>he</u> wakes.
3. Will <u>she</u> play in the recital by (herself, himself)?
4. My (grandfather, grandmother) says <u>he</u> knows best.
5. The (party, parties) was fun. <u>It</u> was held outside.

closer	largest	monthly	really	classes

B. Write the word from the box that completes the sentence and underline the pronoun.
6. Can you move _____ to Tom for the picture?
7. Joey _____ thinks he is too old to sleep in a crib.
8. I call Grandma weekly and visit her _____.
9. The _____ were fun because we learned to cook.
10. Take the _____ apples and put them in the bag.

 TEKS 3.24C Spell high-frequency and compound words from a commonly used list.

The Writing Process: Expository
Writing Directions

PREWRITING
How do you get to the library or to another place in your community? You can find city maps at the library, or you can ask your teacher to help you find city maps on the Internet. As you think about how to get to a certain place, write down the directions from start to finish.

DRAFTING
Use your directions to write a rough draft. Follow your steps as you write sentences. Use as many spelling words as possible. If you don't know how to spell a word, make your best guess.

REVISING
When you have finished your draft, read your directions from beginning to end. Check to see that you have included all of the directions a person would need. Make sure your steps are in order.

EDITING
Use the **Editing Checklist** to proofread your directions. Be sure to use proofreading marks when you make corrections. Circle at least two words that may be misspelled. Use a dictionary or electronic resource to check the spelling. Now, write your final draft.

PUBLISHING
Make a copy of your directions. Draw a map and share it with your readers.

EDITING CHECKLIST

Spelling
- ✓ Circle words that contain the spelling patterns and rules learned in Units 31–35.
- ✓ Check the circled words in your **Spelling Dictionary**.
- ✓ Check for other spelling errors.

Capital Letters
- ✓ Capitalize important words in the title.
- ✓ Capitalize the first word in each sentence.
- ✓ Capitalize proper nouns.

Punctuation
- ✓ End each sentence with the correct punctuation.
- ✓ Use commas, apostrophes, and quotation marks correctly.

Grammar, Usage, and Mechanics
- ✓ Use singular and plural pronouns correctly.

 TEKS 3.24A Use knowledge of letter sounds, word parts, word segmentation, and syllabication to spell.
3.24G Use print and electronic resources to find and check correct spellings.

241

Spelling and the Writing Process

When you write anything—a friendly letter, a paper for school—you should follow the writing process. The writing process has five steps. It might look like this:

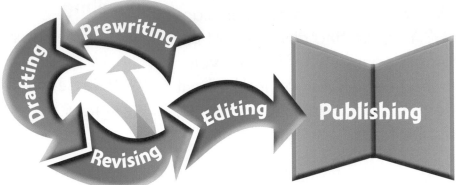

Part of the writing process forms a loop. That is because not every writing task is the same. It is also because writers often jump back and forth between the steps as they change their minds and think of new ideas.

Here is what you do in each step:

PREWRITING Think about your audience and your purpose for writing. Brainstorm ideas for writing. Use a graphic organizer to record your ideas.

DRAFTING Get your ideas down on paper. Try to spell correctly, but if you don't know a spelling, make your best guess. You can fix any mistakes later.

REVISING Improve your draft. Rewrite, change, and add words to make your message clear and descriptive.

EDITING Proofread your paper for spelling, grammar, and punctuation errors. Be sure to use a print or online dictionary to check your spelling.

PUBLISHING Make a copy of your writing and share it with your readers. Put your writing in a form that your readers will enjoy.

Confident spellers are better writers. Confident writers understand the writing process better. Know how these five steps best fit the way you write.

Spelling and Writing Ideas

Being a good speller can help make you a more confident writer. Writing often can make you a better writer. Here are descriptions of each type of writing and some ideas to get you started.

Descriptive writing describes something.

You might…

- describe something small and something big.
- describe something from the point of view of a zoo animal. Look at books about animals for ideas.

Narrative writing tells a story.

You might…

- write a story about your first visit to someplace new. Make a timeline to help you remember events in the order in which they happened.
- write a story with your best friend as the main character.

Persuasive writing tries to persuade the reader to think or do something.

You might…

- try to persuade your teacher to change a class rule.
- try to persuade your classmates to read a book you like. Skim the book again to remind yourself what you liked about it.

Expository writing explains something.

You might…

- write a report about the cause and effect of watching television while studying.
- find out how your local government works and write a report. Ask an adult to help you find articles about your town or city government in a local newspaper.
- interview an animal caregiver and write a report about the job.
- inform your classmates how to create a craft project.

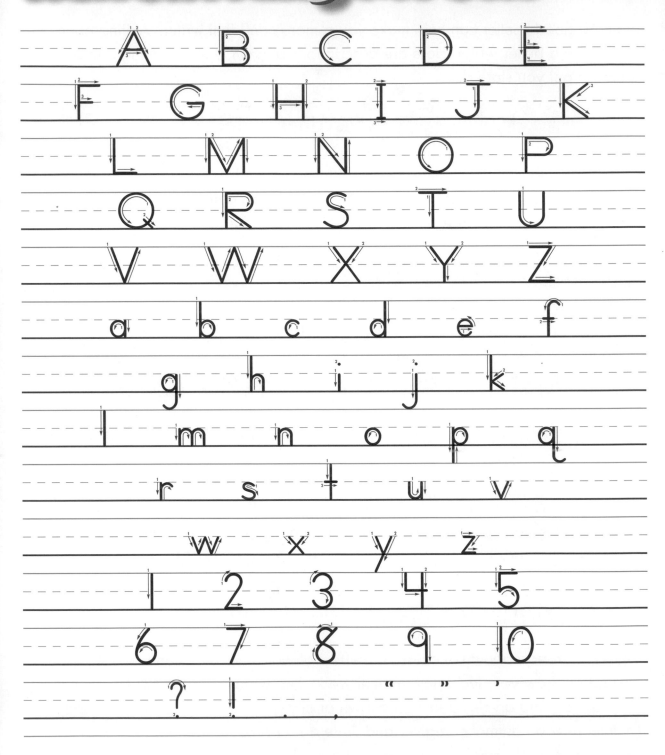

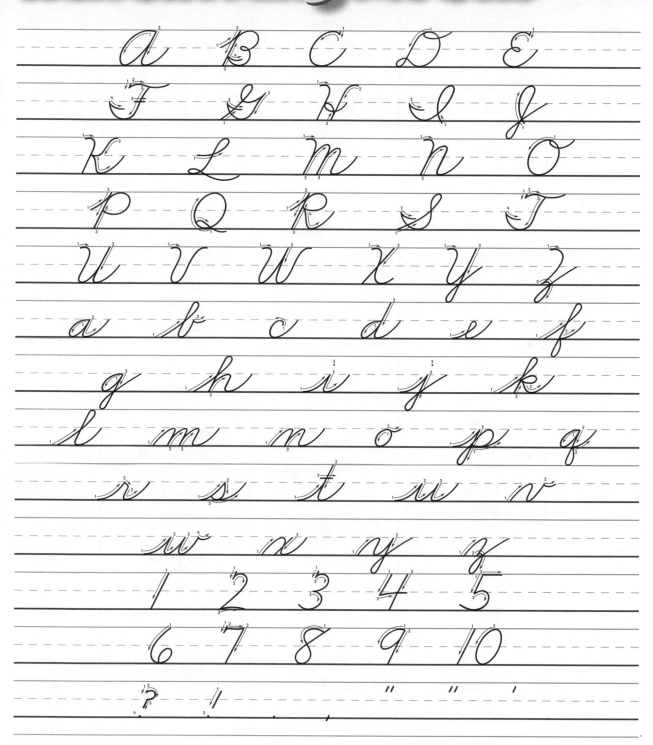

High Frequency Writing Words

A

a
about
afraid
after
again
air
all
almost
also
always
am
America
an
and
animal
animals
another
any
anything
are
around
as
ask
asked
at
ate
away

B

baby
back
bad
ball
balloons
baseball

basketball
be
bear
beautiful
because
become
bed
been
before
being
believe
best
better
big
bike
black
boat
book
books
both
boy
boys
bring
broke
brother
build
bus
but
buy
by

C

call
called
came
can
candy

can't
car
care
cars
cat
catch
caught
change
charge
children
Christmas
circus
city
class
clean
clothes
come
comes
coming
could
couldn't
country
cut

D

Dad
day
days
decided
did
didn't
died
different
dinner
do
does
doesn't

dog
dogs
doing
done
don't
door
down
dream

E

each
earth
eat
eighth
else
end
enough
even
every
everybody
everyone
everything
except
eyes

F

family
fast
father
favorite
feel
feet
fell
few
field
fight

finally
find
fire
first
fish
five
fix
food
football
for
found
four
free
Friday
friend
friends
from
front
fun
funny
future

G

game
games
gas
gave
get
gets
getting
girl
girls
give
go
God
goes
going

good
got
grade
grader
great
ground
grow

had
hair
half
happened
happy
hard
has
have
having
he
head
heard
help
her
here
he's
high
hill
him
his
hit
home
homework
hope
horse
horses
hot
hour
house

how
hurt

I
I'd
if
I'm
important
in
into
is
it
its
it's

job
jump
just

keep
kept
kids
killed
kind
knew
know

lady
land
last
later
learn
leave

left
let
let's
life
like
liked
likes
little
live
lived
lives
long
look
looked
looking
lost
lot
lots
love
lunch

mad
made
make
making
man
many
math
may
maybe
me
mean
men
might
miss
Mom
money

more
morning
most
mother
mouse
move
Mr.
Mrs.
much
music
must
my
myself

name
named
need
never
new
next
nice
night
no
not
nothing
now

of
off
oh
OK
old
on
once
one

only
or
other
our
out
outside
over
own

parents
park
party
people
person
pick
place
planet
play
played
playing
police
president
pretty
probably
problem
put

R

ran
read
ready
real
really
reason
red
responsibilities

rest
ride
riding
right
room
rules
run
running

S

said
same
saw
say
scared
school
schools
sea
second
see
seen
set
seventh
she
ship
shot
should
show
sick
since
sister
sit
sleep
small
snow
so

some
someone
something
sometimes
soon
space
sport
sports
start
started
states
stay
still
stop
stopped
store
story
street
stuff
such
sudden
suddenly
summer
sure
swimming

T

take
talk
talking
teach
teacher
teachers
team
tell
than

Thanksgiving
that
that's
the
their
them
then
there
these
they
they're
thing
things
think
this
thought
three
through
throw
time
times
to
today
together
told
too
took
top
tree
trees
tried
trip
trouble
try
trying
turn
turned

TV
two

U

united
until
up
upon
us
use
used

V

very

W

walk
walked
walking
want
wanted
war
was
wasn't
watch
water
way
we
week
weeks
well
went
were
what
when

where
which
while
white
who
whole
why
will
win
winter
wish
with
without
woke
won
won't
work
world
would
wouldn't

Y

yard
year
years
yes
you
your
you're

Using the Dictionary

Guide Words

The **guide words** at the top of each dictionary page can help you find the word you want quickly. The first guide word tells you the first word on that page. The second guide word tells you the last word on that page. The entries on the page fall in alphabetical order between these two guide words.

Entries

Words in the dictionary are called entries. Entries provide a lot of information besides the correct spelling. Look at the sample entry below.

Tips for Finding a Word in a Dictionary

- Practice using guide words in a dictionary. Think of words to spell. Then use the guide words to find each word's entry. Do this again and again until you can use guide words easily.

- Some spellings are listed with the base word. To find **easiest,** you would look up **easy**. To find **remaining,** you would look up **remain**. To find **histories,** you would look up **history**.

- If you do not know how to spell a word, guess the spelling before looking it up. Try to find the first three letters of the word. (If you use just the first letter, it will probably take too long to find the word.)

- If you can't find a word, think of how else it might be spelled. For example, if a word starts with the /**k**/ sound, the spelling might begin with **k, c,** or even **ch**.

entry the correct spelling, sometimes broken into syllables

pronunciation

other spellings other word forms, including plurals that change the spelling of the base word

pup·py /pŭp′ ē/ *n.* (pup•pies *pl.*) a young dog; a pup. *The silly puppy tried to chase its own tail.*

definition to be sure you have the correct entry word

sample sentence to make the definition clearer

a·bout[1] /ə **bout**′/ *prep.* of; having to do with; concerning. *Let me tell you something about baseball.*

a·bout[2] /ə **bout**′/ *adv.* somewhere near. *She guessed it was about seven o'clock.*

a·bove[1] /ə **bŭv**′/ *adv.* in a higher place. *The plane was flying far above.*

a·bove[2] /ə **bŭv**′/ *prep.* higher than; over. *The plane went above the clouds.*

a·cross[1] /ə **krôs**′/ or /ə **krŏs**′/ *adv.* from side to side. *The room is twenty feet across.*

a·cross[2] /ə **krôs**′/ or /ə **krŏs**′/ *prep.* to the other side of. *The bridge goes across the river.*

act[1] /ăkt/ *n.* a division of a play. *Most plays today have three acts.*

act[2] /ăkt/ *v.* to perform. *Many girls would like to act in the movies.*

a·fraid /ə **frād**′/ *adj.* frightened; filled with fear. *Some people are afraid of falling from high places.*

af·ter /**ăf**′ tər/ *prep.* **a.** behind. *Don't forget that you come after me in the parade!* **b.** following; later in time than. *After lunch, let's go on with the game.*

af·ter·noon /**ăf**′ tər **noon**′/ *n.* the part of the day that follows noon and lasts until evening. *Little children often take naps in the afternoon.*

a·gain /ə **gĕn**′/ *adv.* once more. *When no one answered the door, the mailman rang the bell again.*

age /āj/ *n.* number of years old. *The baby's age is now two years.*

a·gree /ə **grē**′/ *v.* to have the same opinion. *We all agree that Mr. Jansen would make a good mayor.*

aid[1] /ād/ *v.* to help. *The doctor will aid him promptly.*

aid[2] /ād/ *n.* **a.** assistance. *Send aid at once to the men lost in the cave.* **b.** first aid; quick help for the injured. *Girl Scouts learn first aid.*

air /âr/ *n.* **a.** the mixture of gases surrounding the earth. *All people breathe air.* **b.** the space above Earth. *Birds and airplanes fly in the air.*

air·plane /**âr**′ plān′/ *n.* a machine for flying that has a motor, wings, and a tail. *The airplane will land in ten minutes.*

a·larm /ə **lärm**′/ *n.* a warning signal that danger is near. *The alarm went off moments after the fire started.*

a·live /ə **līv**′/ *adj.* living; not dead. *People sometimes forget that trees are alive.*

al·most /**ôl**′ mōst′/ or /ôl **mōst**′/ *adv.* nearly; just about. *That bus is almost on time; it is only two minutes late.*

a·loud /ə **loud**′/ *adv.* with a speaking voice. *Please read this book aloud to the class.*

al·ways /**ôl**′ wāz/ or /**ôl**′ wēz/ *adv.* all the time; constantly. *At the North Pole, it is always cold.*

an·i·mal /**ăn**′ ə məl/ *n.* a living being that is not a plant. *A fox is a wild animal.*

animal

an·oth·er /ə **nŭ***th*′ ər/ *adj.* **a.** one more. *Let me read another story.* **b.** any other; a different. *I am going to another part of the country.*

an·y /**ĕn**′ ē/ *adj.* **a.** one out of a group. *Read any book you like.* **b.** some. *Would you like any orange juice?*

an·y·bod·y /**ĕn**′ ē bŏd′ ē/ or /**ĕn**′ ē bŭd′ ē/ *pron.* any person. *Did you see anybody that I know at the meeting?*

an•y•one /ĕn′ ē wŭn′/ or /ĕn′ ē wən/ *pron.* anybody; any person. *Does anyone know how to get to the library?*

an•y•thing /ĕn′ ē thĭng′/ *pron.* any thing; something. *We couldn't find anything for Grandma's birthday.*

ap•ple /ăp′ əl/ *n.* (**ap•ples** *pl.*) a fruit for eating, usually round, that grows on a tree. *Green apples are often used in pies.*

arm•chair /ärm′ châr′/ *n.* a chair with sides that support a person's arms or elbows. *Dad likes to sit in his armchair when he reads.*

a•round[1] /ə round′/ *prep.* **a.** in a circular path about. *We rode around the block on our bikes.* **b.** on every side of. *There was nothing but water around us.*

a•round[2] /ə round′/ *adv.* in a circular path. *The merry-go-round went around.*

a•sleep[1] /ə slēp′/ *adj.* not awake; sleeping. *The dog is asleep after a long walk.*

a•sleep[2] /ə slēp′/ *adv.* into a state of sleep. *He fell asleep during the movie.*

a•wake /ə wāk′/ *adj.* alert; not asleep. *She was already awake when the alarm clock rang.*

a•ward /ə wôrd′/ *n.* a prize. *The winner accepted the award.*

a•way /ə wā′/ *adv.* **a.** from a place; to a different place. *Our dog ran away last week.* **b.** aside; out of the way. *He put the dishes away after supper.*

ba•by[1] /bā′ bē/ *n.* (**ba•bies** *pl.*) **a.** a very young child. *The mother pushed her baby in a stroller.* **b.** the youngest member of a family or group. *My brother is the baby of the family.* **c.** a very young animal. *The otter's baby was very cute.*

ba•by[2] /bā′ bē/ *adj.* **a.** of or having to do with a baby. *We gave baby clothes to my mother's friend.* **b.** small in comparison to others. *I love to eat baby carrots.*

Pronunciation Key

ă	pat	ŏ	pot	th	thin
ā	pay	ō	toe	*th*	this
âr	care	ô	paw, for	hw	which
ä	father	oi	noise	zh	vision
ĕ	pet	ou	out	ə	about,
ē	be	o͝o	took		item,
ĭ	pit	o͞o	boot		pencil,
ī	pie	ŭ	cut		gallop,
îr	pier	ûr	urge		circus

bad•ly /băd′ lē/ *adv.* poorly; in a bad manner. *He plays the piano well but sings badly.*

bake /bāk/ *v.* (**bakes, baked, bak•ing**) to cook without applying fire directly; to cook in an oven. *We bake bread every week.*

bake

bal•loon /bə loon′/ *n.* a brightly colored rubber bag that can be filled with air or gas and used as a toy. *Can you blow up this balloon?*

ba•nan•a /bə năn′ ə/ *n.* a tropical, yellow fruit with a slight curve and a peel. *The monkey ate the banana.*

band /bănd/ *n.* **a.** a number of persons who play musical instruments together. *She plays the drums in a band.* **b.** any flat strip of material used for holding something together. *Put a rubber band around each newspaper.*

bare /bâr/ *adj.* **a.** not wearing clothes; not covered. *Should you be walking outside in your bare feet?* **b.** without a covering. *The floor is bare because the rug is being cleaned.*

➤ Bare sounds like **bear.**

bare•foot /bâr′ fŏŏt′/ *adv.* and *adj.* without shoes or socks. *The barefoot boy played in the sand.*

bar•rel /băr′ əl/ *n.* a bulging container with a flat top and bottom. *Oil comes in a barrel.*

base•ball /bās′ bôl′/ *n.* **a.** a game played with a bat and a ball by two teams of nine players each. *Debbie wants to play baseball.* **b.** the ball used in this game. *A baseball is very hard.*

bas•ket•ball /băs′ kĭt bôl′/ *n.* **a.** a game in which points are scored by throwing a ball through a basket. *Basketball is usually played indoors.* **b.** the ball used in this game. *Our basketball had lost all its air.*

bat¹ /băt/ *n.* a heavy stick used to hit a ball. *Mike showed me how to hold the bat.*

bat² /băt/ *v.* (**bats, bat•ted, bat•ting**) to hit something, as a ball, with a heavy stick or other object. *Throw me the ball, and I will bat it.*

bath•room /băth′ rŏŏm′/ *n.* a room usually with a toilet, sink, bathtub, and shower. *We are replacing the tub in our bathroom.*

be /bē/ *v.* (**am, are, is; was, were; been; be•ing**) used as a helping verb in addition to having the following meanings: **a.** to have the identity of; to equal. *Carlos is my cousin.* **b.** to have a particular quality, appearance, or character. *The sand was hot.* **c.** to happen; to take place. *The finals are at two o'clock.*

bean /bēn/ *n.* a seed or pod that can be eaten as a vegetable. *He ate everything but one green bean.*

bear /bâr/ *n.* a large, heavy animal with long, coarse fur, short legs, and a very short tail. *The bear stood on its hind legs.*

➤ Bear sounds like **bare.**

be•cause /bĭ kôz′/ *conj.* for the reason that. *I study because I want to learn.*

be•come /bĭ kŭm′/ *v.* (**be•comes, be•came, be•come, be•com•ing**) to develop into; to come or grow to be. *A caterpillar may become a butterfly or a moth.*

be•com•ing /bĭ kŭm′ ĭng/ *v.* (**be•comes, be•came, be•come, be•com•ing**) turning into. *The caterpillar is becoming a butterfly in the cocoon.*

bee•tle /bēt′ l/ *n.* an insect that has four wings, two of which form a hard, shiny covering. *A ladybug is a small beetle that eats insects that harm garden plants.*

be•fore¹ /bĭ fôr′/ or /bĭ fōr′/ *prep.* at an earlier time than. *I had to be home before six o'clock.*

be•fore² /bĭ fôr′/ or /bĭ fōr′/ *adv.* previously; at an earlier time. *Have you heard this story before?*

be•fore³ /bĭ fôr′/ or /bĭ fōr′/ *conj.* earlier than the time when; previous to the time that. *Before you cross the street, look both ways.*

be•long /bĭ lông′/ or /bĭ lŏng′/ *v.* **a.** to have a proper place. *Pots and pans belong in the kitchen.* **b.** belong to; to be the property of someone. *The dolls belong to Anita.*

be•low¹ /bĭ lō′/ *adv.* beneath; in a lower place. *Far below, we could see the bottom of the pit.*

be•low² /bĭ lō′/ *prep.* in a lower place than; to a lower place than. *Kansas is below Nebraska on the map.*

bench /bĕnch/ *n.* (**bench•es** *pl.*) a long, low, wooden or stone seat that sometimes has a back. *George fell asleep on a bench in the park.*

ber•ry /bĕr′ ē/ *n.* (**ber•ries** *pl.*) **a.** a small, juicy fruit with soft flesh and many seeds. *We had berries and ice cream for dessert.* **b.** the dry seed of certain plants. *The seed used in making coffee is a berry.*

bet•ter /bĕt′ ər/ *adj.* higher in quality; more excellent; finer. *Does anyone have a better plan?*

be•tween /bĭ twēn′/ *prep.* in the space that separates two things. *There were four people between me and the door.*

be•ware /bĭ wâr′/ *v.* to be cautious of. *Beware of the undertow when you swim in the ocean.*

birds /bûrdz/ *n.* plural of **bird**. *The birds flew south together.*

birds

blew /blōō/ *v.* past tense of **blow**.

blind¹ /blīnd/ *adj.* not able to see. *Many blind persons know how to read Braille.*

blind² /blīnd/ *n.* a window shade. *Please raise the blind and let in the sunshine.*

block /blŏk/ *n.* **a.** a solid piece of wood, stone, metal, etc. *Children play with blocks.* **b.** a part of a town or city surrounded by four streets. *The new shopping center covers a city block.*

blow /blō/ *v.* (**blows, blew, blown, blow•ing**) **a.** to move rapidly. *We could hear the wind blow.* **b.** to be moved or stirred by the wind. *The falling leaves are blowing around.* **c.** to cause to make a sound by forcing air through. *Blow the horn again.*

board¹ /bôrd/ or /bōrd/ *n.* **a.** a long, flat piece of sawed wood. *Boards are used in building houses.* **b.** a flat piece of wood or other material used for a special purpose. *The game of checkers is played on a board.*

board² /bôrd/ or /bōrd/ *v.* to get on a plane, train, ship, or bus. *The passengers waited to board the airplane.*

boats /bōts/ *n.* (**boat** *sing.*) small vessels for traveling on water. *They docked the boats at the pier.*

boil /boil/ *v.* **a.** to bubble and send out steam. *When water is heated enough, it boils.* **b.** to heat a liquid until bubbles rise. *He boiled the soup.* **c.** to cook in boiling water. *My mother boiled eggs for breakfast.*

boot /bōōt/ *n.* a cover for the foot and leg. *Sean and I have rubber boots.*

bore•dom /bôr′ dəm/ or /bōr′ dəm/ *n.* a weary feeling because something is not interesting. *He fell asleep from boredom.*

boss /bôs/ or /bŏs/ *n.* (**boss•es** *pl.*) the person in charge; the manager. *A good boss knows how to get along with people.*

bot·tom[1] /bŏt′ əm/ *n.* the lowest part. *The sled flew to the bottom of the hill.*

bot·tom[2] /bŏt′ əm/ *adj.* lowest. *Look on the bottom shelf for your book.*

bought /bôt/ *v.* (**buy, bought, buy·ing**) purchased. *Ava bought a pair of shoes.*

bounce /bouns/ *v.* (**bounc·es, bounced, bounc·ing**) to hit against a surface and spring back. *The rubber ball bounced off the wall.*

braid /brād/ *n.* three or more strands of hair or cloth woven together. *Marie's braid is ten inches long.*

branch /brănch/ *n.* (**branch·es** *pl.*) **a.** a limb of a tree, growing from the trunk or from another limb. *Children climb the branches of large trees.* **b.** a division of a large thing. *This small stream is a branch of the main river.*

brav·er /brāv′ ər/ *adj.* the comparative form of **brave**. having more courage; having less fear. *If you want to swim across the lake, then you are braver than I am.*

brav·est /brāv′ ĭst/ *adj.* the superlative form of **brave**. having the most courage; having the least fear. *Tony is the bravest of all of us.*

break /brāk/ *v.* (**breaks, broke, bro·ken, break·ing**) **a.** to come apart; to separate into pieces. *Fine china breaks easily.* **b.** to fail to keep or carry out. *Don't break the rules.* **c.** to go beyond; to do better than. *Will the runner break the record?*

brick /brĭk/ *n.* a block of baked clay used for building or paving. *Many houses and apartment buildings are built with bricks.*

bridge /brĭj/ *n.* a structure built over a river or a valley for people or vehicles to cross. *Thousands of cars a day cross a bridge over the Mississippi River.*

brief /brēf/ *adj.* short; quick; direct. *Our meeting was brief.*

bright /brīt/ *adj.* **a.** shining; giving light; reflecting light. *See how bright the car is when it is polished.* **b.** clear; brilliant. *She wore a bright red dress.*

bright·ly /brīt′ lē/ *adv.* in a shiny way; in a bright way. *The star shone brightly in the night sky.*

bring /brĭng/ *v.* (**brings, brought, bring·ing**) to carry from somewhere else. *Please bring my book with you.*

broil /broil/ *v.* to cook directly under heat, usually in an oven. *Mom likes to broil our steaks in the oven.*

broke /brōk/ past tense of **break**.

brook /brŏok/ *n.* a small stream of water. *The children waded in the brook.*

brush[1] /brŭsh/ *n.* (**brush·es** *pl.*) the stiff hairs, straw, wire, etc., set in a stiff back or attached to a handle. *I have a new comb and brush.*

brush[2] /brŭsh/ *v.* to smooth or clean with a brush. *Brush your teeth after eating.*

bub·ble /bŭb′ əl/ *n.* a thin, round film of liquid that forms a ball around a pocket of gas or air. *The slightest touch can pop a bubble.*

bubble

buck·et /bŭk′ ĭt/ *n.* a pail; a container for carrying liquids, sand, or other substances. *Please put the mop in the bucket.*

bucket

bud·dy /bŭd′ ē/ *n.* (**bud·dies** *pl.*) **a.** a good friend. *Max is my buddy.* **b.** a partner. *She is my buddy when we swim in pairs.*

bunch /bŭnch/ *n.* (**bunch·es** *pl.*) **a.** a group of things growing close together. *A bunch of grapes grew on the vine.* **b.** a group of things that are alike. *How much is that bunch of flowers?* **c.** a large number. *A bunch of students are in the band.*

bun·ny /bŭn′ ē/ *n.* (**bun·nies** *pl.*) a pet name for a rabbit. *We saw a bunny hiding in the bushes.*

bus /bŭs/ *n.* (**bus·es** *pl.*) a large motor vehicle that can carry many passengers. *We take a bus to school.*

bush /boŏsh/ *n.* (**bush·es** *pl.*) a plant smaller than a tree, with many branches growing near the ground; a shrub. *Roses grow on bushes.*

bus·y /bĭz′ ē/ *adj.* (**bus·i·er, bus·i·est; bus·i·ly** *adv.*) **a.** at work; active. *We will be busy until dark cleaning up the backyard.* **b.** full of work or activity. *The first day of school is always busy.*

but·ter·fly /bŭt′ ər flī′/ *n.* (**but·ter·flies** *pl.*) an insect with a slender body, knobbed antennae, and four broad, usually colorful wings. *The butterfly flew from flower to flower.*

but·ton /bŭt′ n/ *n.* a small, flat, hard, round piece used to fasten two parts of a garment by fitting through a slit. *The top button on my coat is loose.*

buzz[1] /bŭz/ *n.* the humming sound made by some insects. *The country air was still except for the buzz of the bees among the flowers.*

buzz[2] /bŭz/ *v.* to make a humming sound. *The wasps buzz around their nest.*

cake /kāk/ *n.* a sweet, breadlike food made from batter. *The cake is mixed and ready to bake.*

can /kăn/ or /kən/ *v.* (**could**) **a.** to be able to. *A cheetah can run fast.* **b.** to know how to. *Susan can play the drums.*

can·not /kăn′ ŏt/ or /kə nŏt′/ *v.* is or are not able to. *They cannot come with us.*

care[1] /kâr/ *n.* **a.** protection; close attention. *A baby needs loving care.* **b.** anxiety; concern; worry. *Too much care can cause health problems.*

care[2] /kâr/ *v.* (**cares, cared, car•ing**) **a.** to feel anxiety, interest, or worry. *I don't care who wins.* **b.** to love or like someone. *They care deeply for their children.*

care•ful•ly /kâr′ fəl ē/ *adv.* (**care•ful** *adj.*) in a careful way; cautiously. *He carefully crossed the busy street.*

care•less•ly /kâr′ lĭs lē/ *adv.* (**care•less** *adj.*) recklessly; in a careless way. *She carelessly tossed the litter into the street.*

car•rot /kăr′ ət/ *n.* a long, tapering, orange vegetable. *I chopped a carrot for the soup.*

carrot

car•ry /kăr′ ē/ *v.* (**car•ries, car•ried, car•ry•ing**) to take from one place to another. *Will you carry this package home?*

catch[1] /kăch/ or /kĕch/ *v.* (**catch•es, caught, catch•ing**) **a.** to get; to take and hold onto; to seize. *Watch that boy catch the ball!* **b.** to get to in time. *If you run, you can catch the bus.* **c.** to be held by something. *I always catch my coat on that nail.*

catch[2] /kăch/ or /kĕch/ *n.* (**catch•es** *pl.*) **a.** a thing that fastens or holds. *The catch on her dress was broken.* **b.** the act of taking and holding. *The shortstop made a great catch!*

caught /kôt/ *v.* (**catch•es, caught, catch•ing**) seized or retrieved; captured. *Tonight we caught five fireflies.*

cav•i•ty /kăv′ ĭ tē/ *n.* (**cav•i•ties** *pl.*) a small hollow caused by decay in a tooth. *If you brush your teeth properly, you won't have many cavities.*

ce•dar /sē′ dər/ *n.* **a.** a type of tree known for its fragrant wood. **b.** a reddish wood. *Cedar is used to make trunks and closets.*

cell /sĕl/ *n.* **a.** one of the tiny parts of living matter of which all animals and plants are made. *Some organisms are made up of only one cell.* **b.** a small, enclosed space. *Each cell contains data.*

➤ **Cell** sounds like **sell**.

cel•lar /sĕl′ ər/ *n.* an underground room, used for storage. *The family next door fixed up the cellar as a playroom for their children.*

cent /sĕnt/ *n.* the smallest coin of the United States; a penny. *One cent is one hundredth of a dollar.*

➤ **Cent** sounds like **scent** and **sent**.

cen•ter /sĕn′ tər/ *n.* **a.** a point in the middle. *Stand in the center of the circle.* **b.** a main area or place where people gather. *The town has a new shopping center.*

chain /chān/ *n.* **a.** a number of links or rings fastened together. *She strung the beads on a gold chain.* **b.** a series of things that are connected or joined. *The Rocky Mountains are a chain of mountains.*

chair /châr/ *n.* a piece of furniture with legs and a back that holds one seated person. *Let Grandfather sit in the rocking chair.*

chance /chăns/ *n.* a risk. *Sometimes you have to take a chance and try something new.*

change[1] /chānj/ *v.* (**chang•es, changed, chang•ing**) to make or become different. *She will change her mind.*

change² /chānj/ *n.* **a.** making or becoming different. *Watch for a change in the weather tomorrow.* **b.** small coins. *John has a pocketful of change.*

chase¹ /chās/ *v.* (chas•es, chased, chas•ing) **a.** to run after, trying to catch. *The hounds chase the fox.* **b.** to drive away. *She is trying to chase the cat away from the bird's nest.*

chase² /chās/ *n.* a chasing. *It was a fine chase, but the fox got away.*

check¹ /chĕk/ *v.* to make sure of the correctness of. *Be sure to check your test before you hand it in.*

check² /chĕk/ *n.* **a.** a mark (✓) meaning something is satisfactory. *Make a check if the answer is correct.* **b.** a bill in a restaurant. *The check for our dinners was twelve dollars.* **c.** a written order from a bank to pay money to a certain person or place. *Make out a check for twenty dollars.*

cheese /chēz/ *n.* a food made from the thick part of milk. *I like sandwiches made with cheese.*

cher•ry /chĕr′ ē/ *n.* (cher•ries *pl.*) a small, round red or white fruit with a stone or seed in the center. *That cherry tastes sweet.*

cherry

chew /choō/ *v.* to bite and grind with the teeth. *Chew your food well before you swallow it.*

chin /chĭn/ *n.* the part of the face beneath the bottom lip. *You move your chin when you chew.*

chirp /chûrp/ *v.* to make a short, sharp sound. *Some sparrows chirp.*

choice /chois/ *n.* a decision; a selection. *For dinner we will go to a restaurant of your choice.*

choose /cho͞oz/ *v.* (choos•es, chose, chos•en, choos•ing) **a.** to pick out. *Choose the book you want.* **b.** to prefer. *I do not choose to tell you my age.*

chop /chŏp/ *v.* (chops, chopped, chop•ping) to cut by hitting with a sharp tool like an ax. *We need to chop wood for our campfire.*

chuck•le /chŭk′ əl/ *n.* a small, quiet laugh. *His funny speech caused chuckles in the audience.*

church /chûrch/ *n.* (church•es *pl.*) **a.** a building for public worship. *That church has stained-glass windows.* **b.** a religious service. *Church begins at ten o'clock.*

ci•der /sī′ dər/ *n.* the juice made from apples. *Hot apple cider is nice after a day out in the cold.*

cir•cus /sûr′ kəs/ *n.* (cir•cus•es *pl.*) a show featuring acts with animals, clowns, and acrobats. *A circus may be held under a tent.*

cit•y /sĭt′ ē/ *n.* (cit•ies *pl.*) a large and important town. *Some large cities in the United States are New York, Chicago, Los Angeles, Philadelphia, and Detroit.*

clap¹ /klăp/ *v.* (claps, clapped, clap•ping) to strike the hands together. *After the play we all began to clap.*

clap² /klăp/ *n.* a sudden loud noise or crash. *I heard a clap of thunder.*

class /klăs/ *n.* (**class•es** *pl.*) **a.** a group of students meeting regularly with a teacher. *My English class is the first class of the day.* **b.** persons, animals, or things thought of as a group because they are alike. *Dogs belong to the class of mammals.*

clean /klēn/ *adj.* free from dirt. *Put on clean clothes for the party.*

clock /klŏk/ *n.* a device made for telling time. *Can you see the hands move on that clock?*

close¹ /klōz/ *v.* (**clos•es, closed, clos•ing**) to shut. *Close the door when you leave.*

close² /klōs/ *adj.* (**clos•er, clos•est; close•ly** *adv.*) near. *We planted the tree close to the house.*

cloth /klôth/ or /klŏth/ *n.* a material made by weaving threads of cotton, wool, silk, nylon, etc. *Most of our clothes are made of cloth.*

cloud /kloud/ *n.* a large gray or white mass of tiny water drops floating in the sky. *That big cloud may bring rain.*

coast /kōst/ *n.* the seashore; land along the sea or ocean. *There are many beaches along the coast of the Pacific Ocean.*

coat /kōt/ *n.* an outer garment with sleeves. *In winter I wear a heavy coat over my other clothes.*

coin /koin/ *n.* a piece of metal money. *Pennies, nickels, dimes, and quarters are coins.*

col•lar /kŏl′ər/ *n.* an item such as a piece of cloth or leather that circles the neck. *He loosened his tie and his collar.*

col•o•ny /kŏl′ə nē/ *n.* (**col•o•nies** *pl.*) a group of animals or people with similar interests who live in a particular area. *The Pilgrims' colony grew as more people arrived.*

col•or¹ /kŭl′ər/ *n.* (**col•ors** *pl.*) a hue, tint, or shade caused by the effect of light rays on the eyes. *All colors are combinations of red, yellow, and blue.*

col•or² /kŭl′ər/ *v.* to change the color. *The children like to color the pictures in their coloring books.*

come /kŭm/ *v.* (**comes, came, com•ing**) **a.** to move toward. *The dark clouds are coming this way.* **b.** to arrive. *What time does the bus come?*

com•pare /kəm pâr′/ *v.* (**com•pares, com•pared, com•par•ing**) to examine things for similarities or differences. *If you compare prices, you can save money when you shop.*

corn /kôrn/ *n.* a grain that grows in kernels or seeds on large ears. *We ate corn and peas for dinner.*

cor•ner¹ /kôr′nər/ *n.* **a.** the place where two lines, edges, or sides of something come together. *A square has four corners.* **b.** the place where two or more streets come together. *The bus stops at the corner of Sixth and Main.*

cor•ner² /kôr′nər/ *adj.* on or at a corner. *Jerry lives in the corner house.*

cost¹ /kôst/ or /kŏst/ *v.* to be for sale for; to be worth. *How much does one tomato cost?*

cost² /kôst/ or /kŏst/ *n.* the price that is to be paid. *The cost of a meal in a restaurant is going up.*

cot /kŏt/ *n.* a light bed that can be folded up. *Many cots are made of canvas on a metal or wood frame.*

coin

cot·ton[1] /kŏt′n/ *n.* **a.** the soft white fibers that surround the tiny seeds of certain plants. *Cotton is grown mainly to make cloth.* **b.** the thread or cloth made of cotton fibers. *Cotton is spun on large machines in mills.*

cot·ton[2] /kŏt′n/ *adj.* made of cotton. *Cotton shirts are not as warm as wool shirts.*

could /kŏŏd/ **a.** past tense of **can.** **b.** used to suggest possibility. *We could do better.* **c.** used to suggest politeness. *Could you help us with this?*

could·'ve /kŏŏd′ əv/ contraction of **could have.** *If we had been ready, we could've gone on the bus.*

count /kount/ *v.* **a.** to name the numbers in order. *Our baby is learning to count already.* **b.** to add to find the total. *He counted the quarters in his bank.*

cou·ple /kŭp′ əl/ *n.* **a.** two of anything; a pair. *He had only a couple of dollars.* **b.** a man and woman together. *Mary and Jack make an attractive couple.*

cov·er[1] /kŭv′ ər/ *n.* **a.** the outside of a book. *Our math book has a red cover.* **b.** a lid or top. *Put the cover on the pot.* **c.** anything put on to protect, keep warm, etc. *A blanket is a cover for a bed.*

cov·er[2] /kŭv′ ər/ *v.* to put something on or over a person or thing. *We covered our books with heavy paper.*

crawl /krôl/ *v.* **a.** to move slowly along the ground by pulling the body. *Worms and caterpillars crawl.* **b.** to move on hands and knees. *Babies crawl before they walk.* **c.** to move slowly. *The cars crawl along the crowded highway.*

crew /krōō/ *n.* the persons who run a boat, ship, train, or airplane. *A crew takes orders from a captain or other officer.*

crop /krŏp/ *n.* food plants that are grown and harvested. *The farmer plants crops in the spring.*

cross /krôs/ or /krŏs/ *v.* **a.** to draw a line across. *Careful writers cross the letter "t" properly.* **b.** to go from one side to the other. *Wait for the traffic to clear, and then cross the street.*

crouch /krouch/ *v.* (**crouch·es, crouched, crouch·ing**) to bend your legs and get close to the ground. *Crouch down to look under the table.*

cuff /kŭf/ *n.* the fold of material turned over at the end of a sleeve or turned up at the bottom of a trouser leg. *I found the missing coin in my pants cuff.*

cuff

cup /kŭp/ *n.* a small, hollow container used for drinking. *Pour some milk into my cup, please.*

curl[1] /kûrl/ *v.* **a.** to twist or turn into rings or spirals. *The ladies curl their hair every night.* **b.** to coil. *The cowboy's lasso was curled around the saddle.*

curl[2] /kûrl/ *n.* a lock of hair forming a ring. *Her head is covered with curls.*

curve /kûrv/ *n.* a bend in a road; the part of a road that is not straight. *That curve in the road is dangerous!*

curv•ing /kûrv′ ĭng/ *v.* (**curves, curved, curv•ing**) bending; going in a way that is not straight. *The road is curving to the right and then to the left.*

dance[1] /dăns/ *v.* (**danc•es, danced, danc•ing**) to move, walk, step, etc., in time to music. *Can you dance to this song?*

dance[2] /dăns/ *n.* **a.** a particular series of steps done in time to music. *Can you do that new dance?* **b.** a party or gathering of people for dancing. *There will be a dance in the gymnasium on Friday night.*

danc•er /dăns′ ər/ *n.* a person who participates in the various forms of dance. *The ballet dancer twirled on stage.*

dawn /dôn/ *n.* the first appearance of light in the morning. *Dawn came at six o'clock this morning.*

deep•ly /dēp′ lē/ *adv.* having extreme feeling. *The child deeply loved her cat.*

de•frost /dē frôst′/ or /dē frŏst′/ *v.* to remove ice from; to thaw. *Defrost the meat before baking it.*

de•gree /dĭ grē′/ *n.* a unit used to measure temperature. *Water freezes at thirty-two degrees Fahrenheit.*

de•lay[1] /dĭ lā′/ *v.* to put off until a later time; to postpone. *The referee is going to delay the game until it stops raining.*

de•lay[2] /dĭ lā′/ *n.* a putting off until a later time; a postponement. *The train had a two-hour delay.*

depth /dĕpth/ *n.* the distance from the top of something to the bottom of something. *The scientist studied the depth of the ocean.*

desk /dĕsk/ *n.* a piece of furniture somewhat like a table, having a flat top for writing and usually having drawers. *Office workers, teachers, and students have desks.*

dew /do͞o/ or /dyo͞o/ *n.* water droplets that form at night on cool surfaces. *In the morning you may see dew on the leaves.*

dig /dĭg/ *v.* (**digs, dug, dig•ging**) to make a hole in the ground; to break up the soil. *Dogs dig holes with their front paws.*

dime /dīm/ *n.* a silver coin used as money by the United States and by Canada. *A dime is worth ten cents.*

din•ner /dĭn′ ər/ *n.* the main meal of the day. *Some people have dinner at noon, and other people have dinner in the evening.*

dirt /dûrt/ *n.* **a.** mud, dust, soot, or any other thing that can soil skin, clothes, and furniture. *You have a smudge of dirt on your face.* **b.** earth; soil. *We put some dirt into the flowerpot.*

does /dŭz/ *v.* (**does, did, done, do•ing**) **a.** performs or carries out a job. *My dad does the cooking.* **b.** acts or behaves. *She does very well playing quietly.*

dog /dôg/ or /dŏg/ *n.* a four-legged animal that makes a good pet. *Some dogs watch houses or tend sheep.*

dog

down•town[1] /doun′ toun′/ *adv.* in or toward the main business part of a city. *We all went downtown to shop.*

down·town² /doun′ toun′/ *n.* the business part of a city. *The downtown was decorated for the big parade.*

drain¹ /drān/ *v.* (**drains, drained, drain·ing,**) to flow water or waste through a pipe. *Remember to drain the water in the tub after your bath.*

drain² /drān/ *n.* a pipe for flowing water or waste. *The drain in our sink is clogged.*

draw /drô/ *v.* (**draws, drew, drawn, draw·ing**) to make a design, picture, etc. *The artist will draw an outline before he paints the picture.*

draw·er /drô′ ər/ *n.* a box, with handles, that slides in and out of a dresser or desk. *My socks are in the top drawer.*

dream¹ /drēm/ *n.* the thoughts, feelings, and pictures that occur in a person's mind while sleeping. *Her dream was about flying in an airplane.*

dream² /drēm/ *v.* **a.** to have a dream while sleeping. *The kittens dream about chasing mice.* **b.** to suppose or imagine that a thing could happen. *We never dreamed that we'd win.*

dress¹ /drĕs/ *n.* (**dress·es** *pl.*) an outer garment worn by a woman or a girl. *She wore a long white dress for the wedding.*

dress² /drĕs/ *v.* to clothe; to put clothes on. *Mother dressed the baby after his nap.*

drew /drōō/ past tense of **draw.**

drive¹ /drīv′/ *v.* (**drives, drove, driv·en, driv·ing**) to make a car or working animal go. *Who is going to drive me home?*

drive² /drīv′/ *n.* a trip in a car. *We took a drive last Sunday.*

drop¹ /drŏp/ *n.* **a.** a small amount of liquid formed in a rounded mass. *A single drop of water was on the leaf.* **b.** a sudden fall. *After the fire, there was a sharp drop in the value of the house.*

drop² /drŏp/ *v.* (**drops, dropped, drop·ping**) to fall or let fall. *I will try not to drop the dish as I dry it.*

drum /drŭm/ *n.* (**drums** *pl.*) a musical instrument that consists of a hollow cylinder with a skin or fabric stretched taut over one or both ends. *The marchers kept time to the beat of a drum.*

dull /dŭl/ *adj.* **a.** not sharp; not pointed; blunt. *We couldn't chop the wood because the ax was dull.* **b.** uninteresting; boring. *It was such a dull book that I fell asleep reading it.*

dust /dŭst/ *n.* a light powder of dirt. *I could see the dust on the old table.*

ear·ly¹ /ûr′ lē/ *adv.* **a.** at or near the beginning of something. *I became tired very early in the race.* **b.** sooner than usual; before the usual time. *I will have to get up early to go fishing tomorrow.*

ear·ly² /ûr′ lē/ *adj.* (**ear·li·er, ear·li·est**) coming or happening at the beginning of something. *We took the early train.*

earn /ûrn/ *v.* **a.** to receive in return for performing a service, doing work, etc. *I will earn four dollars today for mowing grass.* **b.** to deserve as a result of performing a service, doing work, etc. *After studying for two hours, we will earn a break.*

earth /ûrth/ *n.* **a.** the third planet from the sun; the planet on which we live. *Earth revolves around the sun.* **b.** ground; soil. *Plant these seeds in black earth.*

eas•i•ly /ē′ zə lē/ *adv.* without trying hard; in an easy way. *He easily carried the light box.*

east[1] /ēst/ *n.* the direction to your right as you face north; the direction from which the sun rises. *We saw a glow of light in the east before dawn.*

east[2] /ēst/ *adv.* to the east. *We walked east until we came to the hotel.*

east[3] /ēst/ *adj.* from the east. *An east wind brought rain and colder temperatures.*

ei•ther /ē′ thər/ or /ī′-/ *adj.* one or the other of two. *I couldn't run faster than either one of my friends.*

emp•ty /ĕmp′ tē/ *adj.* (**emp•ti•er, emp•ti•est**) the opposite of full; not having anything or anyone in it. *Put this hat into the empty box.*

en•gine /ĕn′ jĭn/ *n.* a machine that changes fuel and energy into motion. *Most automobile engines use gasoline.*

-er a suffix that means "more" and is used to form comparative adjectives: *greater.*

e•rase /ĭ rās′/ *v.* (**e•ras•es, e•rased, e•ras•ing**) to wipe or rub out. *Will you please erase the board?*

-est a suffix that means "most" and is used to form superlative adjectives: *greatest.*

ev•er /ĕv′ ər/ *adv.* at any time. *Have you ever traveled to Europe?*

eve•ry /ĕv′ rē/ *adj.* each; all of a group. *Every child should visit the dentist regularly.*

eve•ry•day /ĕv′ rē dā′/ *adj.* ordinary; all right for the usual day or event. *You should wear your everyday clothes to play outside.*

eve•ry•thing /ĕv′ rē thĭng′/ *pron.* all things; each thing. *Everything is going right for me.*

eve•ry•where /ĕv′ rē hwâr′/ or /ĕv′ rē wâr′/ *adv.* in all places. *The birdwatcher saw birds everywhere.*

face[1] /fās/ *n.* the front part of the head; that part of the head on which the eyes, nose, and mouth are located. *Her face was covered by a funny mask.*

face[2] /fās/ *v.* (**fac•es, faced, fac•ing**) to be turned toward; to have the front toward. *Our classrooms face the street.*

fac•ing /fā′ sĭng/ *v.* (**fac•es, faced, fac•ing**) **a.** looking in a certain direction. *Our beach house is facing the sea.* **b.** meeting a situation; confronting. *I will be facing the contest judges tomorrow.*

fac•to•ry /făk′ tə rē/ *n.* (**fac•to•ries** *pl.*) a building or a group of buildings in which something is manufactured. *He worked in a factory that makes farm machinery.*

fair[1] /fâr/ *adj.* **a.** in keeping with the rules; according to what is accepted as right. *If you want to play on the team, you must learn fair play.* **b.** light in color. *She has fair hair and dark eyes.*

fair[2] /fâr/ *n.* an event or exhibition, usually for farm products or animals. *We showed our rabbits at the county fair.*

➤ **Fair** sounds like **fare.**

fair•y /fâr′ ē/ *n.* (**fair•ies** *pl.*) A tiny imaginary being in human form, depicted as clever, mischievous, and possessing magical powers. *We pretended that fairies lived in that garden.*

fair•y tale /fâr′ ē tāl′/ *n.* a made-up story, usually with fairies, elves, or other magical characters. *Cinderella is a famous fairy tale.*

fan /făn/ *n.* anything used to move the air. *When it got hot I turned on the fan.*

fare /fâr/ *n.* money charged for a trip. *You pay a fare to ride in a bus, taxi, train, or airplane.*

➤ **Fare** sounds like **fair.**

fare•well /fâr wĕl′/ *n.* a wish of well-being at parting; a good-bye. *On my last day at work, I was given a warm farewell.*

fa•ther /fä′ thər/ *n.* the male parent. *My father is a very kind man.*

fence /fĕns/ *n.* a barrier or enclosure of wood, wire, stone, etc., to keep people or animals from going into or out of a certain property. *Fences prevent animals from wandering off.*

fer•ry /fĕr′ ē/ *n.* (**fer•ries** *pl.*) a boat used to transport people or goods across a narrow body of water. *The ferry takes cars across the channel every day.*

fight[1] /fīt/ *n.* a struggle to beat or overcome someone or something by force. *The boys stopped the fight between the two dogs.*

fight[2] /fīt/ *v.* (**fights, fought, fight•ing**) **a.** to try to overcome by force. *Boxers wear padded gloves when they fight.* **b.** to work hard in helping overcome. *Doctors fight disease.*

find /fīnd/ *v.* (**finds, found, find•ing**) **a.** to come upon accidentally; to locate an object by chance. *You may find my brother at the supermarket.* **b.** to look for and get back a lost object. *We will find my watch.*

fin•ish /fĭn′ ĭsh/ *v.* to come or bring to an end; to complete or become completed. *The movie will finish at 9:30.*

firm /fûrm/ *adj.* hard; solid. *They left the muddy road and walked on firm ground.*

flag /flăg/ *n.* (**flags** *pl.*) **a.** a piece of cloth with certain colors and designs. *A flag may stand for a country, a state, a city, or an organization.* **b.** a piece of cloth used as a signal. *A red flag often means "danger."*

flag

flame[1] /flām/ *n.* the glow of burning; the visible part of the fire. *The flames from the forest fire shot upward.*

flame[2] /flām/ *v.* (**flames, flamed, flam•ing**) to burn with a flame; to blaze. *The campfire flamed when we added a sheet of paper.*

flash[1] /flăsh/ *n.* (**flash•es** *pl.*) **a.** a light that appears suddenly and briefly. *A flash of lightning appeared in the distance.* **b.** a very short time. *I'll be there in a flash.*

flash[2] /flăsh/ *v.* to give off a sudden, brief light. *The light on an answering machine will flash when there is a message.*

flat•ter /flăt′ ər/ *adj.* the comparative form of **flat**; smoother and more level. *This rock is flatter than that rock.*

flat•test /flăt′ ĭst/ *adj.* the superlative form of **flat**; the smoothest and the most level. *The desert is the flattest place around here.*

flight /flīt/ *n.* a scheduled trip on an airplane. *The next flight to Chicago departs at 3:05.*

float[1] /flōt/ *v.* to stay or move in or on top of air, water, or other liquid. *Icebergs float in water.*

float[2] /flōt/ *n.* **a.** something that floats. *The float on a fishing line bobs up and down.* **b.** a decorated truck or wagon used in a parade. *Elena rode on the float.*

flock[1] /flŏk/ *n.* a group of animals or birds that stay together. *There are fifty sheep in the flock.*

flock[2] /flŏk/ v. to gather in large numbers. *People flock to see the movie star.*

flow[1] /flō/ v. to move in a stream, as water does. *Many rivers flow to the ocean.*

flow[2] /flō/ n. a smooth, even, steady movement. *The flow of the sea is restful to watch.*

fluff•y /flŭf' ē/ adj. (fluff•i•er, fluff•i•est) light and soft. *I like fluffy pillows.*

foam /fōm/ n. a quantity of small bubbles. *The big waves of the ocean have foam on top.*

fold /fōld/ v. to close or bend parts of something together in order to fit it into a smaller space. *When we take down the flag, we fold it into the shape of a triangle.*

fol•low /fŏl' ō/ v. **a.** to go or come after. *Please follow me to your table.* **b.** to walk or move along. *Follow this path to the park.*

fool /fool/ v. to trick or attempt to trick someone. *She hoped her costume would fool me into thinking she was someone else.*

for /fôr/ prep. **a.** with the purpose of. *We are going for a bike ride.* **b.** sent or given to. *This letter is for you.* **c.** because of. *We jumped for joy.* **d.** in favor of. *Everyone voted for the trip to the zoo.*

➤ **For** sounds like **four**.

for•est /fôr' ĭst/ n. an area covered with trees; a woods. *We found pine cones in the forest.*

for•get /fər gĕt'/ or /fôr gĕt'/ v. (for•gets, for•got, for•got•ten or for•got, for•get•ting) **a.** to have no memory of; to be unable to recall. *I forget where I left my books.* **b.** to neglect because of carelessness, lack of interest, etc. *Did I forget to do my homework last night?*

form[1] /fôrm/ n. **a.** the shape of something. *We saw a cloud in the form of an elephant.* **b.** a particular kind or variety of something. *Steam is a form of water.* **c.** a paper containing blank spaces to be filled in. *Mark your answers on the answer form, not in the test book.*

form[2] /fôrm/ v. to give a shape to something. *Potters form dishes out of clay.*

for•ty /fôr' tē/ n. one more than thirty-nine; four times ten; 40. *Her father is forty years old.*

foul /foul/ adj. (foul•er, foul•est) being outside the game lines, as in baseball. *The foul ball flew into the dugout.*

➤ **Foul** sounds like **fowl**.

found /found/ past tense of **find**.

four /fôr/ or /fōr/ n. one more than three; 4. *We need four to play this game.*

➤ **Four** sounds like **for**.

fowl /foul/ n. (**fowl** or **fowls** pl.) large birds used as food, such as turkeys, chickens, and ducks. *The county fair has a building that houses several types of fowl.*

➤ **Fowl** sounds like **foul**.

fox•es /fŏks' ĭz/ n. (**fox** sing.) wild animals like dogs but with bushy tails. *The hiker uncovered where the foxes like to hide.*

fresh /frĕsh/ adj. **a.** newly made, grown, or gathered. *Mother baked fresh bread this morning.* **b.** clean. *Breathe this fresh air.*

friend /frĕnd/ n. a person that one likes. *Julio is a good friend who is always ready to cheer me up.*

friends /frĕndz/ n. plural of **friend**. *My friends are coming over this weekend for a slumber party.*

fun•ny /fŭn' ē/ adj. (fun•ni•er, fun•ni•est; fun•ni•ly adv.) **a.** comical; causing laughs; humorous. *The movie was so funny that our sides hurt from laughing so much.* **b.** strange; unusual; peculiar. *That is a funny way to act.*

fur /fûr/ n. the thick, soft hair that is on the bodies of many animals. *We brush the cat's fur to keep it shiny.*

fur•ry /fûr' ē/ or /fŭr' ē/ adj. covered with fur. *A mouse is a small furry animal.*

fuzz•y /fŭz' ē/ adj. (fuzz•i•er, fuzz•i•est) **a.** having a furry texture. *These young chicks are fuzzy.* **b.** blurred; out of focus. *Hold still while I take the picture so it won't be fuzzy.*

gadg•et /găj′ ĭt/ *n.* a small mechanical object with a practical use but often thought of as a novelty. *This gadget is used to open a can.*

girls /gûrlz/ *n.* plural of **girl**. *The girls sang "Happy Birthday" to their older brother.*

give /gĭv/ *v.* (**gives, gave, giv•en, giv•ing**) **a.** to hand over to another as a present. *I will give her a watch.* **b.** to let have. *Give me your hand and I'll pull you up.* **c.** to provide. *Let's give a show for parents' night.*

glad•ly /glăd′ lē/ *adv.* in a happy or joyful manner. *He gladly accepted the award.*

globe /glōb/ *n.* a round model of Earth with a map on the outside showing oceans, countries, etc. *The children pointed out on the globe the route by which Columbus reached America.*

glo•ry /glôr′ ē/ or /glŏr′ ē / *n.* (**glo•ries** *pl.*) great honor or praise. *The winner was embarrassed by all the glory.*

gloss•y /glô′ sē/ or /glŏs′ ē / *adj.* (**gloss•i•er, gloss•i•est**) smooth and shiny. *The glossy paper is really smooth.*

goat /gōt/ *n.* a horned animal about the size of a sheep. *The mountain goat is wild and very quick in climbing rocks.*

go•ril•la /gə rĭl′ ə/ *n.* an ape related to the chimpanzee, but less erect and much larger. *The gorilla named Coco learned sign language.*

grab /grăb/ *v.* (**grabs, grabbed, grab•bing**) to take or grasp suddenly. *The cat scratched me because I grabbed its tail.*

grace /grās/ *n.* beauty and ease of movement. *Ballet dancers need to have grace and flexibility.*

grade /grād/ *v.* (**grades, grad•ed, grad•ing**) to check over; to evaluate. *He took the homework papers home to grade.*

grand /grănd/ *adj.* **a.** large; beautiful; impressive. *The queen lived in a grand palace.* **b.** fine; wonderful. *You'll have a grand time at the party.*

grand•fa•ther /grănd′ fä′ thər/ or /grăn′ fä′ thər/ *n.* the father of one's mother or father. *One of my grandfathers lives here in town; my other grandfather lives in the country.*

grandfather

grand•moth•er /grănd′ mŭ*th*′ ər/ or /grăn′ mŭ*th*′ ər/ *n.* the mother of one's father or mother. *My grandmother is coming to my birthday party.*

grasp /grăsp/ *v.* to clasp or embrace with the fingers or hands. *Grasp my hand and I will help you out of the pool.*

grate /grāt/ *v.* (**grates, grat•ed, grat•ing**) to break something down into small pieces by rubbing it against a rough surface. *We usually grate the onions and mix them with the meat.*

➤ **Grate** sounds like **great**.

great /grāt/ *adj.* (**great•er, great•est; great•ly** *adv.*) **a.** large in size or number; big. *A great crowd of people was at the carnival.* **b.** more than is ordinary or expected. *You did a great job in cutting down the tree.* **c.** important; skilled; famous. *There have been many great presidents in our history.*

➤ **Great** sounds like **grate**.

great•ly /grāt′ lē/ *adv.* very much. *I greatly appreciate your help.*

greet /grēt/ *v.* to welcome in a friendly way. *A taxi driver will greet us at the airport.*

grew /grōō/ *v.* past tense of **grow**. *The strawberries grew all over our backyard.*

grind /grīnd/ *v.* (**grinds, ground, grind•ing**) to crush into bits or small pieces. *I'll grind this tablet into powder.*

ground /ground/ *n.* **a.** the surface of the earth. *The model airplane crashed to the ground when it ran out of gas.* **b.** soil; earth. *The ground in this field is rich and fertile.*

grow /grō/ *v.* (**grows, grew, grown, grow•ing**) **a.** to become larger; to increase. *Our baby is growing so fast!* **b.** to live in a certain place. *Palm trees grow in the tropics.* **c.** to raise by planting seeds and caring for. *We grow tomatoes in our garden.*

gulf /gŭlf/ *n.* (**gulfs** *pl.*) a large bay, or part of a sea or an ocean, that is partly enclosed by land. *The Gulf of Mexico is a part of the Atlantic Ocean.*

hair /hâr/ *n.* **a.** the mass of thin, threadlike strands that grow on a person's or an animal's skin. *Elizabeth has beautiful hair; she brushes it often.* **b.** any one of these strands. *Look at the hairs that dog left on the chair!*

➤ **Hair** sounds like **hare**.

hand•writ•ing /hănd′ rī tĭng/ *n.* writing done by hand with a pen or a pencil. *Neat handwriting always makes a good impression.*

hap•pen /hăp′ ən/ *v.* to take place; to occur. *Do you think something will happen tomorrow afternoon?*

hap•pi•ly /hăp′ ə lē/ *adv.* with joy or gladness; in a happy way. *The children happily played in the yard.*

hap•py /hăp′ ē/ *adj.* (**hap•pi•er, hap•pi•est; hap•pi•ly** *adv.*) feeling or showing pleasure; joyful. *The happy man whistled all day.*

hard•ware /hard′ wâr′/ *n.* **a.** things made of metal, such as tools. *All of our hardware is in the toolshed.* **b.** equipment used for a special purpose, such as computers. *A monitor, CPU, and keyboard are computer hardware.*

hare /hâr/ *n.* an animal like a rabbit, but much larger. *A hare has strong legs and can run fast.*

➤ **Hare** sounds like **hair**.

hare

hatch /hăch/ *v.* (**hatch•es, hatched, hatch•ing**) to emerge from an egg or cocoon. *The bird's egg might hatch today.*

haul /hôl/ *v.* to pull with force; to drag. *We watched the girls haul their rowboat out of the water.*

have /hăv/ *v.* (**has, had, hav•ing**) used as a helping verb in addition to having the following meanings: **a.** to own; to possess. *They have a new house.* **b.** to accept; to take. *Have a piece of pie.* **c.** to be forced; to feel obliged. *I have to do my homework now.*

heal /hēl/ *v.* to restore to health; to return to a healthy state. *Tim's broken finger should heal quickly.*

➤ **Heal** sounds like **heel** and **he'll**.

hear /hîr/ *v.* (**hears, heard, hear•ing**) **a.** to take in sound through the ears. *We could hear every word clearly.* **b.** to listen to; to pay attention to. *Did you hear the principal's announcement?*

heard /hûrd/ past tense of **hear**.

heat[1] /hēt/ *n.* hotness; great warmth. *Fire gives off heat.*

heat[2] /hēt/ *v.* to make or become warm. *The furnace heats the house.*

he'd /hēd/ contraction of **he would** or **he had**.

heel /hēl/ *n.* the rounded part at the back of a human foot, sock, or shoe. *Someone stepped on the heel of my shoe.*

➤ **Heel** sounds like **he'll** and **heal**.

he'll /hēl/ contraction of **he will**.

➤ **He'll** sounds like **heel** and **heal**.

her•self /hûr sĕlf′/ *pron.* **a.** her own self. *Jennifer fell down and hurt herself.* **b.** the person or self she usually is. *Beth isn't acting like herself today.*

hic•cup /hĭk′ əp/ *n.* an uncontrollable intake of breath that causes a clicking sound. *Amy covered her mouth to muffle her hiccup.*

high[1] /hī/ *adj.* **a.** tall; far above the ground. *Walnuts fell from a high branch.* **b.** greater than usual; more than normal. *Prices at this store are high.*

Pronunciation Key

ă	pat	ŏ	pot	th	**th**in
ā	pay	ō	toe	*th*	**th**is
âr	care	ô	paw, for	hw	**wh**ich
ä	father	oi	n**oi**se	zh	vi**s**ion
ĕ	pet	ou	**ou**t	ə	**a**bout,
ē	be	ŏŏ	t**oo**k		it**e**m,
ĭ	pit	ōō	b**oo**t		penc**i**l,
ī	pie	ŭ	cut		gall**o**p,
îr	p**ie**r	ûr	**ur**ge		circ**u**s

---

high[2] /hī/ *n.* a high amount, as in temperature. *Yesterday's high was ninety-eight degrees.*

high•light /hī′ līt′/ *n.* the best part of something. *Swimming was the highlight of our day.*

him•self /hĭm sĕlf′/ *pron.* **a.** his own self. *My little brother tied his shoes all by himself.* **b.** the person or self he usually is. *Jason looked more like himself after the doctor took the cast off his arm.*

hoarse /hôrs/ or /hōrs/ *adj.* (**hoars•er, hoars•est**) low or rough in sound or voice. *My voice was hoarse from cheering so loudly at the football game.*

➤ **Hoarse** sounds like **horse**.

hob•by /hŏb′ ē/ *n.* (**hob•bies** *pl.*) something you do for fun. *Sue's favorite hobby is sewing.*

hol•i•day /hŏl′ ĭ dā′/ *n.* a day on which a special event is celebrated. *Independence Day is the favorite holiday of many people.*

hol•ly /hŏl′ ē/ *n.* (**hol•lies** *pl.*) a shrub or tree that has evergreen leaves and red berries. *This holiday wreath is made of holly.*

hop /hŏp/ *v.* (**hops, hopped, hop•ping**) to move by jumping. *Rabbits hop from place to place.*

hope /hōp/ *v.* (**hopes, hoped, hop•ing**) to expect and desire; to wish. *We hope Brad will win.*

horse /hôrs/ *n.* a large, hoofed animal used for riding and pulling loads. *A colt is a young horse.*

➤ **Horse** sounds like **hoarse**.

horse

hot /hŏt/ *adj.* (**hot•ter, hot•test**) **a.** very warm; having a high temperature. *I like taking hot baths.* **b.** sharp to the taste; peppery, spicy. *Do you prefer hot or mild sauce?*

hour•ly¹ /our′ lē/ *adv.* every hour. *The bells in our school ring hourly.*

hour•ly² /our′ lē/ *adj.* for every hour. *She receives an hourly wage of six dollars.*

house /hous/ *n.* a building in which to live. *The fine old house is for sale.*

how•ev•er /hou ĕv′ ər/ *conj.* nevertheless. *I've never tasted eggplant before; however, it looks delicious.*

how'd /houd/ contraction of **how would** or **how did.**

hug /hŭg/ *v.* (**hugs, hugged, hug•ging**) to press tightly, especially in the arms. *Sarah hugged her teddy bear.*

hun•ger /hŭng′ gər/ *v.* **a.** to want for food. *During our long hiking trip, we began to hunger for home-cooked meals.* **b.** to want for knowledge.

hunt•er /hŭn′ tər/ *n.* a person or animal who hunts. *The hawk's keen eyesight makes it a good hunter.*

hur•ry¹ /hûr′ ē/ or /hŭr′ ē/ *v.* (**hur•ries, hur•ried, hur•ry•ing**) to act quickly; to move fast. *Hurry or you'll be late!*

hur•ry² /hûr′ ē/ or /hŭr′ ē/ *n.* haste; a rush; a fast action. *Why are you in such a hurry?*

hurt /hûrt/ *v.* (**hurts, hurt, hurt•ing**) **a.** to cause pain to. *The sting of the bee hurt his arm.* **b.** to suffer pain. *Does your head hurt?*

ice /īs/ *n.* water that has been frozen solid by cold. *Ice keeps food and drinks cool.*

I'll /īl/ contraction of **I shall** or **I will.**

inch /ĭnch/ *n.* (**inch•es** *pl.*) a measure of length equal to one-twelfth of one foot. *Michelle is forty-six inches tall.*

it•'d /ĭt′ əd/ contraction of **it had** or **it would.**

it•'ll /ĭt′ əl/ contraction of **it will.**

its /ĭts/ *pron.* of or belonging to it. *The bird left its nest.*

➤ **Its** sounds like **it's.**

it's /ĭts/ contraction of **it is** or **it has.**

➤ **It's** sounds like **its.**

I've /īv/ contraction of **I have.**

i•vo•ry /ī′ və rē/ or /īv′ rē/ *n.* (**i•vo•ries** *pl.*) **a.** a hard, white substance, like the tusks of an elephant. *The tabletop is made of ivory.* **b.** a creamy-white color. *Ivory is a nice color for my living room.*

jaw /jô/ *n.* the lowest part of the face; the part that holds the teeth. *When you yawn, your jaw drops.*

jel·ly /jĕl′ ē/ *n.* (**jel·lies** *pl.*) a food made by boiling fruit juices and sugar. *I like grape jelly.*

jig·saw /jĭg′ sô′/ *n.* a saw with a narrow blade for cutting curved and ornamental patterns. *Dad used a jigsaw to make the fancy shelf.*

jog·ging /jŏg′ ĭng/ *v.* (**jogs, jogged, jog·ging**) running at a slow, regular pace. *I like jogging early in the morning before it gets hot outside.*

join /join/ *v.* **a.** to put together; to connect. *They will join the caboose to the last car of the train.* **b.** to become a member of. *Next year I will be able to join the Boy Scouts.* **c.** to combine with a group in doing something. *Would you like to join our game?*

joke /jōk/ *n.* something said or done to make someone laugh. *Rob told a funny joke.*

jump /jŭmp/ *v.* to leap off the ground. *It was fun to watch the horses jump over the fences.*

kan·ga·roo /kăng′ gə roo′/ *n.* a mammal found in Australia and surrounding islands with a small head, large ears, long powerful hind legs, and a long thick tail. *The mother kangaroo carries her young in a pouch.*

keen·ly /kēn′ lē/ *adv.* with great interest; eagerly. *We keenly looked forward to learning the new computer game.*

kept /kĕpt/ *v.* (**keeps, kept, keep·ing**) stored; put away; saved. *I kept all of my old homework.*

kind¹ /kīnd/ *adj.* gentle and caring. *They are always very kind to animals.*

kind² /kīnd/ *n.* type; sort; variety. *Which kind of ice cream would you like?*

kit·ten /kĭt′ n/ *n.* a young cat. *The kitten chased a butterfly around the garden.*

kitten

knew /n o͞o/ or /ny o͞o/ past tense of **know**.

knight /nīt/ *n.* during the Middle Ages, a warrior who was honored with a military rank by a king or lord. *The king called his knights together to plan the battle.*

➤ **Knight** sounds like **night**.

knit·ting /nĭt′ ĭng/ *v.* (**knits, knit** or **knit·ted, knit·ting**) making by weaving yarn with long needles. *My mother is knitting a hat for me.*

know /nō/ *v.* (**knows, knew, known, know·ing**) **a.** to understand; to have information about. *Do you know how fossils are made?* **b.** to be aware; to be sure. *We knew we had heard a noise.* **c.** to be acquainted with. *I've known them for years.* **d.** to have skill in. *Who knows how to play the piano?*

lad·der /lăd′ ər/ *n.* a series of steps placed between two long sidepieces, used for climbing. *The painter leaned the ladder against the wall.*

la·dy /lā′ dē/ *n.* (**la·dies** *pl.*) **a.** a woman or girl who has very good manners. *She is a very thoughtful young lady.* **b.** a woman who is the head of a household. *Are you the lady of the house?* **c.** a woman, especially when spoken of in a polite way. *Ask the lady if she dropped her purse.*

laid /lād/ past tense of **lay.**

land /lănd/ *n.* **a.** the part of the earth that is not water. *After the plane went up through the clouds, we could no longer see the land.* **b.** ground; earth; soil. *This rich land is good for planting corn.*

large /lärj/ *adj.* (**larg·er, larg·est; large·ly** *adv.*) big. *A whale is large.*

last /lăst/ *adj.* **a.** coming after all others; final. *The last train leaves at six o'clock.* **b.** before the present time; most recent. *I read this book last year.*

last·ly /lăst′ lē/ *adv.* at the end; finally. *Lastly pour the batter into a cake pan and put it into the oven.*

late[1] /lāt/ *adj.* (**la·ter, la·test**) **a.** happening after the usual time. *We had a late summer this year.* **b.** near the end of a certain time. *Our tomatoes ripen in late summer.*

late[2] /lāt/ *adv.* after the usual or proper time. *The bus came late.*

late·ly /lāt′ lē/ *adv.* not long ago; recently. *Edna has lately been working harder than ever.*

lat·er /lā′ tər/ *adv.* at a time in the future. *Dinah will arrive later.*

lat·est /lā′ tĭst/ *adj.* most recent; up-to-date. *Have you read the latest news?*

law /lô/ *n.* a rule. *Every state has a law against stealing.*

lawn /lôn/ *n.* ground covered with grass that is kept cut short. *Mr. Griffin's lawn is smooth and green.*

lawn

lay /lā/ *v.* (**lays, laid, lay·ing**) **a.** to put or place. *You can lay your book on the table.* **b.** to produce eggs. *Hens lay eggs.*

learn /lûrn/ *v.* **a.** to gain skill or knowledge in. *We learn spelling in school.* **b.** to memorize. *Can you learn this poem?* **c.** to find out. *When will we learn the results of the election?*

leave /lēv/ *v.* (**leaves, left, leav·ing**) **a.** to go away; to go from. *The train will leave in ten minutes.* **b.** to let stay or be. *Leave your packages here while you shop.*

left[1] /lĕft/ past tense of **leave.**

left[2] /lĕft/ *adj.* located closer to the side; opposite the right. *We took a left turn at the corner.*

left[3] /lĕft/ *n.* the left side. *Her house is the one on the left.*

left[4] /lĕft/ *adv.* in the direction to the left. *Go left after you reach the stoplight.*

lem·on /lĕm′ ən/ *n.* a juicy, yellow, sour fruit. *The lemon made Alex pucker.*

les·son /lĕs′ ən/ *n.* something to be taught or learned. *My brother is taking a violin lesson.*

let·ter /lĕt′ ər/ *n.* (**let·ters** *pl.*) **a.** a symbol for a sound. *The last letter in our alphabet is z.* **b.** a written or typed message sent by mail. *Mail your letter at the post office.*

li·brar·y /lī′ brĕr′ ē/ *n.* (**li·brar·ies** *pl.*) a room or building containing books that may be read or borrowed. *A library is also used for research and studying.*

lift /lĭft/ *v.* to raise from a lower to a higher position. *This box is too heavy for me to lift.*

light[1] /līt/ *n.* **a.** rays of energy that help us see; the opposite of dark. *The sun gives light.* **b.** anything that gives light. *Turn off the light when you leave the room.*

light[2] /līt/ *adj.* not heavy; not having much weight. *In the summer we wear light clothes.*

li·on /lī′ ən/ *n.* a large, powerful, brownish-yellow member of the cat family. *A group of lions is called a pride.*

list[1] /lĭst/ *n.* a column of names, words, or numbers. *I need to write a grocery list.*

list[2] /lĭst/ *v.* to write or print in a column or columns. *List the spelling words on your paper.*

lit·tle[1] /lĭt′ l/ *adj.* **a.** small. *An elephant is big and an ant is little.* **b.** not much. *There is little food in the house.*

lit·tle[2] /lĭt′ l/ *n.* a small amount. *Patricia showed the teacher a little of her poetry.*

live /lĭv/ *v.* (**lives, lived, liv·ing**) **a.** to be alive; to exist. *We live on the planet Earth.* **b.** to have one's home; to dwell. *Our aunt lives in Texas.*

liv·ing /lĭv′ ĭng/ *adj.* alive; not dead. *Biology is the study of living things.*

load[1] /lōd/ *n.* something that is carried. *The load was too heavy for the small car.*

load[2] /lōd/ *v.* to fill with something to be carried. *Load the truck with bricks.*

loaf /lōf/ *n.* (**loaves** *pl.*) a shaped or molded mass of bread; food baked in one large piece. *Grandma baked a loaf of bread.*

loaf

lob·by /lŏb′ ē/ *n.* (**lob·bies** *pl.*) a hall or waiting room in a hotel or other building. *Let's sit in the lobby and wait for Tanisha.*

long·er /lông′ gər/ or /lŏng′ gər/ *adj.* having a greater length than something else. *This string is longer than that one.*

long·est /lông′ gĭst/ or /lŏng′ gĭst/ *adj.* having the greatest length than anything else. *She has the longest hair of anyone in her class.*

loop /lo͞op/ *n.* the curved shape of a line that dips and crosses itself. *We hung the crepe paper in loops.*

loose /lo͞os/ *adj.* (**loos·er, loos·est; loose·ly** *adv.*) not fastened tightly. *The bottom step is loose.*

lose /lo͞oz/ *v.* (**los·es, lost, los·ing**) **a.** to be unable to find. *Don't lose your key.* **b.** to fail to win. *Our team almost lost the game.*

lost[1] /lôst/ or /lŏst/ *v.* past tense of **lose.**

lost[2] /lôst/ or /lŏst/ *adj.* **a.** missing. *The children found the lost cat.* **b.** destroyed; ruined. *The lost trees will take years to replace.*

loud /loud/ *adj.* (**loud·er, loud·est, loud·ly**) **a.** strong in sound; not soft or quiet. *My alarm clock is loud.* **b.** noisy. *The people in the next apartment have loud parties.*

love[1] /lŭv/ *n.* **a.** a deep, fond, affectionate feeling. *Helping people is a way of showing love.* **b.** a great liking. *He has a love of books.*

love[2] /lŭv/ *v.* (**loves, loved, lov•ing**) **a.** to have a deep affection for. *My parents love me.* **b.** to like very much. *Emily loves to play soccer.*

lov•ing /lŭv′ ĭng/ *adj.* caring; fond; showing love. *The loving mother held the baby.*

lunch /lŭnch/ *n.* (**lunch•es** *pl.*) a light meal eaten around the middle of the day. *We have lunch at noon.*

-ly **a.** a suffix that means "in a certain manner" and is used to form adverbs and sometimes adjectives: *wisely, friendly.* **b.** a suffix that means "at a particular interval of time": *monthly.*

mag•net /măg′ nĭt/ *n.* an iron, steel, or alloy object that attracts iron. *He used a magnet to pick up the nails.*

mail[1] /māl/ *n.* packages, letters, postcards, etc., that are delivered through the post office. *Has the mail come yet?*

mail[2] /māl/ *v.* to send by mail; to place in a mailbox. *Did you mail my letter?*

main /mān/ *adj.* most important; chief; major. *Roast beef was the main course.*

main•ly /mān′ lē/ *adv.* for the most part; chiefly. *The book was mainly about history.*

make /māk/ *v.* (**makes, made, mak•ing**) **a.** to put together; to build; to create. *Let's make a tent out of blankets.* **b.** to cause; to bring about. *A horn makes a loud noise.* **c.** to equal; to add up to. *Two and three make five.*

may•be /mā′ bē/ *adv.* perhaps. *Maybe he hasn't left the train yet, and we can still find him.*

mean[1] /mēn/ *v.* (**means, meant, mean•ing**) **a.** to indicate the idea of. *What does this word mean?* **b.** to have in mind as a purpose. *She didn't mean to get angry.*

mean[2] /mēn/ *adj.* unkind; wicked. *The man was mean to the children who walked on his lawn.*

meat /mēt/ *n.* the flesh of an animal used as food. *Lean meat is better for you.*

➤ **Meat** sounds like **meet.**

meet /mēt/ *v.* (**meets, met, meet•ing**) **a.** to come face to face with; to come together. *I'll meet you at the corner.* **b.** to be introduced to. *How did you meet her?* **c.** to gather as a group or club. *Our dance class meets on Tuesdays.*

➤ **Meet** sounds like **meat.**

mer•ry /mĕr′ ē/ *adj.* (**mer•ri•er, mer•ri•est; mer•ri•ly** *adv.*) full of happiness and cheer; joyful. *There was a merry crowd at the football game.*

mess•y /mĕs′ ē/ *adj.* untidy or dirty. *Felix has a very messy room.*

might /mīt/ (**may**) *v.* **a.** be allowed to. *Might we go tonight?* **b.** to be possible that. *I might buy the book.*

might•'ve /mīt′ əv/ contraction of **might have.**

mild /mīld/ *adj.* **a.** not harsh; not severe; warm rather than cold. *We had a mild winter last year.* **b.** not sharp or biting to the taste. *We ordered mild sauce on our food.*

miss /mĭs/ *v.* (**miss•es, missed, miss•ing**) to fail to hit, reach, or get. *Her arrow missed the target by ten feet.*

mit•ten /mĭt′ n/ *n.* a glove worn in winter with a single covering for the fingers and a separate covering for the thumb. *Mittens keep our fingers warm.*

mod•el[1] /mŏd′ l/ *n.* **a.** a small copy of something. *Mr. Hill made a model of the bridge.* **b.** a person who wears clothes to show to others. *The model will look great in a blue suit.*

mod•el[2] /mŏd′ l/ *v.* to wear clothes to show to others. *Pam was asked to model a new coat.*

month /mŭnth/ *n.* one of the twelve parts into which a year is divided. *The first month is January.*

month·ly¹ /mŭnth′ lē/ *adj.* happening once a month. *Did you pay the monthly bills?*

month·ly² /mŭnth′ lē/ *adv.* once each month. *This magazine is published monthly.*

more /môr/ or /mōr/ *adj.* greater in number or amount. *You have more crayons than I do.*

morn·ing /môr′ nĭng/ *n.* the earliest part of the day, ending at noon. *We eat breakfast every morning.*

moss·y /mô′ sē/ or /mŏs′ ē/ *adj.* (**moss·i·er, moss·i·est**) covered with a soft, green plant (moss), or something like it. *There are mossy stones in the forest.*

most¹ /mōst/ *adj.* greatest in amount, number, etc. *The team from Atlanta scored the most points.*

most² /mōst/ *pron.* the greater or larger part. *Most of the students are girls.*

most³ /mōst/ *adv.* to the highest degree. *It was the most unique toy.*

moth /môth/ or /mŏth/ *n.* an insect that usually flies at night and is very much like a butterfly. *A moth fluttered around the porch light.*

moth

moth·er /mŭ*th*′ ər/ *n.* the female parent. *The teacher wants to see my father and mother.*

mouse /mous/ *n.* (**mice** *pl.*) a small animal with white, gray, or brown fur, a long tail, and long, sharp front teeth. *Field mice make nests in the ground.*

mouth /mouth/ *n.* the opening in the head that contains the tongue and teeth and is used for taking in food and making sounds. *When you yawn, your mouth opens wide.*

mud·dy /mŭd′ ē/ *adj.* (**mud·di·er, mud·di·est**) covered with mud. *Take your muddy shoes off before you come inside.*

mule /myōōl/ *n.* a work animal that is part horse and part donkey. *A mule can carry heavy loads.*

mush·room /mŭsh′ rōōm′/ or /mŭsh′ rŏŏm′/ *n.* an umbrella-shaped fungus. *Some mushrooms are edible, but some are poisonous.*

must·'ve /must′ əv/ contraction of **must have.**

my·self /mī sĕlf′/ *pron.* (**our·selves** *pl.*) **a.** one's own self. *I guessed the answer by myself.* **b.** one's usual self. *When I was sick I didn't feel like myself.*

mys·ter·y /mĭs′ tə rē/ *n.* (**mys·ter·ies** *pl.*) **a.** something that is not fully understood. *What the book is doing here is a mystery.* **b.** a work of fiction, a drama, or a film that deals with a puzzling situation. *I like figuring out the solution when I read a mystery.*

neat·ly /nēt′ lē/ *adv.* in an orderly way. *He neatly folded his shirts.*

neck·lace /nĕk′ lĭs/ *n.* an ornament worn around the neck. *She wore a pearl necklace with her dress.*

need /nēd/ *v.* to require; to have to have. *Most plants need lots of sunshine to grow.*

nest[1] /nĕst/ *n.* **a.** a place built by a bird for laying eggs. *The robin built its nest outside my window.* **b.** a place where insects or animals live. *Wasps build nests.*

nest

nest[2] /nĕst/ *v.* to build and use a nest. *Birds nest in trees.*

nev·er /nĕv′ ər/ *adv.* not ever; not at any time. *Maria has never been late to school; she is always early.*

news /nōōz/ or /nyōōz/ *n.* **a.** information; things that a person has not heard about. *What is the news about your brother's new job?* **b.** recent happenings reported in newspapers and over television and radio. *We read the news in the paper.*

news·pa·per /nōōz′ pā′ pər/ or /nyōōz′-/ *n.* a printed paper that contains news, advertisements, cartoons, etc. *My grandfather likes to work the crossword puzzles in the newspaper.*

nice /nīs/ *adj.* (**nic·er, nic·est**) **a.** agreeable; pleasant. *Did you have a nice time at the picnic?* **b.** showing skill and care. *Kathy does a nice job of painting.*

night /nīt/ *n.* the time between evening and morning; the time from sunset to sunrise when it is dark. *The stars shine at night.*

➤ **Night** sounds like **knight**.

night·mare /nīt′ mâr′/ *n.* a scary dream that usually wakes up the sleeper. *Mike had a nightmare about falling off his bike.*

no·bod·y /nō′ bŏd′ ē/ or /nō′ bə dē/ *pron.* no one; no person. *Nobody is here at this time of day.*

nod /nŏd/ *v.* (**nods, nod·ded, nod·ding**) to bow the head and raise it quickly to say "yes" or "hello." *He nodded and waved to his friend.*

noise /noiz/ *n.* a sound, especially one that is loud and harsh. *The noise of the alarm clock startled me.*

noise

none /nŭn/ *pron.* not any; not one. *None of us had the bus fare, so we walked.*

noon /nōōn/ *n.* the middle of the day; twelve o'clock in the daytime. *Our school serves lunch at noon.*

north[1] /nôrth/ *n.* the direction to your right when you face the sunset. *Cold winds blow from the north.*

north² /nôrth/ *adj.* to the north. *The north side of the house faces the highway.*

north³ /nôrth/ *adv.* toward the north. *Birds fly north in the spring.*

note•book /nōt′ bŏŏk′/ *n.* a book for notes of things to be learned or remembered. *I always carry a notebook to class.*

noth•ing /nŭth′ ĭng/ *n.* **a.** not anything. *We saw nothing we liked in that shop.* **b.** zero. *Six taken from six leaves nothing.*

no•where /nō′ hwâr′/ or /nō′ wâr′/ *adv.* not anywhere. *My shoes are nowhere to be found.*

nudge /nŭj/ *n.* a little push with the elbow. *Mom woke me up by giving me a nudge in my side.*

nurse /nûrs/ *n.* a person who cares for people who are sick or who need help. *Nurses work with doctors to help people stay well.*

o′•clock /ə klŏk′/ *adv.* of or according to the clock. *Our school day ends at three o'clock.*

o•dor /ō′ dər/ *n.* a strong smell. *The garbage had a bad odor.*

oh /ō/ *interj.* a sound that expresses surprise, interest, or sorrow. *Oh, no! I forgot my keys!*
➤ **Oh** sounds like **owe.**

oil /oil/ *n.* a greasy liquid obtained from animals, plants, or minerals. *Olive oil is used for salads.*

oint•ment /oint′ mənt/ *n.* a lotion for the skin. *This ointment will soothe your sunburn.*

once /wŭns/ *adv.* **a.** one time. *We met only once.* **b.** formerly. *Horses once were used to plow fields.*

o•pen¹ /ō′ pən/ *v.* **a.** to move from a shut position. *Open the door.* **b.** to remove the outer cover. *Open the envelope.*

o•pen² /ō′ pən/ *adj.* not closed or shut. *The cat climbed out an open window.*

Pronunciation Key

ă	pat	ŏ	pot	th	thin
ā	pay	ō	toe	*th*	this
âr	care	ô	paw, for	hw	which
ä	father	oi	noise	zh	vision
ĕ	pet	ou	out	ə	about,
ē	be	ŏŏ	took		item,
ĭ	pit	ōō	boot		pencil,
ī	pie	ŭ	cut		gallop,
îr	pier	ûr	urge		circus

or•ange /ôr′ ĭnj/ or /ŏr′ ĭnj/ *n.* a round, reddish-yellow, juicy fruit. *I ate an orange from Florida.*

or•der /ôr′ dər/ *n.* **a.** a command; an instruction. *The sailors obeyed the captain's order.* **b.** the way in which things follow one another. *These names are in alphabetical order.*

oth•er¹ /ŭth′ ər/ *adj.* **a.** different. *I asked the salesman to call some other day.* **b.** remaining. *Can you write with your other hand?*

oth•er² /ŭth′ ər/ *pron.* the remaining one; the other one. *Raise one hand, and then raise the other.*

out•fit /out′ fĭt′/ *n.* the clothing and accessories for an event. *What do you think of my party outfit?*

o•ver¹ /ō′ vər/ *prep.* **a.** above. *The reading lamp is over the bed.* **b.** on top of. *Put the cover over the basket.* **c.** more than. *The flight took over three hours.*

o•ver² /ō′ vər/ *adv.* again. *Do this exercise over.*

o•ver³ /ō′ vər/ *adj.* ended. *The rain is over.*

owe /ō/ *v.* (**owes, owed, ow•ing**) to have to pay or repay in return for something. *We owe Jon a dollar.*
➤ **Owe** sounds like **oh.**

pack·et /păk′ ĭt/ *n.* a small bundle or parcel. *Mom carries a packet of tissues in her purse.*

page /pāj/ *n.* one side of a sheet of paper in a book, magazine, newspaper, or letter. *Kurt knew from the first page that he would like the book.*

paid /pād/ past tense of **pay**.

pail /pāl/ *n.* a round bucket with a handle. *She filled the pail with water.*

paint¹ /pānt/ *n.* a mixture used to color a surface. *Where's the jar of blue paint?*

paint

paint² /pānt/ *v.* **a.** to cover a surface with paint. *They must paint the fence.* **b.** to make a picture with paints. *Ms. Lindquist paints landscapes in her spare time.*

paint·brush /pānt′ brŭsh′/ *n.* (**paint·brush·es** *pl.*) a brush for applying paint. *Please use the big paintbrush to paint the door.*

pair /pâr/ *n.* **a.** two things of the same kind that go together; a set of two. *Carlos has a new pair of shoes.* **b.** a couple. *A pair of robins built their nest in a tree.*

➤ **Pair** sounds like **pear**.

pan·ther /păn′ thər/ *n.* a black leopard. *The panther belongs to the feline family.*

part·ly /pärt′ lē/ *adv.* in part; not completely. *My test is partly finished.*

par·ty¹ /pär′ tē/ *n.* (**par·ties** *pl.*) **a.** a social gathering. *We had fun at the party for our teacher.* **b.** a group of people who gather for a reason. *Are you with the rock-climbing party?*

par·ty² /pär′ tē/ *adj.* suitable for use at a social gathering. *I wore my party shoes to Grandpa's house.*

patch /păch/ *n.* (**patch·es** *pl.*) a piece of cloth sewn over a hole or a tear. *My old pants have a patch on them.*

pave /pāv/ *v.* (**paves, paved, pav·ing**) to cover a road, street, etc., with a smooth, hard surface. *They will pave the dirt road next week.*

pay /pā/ *v.* (**pays, paid, pay·ing**) to give money to someone for goods or for something done. *Kim paid three dollars for her lunch.*

peace /pēs/ *n.* **a.** quiet and calm; stillness. *We like the peace of the country.* **b.** freedom from war. *Every thinking person wants peace.*

➤ **Peace** sounds like **piece**.

pea·cock /pē′ kŏk′/ *n.* a large bird that spreads its beautiful green, blue, and gold feathers. *The peacock's feathers look like a fan.*

pea·nut /pē′ nŭt′/ *n.* an edible seed. *I can't eat this peanut because I am allergic to it.*

pear /pâr/ *n.* a juicy fruit with a mild flavor. *A pear is usually larger at the bottom end.*

➤ **Pear** sounds like **pair**.

pearl /pûrl/ *n.* a white or off-white gem found in oysters. *The pearl on Jane's ring is very smooth.*

pen·cil /pĕn′ səl/ *n.* a long, slender piece of wood with a center of black or colored writing material. *Pencils are used for writing and for drawing.*

pen·ny /pĕn′ ē/ *n.* (**pen·nies** *pl.*) a cent. *One hundred pennies make a dollar.*

peo·ple /pē′ pəl/ *n.* human beings; persons; men, women, boys, and girls. *People of all ages attended the fair.*

pep·per /pĕp′ ər/ *n.* a hot-tasting powdered spice. *Pepper is used to season foods.*

pie /pī/ *n.* (**pies** *pl.*) a baked food made of fruit, meat, or pudding within a crust. *Apple pie is his favorite food.*

piece /pēs/ *n.* a part; a segment. *Would you like a piece of my orange?*

➤ **Piece** sounds like **peace**.

pil·low /pĭl′ ō/ *n.* a support used for the head in resting or sleeping; a cushion. *Do you like to sleep on a feather pillow?*

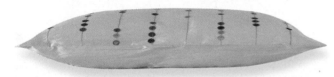

pillow

place¹ /plās/ *n.* **a.** a certain point; a spot. *The coolest place in town is near the river.* **b.** a space where something belongs. *Put the chair back in its place.* **c.** a seat or space for a person. *If you get there early, save me a place.*

place² /plās/ *v.* (**plac·es, placed, plac·ing**) to put in a particular position; to set. *Place your pencil on the desk.*

plain /plān/ *adj.* (**plain·ly** *adv.*) **a.** easy to see; clear. *The directions are plain.* **b.** simple; not fancy in appearance. *Tracy wore a plain dress.*

➤ **Plain** sounds like **plane**.

plan¹ /plăn/ *n.* a way of doing something that is thought out in advance; a scheme. *Mark is excited about his plan for a vacation in California.*

plan² /plăn/ *v.* (**plans, planned, plan·ning**) to think out in advance. *Amy helped us plan the bake sale.*

plane /plān/ *n.* an airplane. *The big planes take off from the airport one minute apart.*

➤ **Plane** sounds like **plain**.

plan·ning /plăn′ ĭng/ *v.* (**plans, planned, plan·ning**) thinking beforehand about how something should be done. *Will you be planning a party soon?*

plant·ed /plănt′ tĭd/ *v.* put into the ground so that it will grow. *We planted a lilac bush in our front yard.*

plat·ter /plăt′ ər/ *n.* a large dish used for serving food. *The platter held three baked fish.*

play /plā/ *v.* **a.** to take part in a game or activity for fun. *Children like to play tag.* **b.** to perform on a musical instrument. *I can play the piano.* **c.** to act on the stage. *Jennifer wants to play the queen.*

plot /plŏt/ *n.* **a.** a small section of ground. *Kevin and Jason each has his own plot.* **b.** the main events in a story. *The plot of the book was mysterious.*

plunge /plŭnj/ *v.* (**plung·es, plunged, plung·ing**) to jump into; to rush into; to thrust oneself into water. *Greg always likes to plunge into our pool.*

pock·et /pŏk′ ĭt/ *n.* a small bag sewn into clothing. *I carry my wallet in the pocket of my pants.*

point¹ /point/ *n.* **a.** a sharp end. *I like a pencil with a fine point.* **b.** a position; a place. *We are at this point on the map.* **c.** a unit of scoring. *She won the game by two points.*

point² /point/ *v.* to aim. *He meant to point his arrow at the target.*

pool /pool/ *n.* a tank filled with water and used for swimming. *Peter swam across the pool.*

poor /poor/ *adj.* (**poor•er, poor•est**) not of good quality; not good enough. *The furniture fell apart because its quality was poor.*

po•ta•to /pə tā′ tō/ *n.* (**po•ta•toes** *pl.*) an oval or round vegetable grown underground. *The sweet potato is also called a yam.*

pounce /pouns/ *v.* (**pounc•es, pounced, pounc•ing**) to suddenly swoop or jump. *When the cat sees the mouse, it may pounce on it.*

pret•ty /prĭt′ ē/ *adj.* (**pret•ti•er, pret•ti•est; pret•ti•ly** *adv.*) lovely; pleasing; pleasant to look at or to hear. *The garden was filled with pretty flowers.*

price /prīs/ *n.* the cost in money; the amount of money for which something is sold. *The price should be clearly labeled.*

prize /prīz/ *n.* a thing won in a contest. *Tony won the prize for spelling the most words correctly.*

proof /proof/ *n.* convincing evidence that something is true or not true. *Do you have proof that he took your toy?*

proud /proud/ *adj.* **a.** having a proper regard for oneself. *Mr. Collins is a proud man who likes to do his job well.* **b.** having satisfaction and pleasure. *The proud mother watched her daughter graduate.*

pup•py /pŭp′ ē/ *n.* (**pup•pies** *pl.*) a young dog; a pup. *The silly puppy tried to chase its own tail.*

put /poot/ *v.* (**puts, put, put•ting**) **a.** to place; to set. *Put the books on the desk.* **b.** to bring into a certain state. *Put the room in order.*

puz•zle /pŭz′ əl/ *n.* a game with a problem to be worked out. *We do word puzzles in school.*

race /rās/ *n.* a contest of speed. *During the summer we went to the boat race.*

rail•way /rāl′ wā′/ *n.* a railroad. *Many people travel to work each day by railway.*

rain•bow /rān′ bō′/ *n.* a curved band of colored light in the sky, caused by the rays of the sun passing through drops of rain, mist, or spray. *We saw a rainbow where the waves broke against the rocks.*

rainbow

rare /râr/ *adj.* not often found or seen. *My uncle saves rare postage stamps.*

rat•tle /răt′ l/ *v.* (**rat•tles, rat•tled, rat•tling**) **a.** to make a number of short, sharp sounds. *The windows rattle when the wind blows.* **b.** to move with short, sharp sounds. *The old car rattled over the bumpy road.*

raw /rô/ *adj.* not cooked. *Strawberries and radishes can be eaten raw.*

real /rē′ əl/ or /rēl/ *adj.* **a.** actual; true; not imagined; not made up. *My uncle told us a real story about his trip to Brazil.* **b.** genuine. *Her necklace is made of real pearls.*

re•al•ly /rē′ ə lē/ or /rē′ lē/ *adv.* truly; in fact. *Nancy can really run fast.*

rea•son[1] /rē′ zən/ *n.* **a.** a cause or explanation. *Your parents will write the reason for your absence.* **b.** logic; the power to think. *Use reason to solve the problem.*

rea·son² /rē′ zən/ *v.* to think in a sensible way; to use logic. *See if you can reason out the meaning of the word.*

red /rĕd/ *adj.* (**red·der, red·dest**) a bright color like that of a ruby or a strawberry. *Stop signs are always red.*

re·main /rĭ mān′/ *v.* **a.** to continue without change; to stay. *The nurse reported that the patient's condition remained good.* **b.** to be left over. *After the picnic only a few sandwiches remain.*

re·port /rĭ pôrt′/ or /-pōrt′/ *n.* a detailed written or spoken account. *The newspaper report of the election listed the winners.*

re·turn /rĭ tûrn′/ *v.* **a.** to come or go back. *We will return after the game is over.* **b.** to bring, send, or give back. *Return the book when you have finished reading it.*

re·wind /rē wīnd′/ *v.* (**re·winds, re·wound, re·wind·ing**) to turn back. *Please rewind the videotape after you have finished watching the movie.*

rib·bon /rĭb′ ən/ *n.* a narrow strip of fabric, especially one used as a decoration. *She wore a yellow ribbon in her hair.*

right¹ /rīt/ *adj.* **a.** just; good. *Obeying the law is the right thing to do.* **b.** correct; true; accurate. *Allan's answers were all right.* **c.** located on the side opposite to left. *Raise your right hand.*

right² /rīt/ *adv.* **a.** correctly; accurately. *Do your work right.* **b.** straight on; directly. *He looked right at me.* **c.** to the right side. *Turn right at the second stop light.*

➤ **Right** sounds like **write**.

rip·en /rī′ pən/ *v.* to become fully grown or developed. *The fruit will ripen in a few days.*

rise /rīz/ *v.* (**ris·es, rose, ris·en, ris·ing**) **a.** to assume a standing position after lying, sitting, or kneeling. *Please rise for the National Anthem.* **b.** to get out of bed. *We like to rise at 7:00 A.M.* **c.** to increase in size, number, or force. *If it continues to rain, the river will rise.*

road /rōd/ *n.* a way or path between places; highway. *This is the road to my friend's house.*

road

role /rōl/ *n.* a part or a character in a play. *Who will play the role of Peter Pan?*

➤ **Role** sounds like **roll**.

roll /rōl/ *v.* **a.** to move by turning over and over. *The boys let the ball roll down the hill.* **b.** to wrap something around itself. *She will roll the yarn into a ball and put it in a drawer.*

➤ **Roll** sounds like **role**.

roof /rōōf/ or /rŏŏf/ *n.* (**roofs** *pl.*) **a.** the part that covers the top of a house or building. *Many houses have sloping roofs.* **b.** anything like a roof. *The peanut butter stuck to the roof of her mouth.*

round /round/ *adj.* **a.** shaped like a ball. *Earth is round.* **b.** shaped like a circle. *Our swimming pool is square, but theirs is round.*

row¹ /rō/ *n.* a line formed by a number of persons or things. *Who is sitting in the last row?*

row² /rō/ *v.* to move a boat by using oars. *He will row across the lake and back.*

rub /rŭb/ *v.* (**rubs, rubbed, rub•bing**) to move something back and forth against another surface. *We had to rub hard to get all the dirt off.*

ru•by¹ /rōō′ bē/ *n.* (**ru•bies** *pl.*) a deep red mineral that is highly valued as a precious stone. *The stone in that ring is a valuable ruby.*

ru•by² /rōō′ bē/ *adj.* having a deep red color. *The shirt was a ruby color.*

run /rŭn/ *v.* (**runs, ran, run•ning**) **a.** to move by lifting the legs quickly off the ground one after the other. *When she hits the ball, Teresa can run to first base.* **b.** to go along a certain path. *The roads run past the lake.* **c.** to flow. *Water runs downhill.*

sad /săd/ *adj.* (**sad•der, sad•dest; sad•ly** *adv.*) **a.** unhappy. *We were sad when our team lost.* **b.** causing unhappiness. *Do you cry when you read a sad book?*

safe /sāf/ *adj.* (**saf•er, saf•est**) free from risk or harm. *The sidewalk is a safe place to walk.*

said /sĕd/ *v.* (**says, said, say•ing**) **a.** spoke; put into words. *He didn't hear what I said.* **b.** to give as an opinion. *I can't tell you what he said about your teacher.*

sail¹ /sāl/ *n.* a large sheet of heavy cloth used to move a boat through water by catching the wind. *The largest ships used to have thirty sails.*

sail² /sāl/ *v.* to move swiftly, especially in air or on water. *The ships sail down the river.*
➤ **Sail** sounds like **sale**.

sale /sāl/ *n.* **a.** the selling of something; an exchanging of goods for money. *How much money would the sale of the house bring?* **b.** a special selling at prices lower than usual. *The store was crowded during the sale.*
➤ **Sale** sounds like **sail**.

sand /sănd/ *n.* tiny bits of stone in large amounts, found in the deserts and on shores along oceans, lakes, and rivers. *This beach has smooth sand.*

sand•wich /sănd′ wĭch/ or /săn′/ *n.* (**sand•wich•es** *pl.*) two or more slices of bread, with a layer of meat, cheese, or other food placed between them. *I like a sandwich made of peanut butter and bananas.*

sandwich

save /sāv/ *v.* (**saves, saved, sav•ing**) **a.** to rescue; to make safe from danger. *We saved the cat that was up in the tree.* **b.** to put away; keep. *I save stamps for my collection.*

sav•ing /sāv′ ĭng/ *v.* (**saves, saved, sav•ing**) putting aside or keeping. *Carla is saving money to buy a new coat.*

saw¹ /sô/ *n.* a tool or machine used to cut. *Dad used his saw to build a birdhouse.*

saw² /sô/ *v.* past tense of **see**. *I saw the Big Dipper last night.*

scarf /skärf/ *n.* (**scarfs, scarves** *pl.*) broad bands of material worn around the shoulders, neck, or head. *The women wore red scarfs to protect their heads.*

scene /sēn/ *n.* **a.** the time and place of a story or play. *The scene of the play is a mining town in the old West.* **b.** a division of an act of a play. *I appear in the second scene of the first act of the play.*

scent /sĕnt/ *n.* an odor; a smell. *The dogs followed the scent of the fox.*

➤ Scent sounds like **cent** and **sent**.

school /skool/ *n.* **a.** a place for teaching and learning. *Children learn how to read in school.* **b.** the regular time when teaching and learning take place. *We had no school because of the storm.*

scoop¹ /skoop/ *n.* a utensil for digging, dipping, or shoveling. *He used a scoop to get ice cream out of the tub.*

scoop² /skoop/ *v.* to take out with a scoop. *I scoop ice cream at the corner store.*

score /skôr/ or /skōr/ *n.* **a.** the number of points made in a game. *The final score in the baseball game was 5 to 0.* **b.** a grade. *His score on the test was 93.*

scout /skout/ *v.* to explore; to make a search. *The hiker will scout a new trail.*

scrape /skrāp/ *v.* to scratch the surface of. *The basketball player scraped his knee when he fell.*

scratch¹ /skrăch/ *v.* (**scratch•es, scratched, scratch•ing**) to cut or scrape a surface. *You can tell that a diamond is genuine if it scratches glass.*

scratch² /skrăch/ *n.* (**scratch•es** *pl.*) a thin cut or mark. *The top of this old desk has many scratches.*

scream /skrēm/ *v.* to voice a sudden sharp cry; to produce harsh, high tones. *The scary movie made me scream.*

scrub /skrŭb/ *v.* (**scrubs, scrubbed, scrub•bing**) to wash or clean by rubbing hard. *At camp we had to scrub and mop the floors.*

Pronunciation Key

ă	pat	ŏ	pot	th	**th**in
ā	pay	ō	toe	*th*	**th**is
âr	care	ô	paw, for	hw	**wh**ich
ä	father	oi	n**oi**se	zh	vi**s**ion
ĕ	pet	ou	**ou**t	ə	**a**bout,
ē	be	oo	t**oo**k		it**e**m,
ĭ	pit	oo	b**oo**t		penc**i**l,
ī	pie	ŭ	c**u**t		gall**o**p,
îr	p**ier**	ûr	**ur**ge		circ**u**s

---

sea•shore /sē' shôr'/ or /sē' shōr'/ *n.* the land where the sea meets the shore. *Our family collected shells at the seashore.*

seat belt /sēt' bĕlt'/ *n.* a safety strap designed to hold a person securely in a seat. *The flight attendant asked the man to fasten his seat belt.*

se•cret /sē' krĭt/ *n.* something kept from other people. *Please don't share my secret with anyone.*

se•cret•ly /sē' krĭt lē/ *adv.* in a secret or hidden way. *Mr. Grant secretly bought his wife a gift.*

seem /sēm/ *v.* to look like; to appear to be. *The new kids next door seem very nice.*

sell /sĕl/ *v.* (**sells, sold, sell•ing**) **a.** to exchange for money or other payment. *Matt wants to sell his old radio for five dollars.* **b.** to keep for sale; to deal in. *Bakeries sell bread, rolls, cookies, and cakes.*

➤ Sell sounds like **cell**.

send /sĕnd/ *v.* (**sends, sent, send•ing**) to cause or order to go. *The principal decided to send the children home early because of the storm.*

sent /sĕnt/ past tense of **send**.

➤ Sent sounds like **cent** and **scent**.

sev•en /sĕv' ən/ *n.* the next number after six; six plus one; 7. *I added seven and three.*

sev·er·al /sĕv′ ər əl/ or /sĕv′ rəl/ *pron. pl.* an indefinite number more than two and fewer than many. *Several of my friends have brown hair.*

shade[1] /shād/ *n.* shelter from heat or sun. *The shade made me feel cooler.*

shade[2] /shād/ *v.* (**shades, shad·ed, shad·ing**) to shelter from heat or sun. *I'd like to shade my deck with an awning.*

shag·gy /shăg′ ē/ *adj.* (**shag·gi·er, shag·gi·est**) covered with long, coarse, or tangled hair. *We washed the shaggy dog with lots of shampoo.*

shake /shāk/ *v.* (**shakes, shook, shak·en, shak·ing**) to move quickly up and down or from side to side. *Shake the can of orange juice before you open it.*

shall /shăl/ *v.* (**should**) **a.** am, is, or are going to. *I shall be there tomorrow.* **b.** must; am, is, or are obliged to. *You shall do your duty.*

shape /shāp/ *n.* **a.** form; appearance. *The shape of an apple is round.* **b.** condition. *Regular exercise will keep you in good shape.*

sharp /shärp/ *adj.* (**sharp·er, sharp·est; sharp·ly** *adv.*) **a.** having a fine point or a thin edge for cutting. *The knife blade is sharp.* **b.** abrupt; sudden; not gradual. *Slow down the car for the sharp turn just ahead.*

she'd /shĕd/ contraction of **she had** or **she would**.

sheep /shēp/ *n.* (**sheep** *pl.*) a hoofed animal with a thick, woolly coat. *Farmers raise sheep both for meat and for wool.*

she'll /shēl/ contraction of **she will**.

shine /shīn/ *v.* (**shines, shone** or **shined, shin·ing**) **a.** to give off light. *Those lights shine right in my eyes.* **b.** to make bright; to polish. *I helped my sister shine the pots and pans.*

shin·y /shī′ nē/ *adj.* (**shin·i·er, shin·i·est**) bright. *We saw the shiny car quickly.*

ship·wreck /shĭp′ rĕk′/ *n.* a wrecked ship or its parts. *Pieces of the shipwreck were floating in the ocean.*

shirt /shûrt/ *n.* a garment for the upper part of the body. *A shirt usually has a collar and sleeves.*

shirt

shoe·lace /shoo′ lās′/ *n.* a strip of leather or other material for tying a shoe. *I have red shoelaces in my new shoes.*

shone /shōn/ past tense of **shine**. *The light shone on the painting.*

shook /shook/ past tense of **shake**.

shoot /shoot/ *v.* (**shoots, shot, shoot·ing**) **a.** to fire a gun. *Mrs. Hill will shoot a pistol to start the race.* **b.** to send out swiftly. *Watch the archer shoot an arrow at the target.*

shop·ping /shŏp′ ĭng/ *v.* (**shops, shopped, shop·ping**) buying things. *We are shopping for shoes.*

short /shôrt/ *adj.* **a.** not long or tall. *I look short next to my big brother.*

short·ly /shôrt′ lē/ *adv.* in a short time; soon. *We will go home shortly.*

should /shood/ *v.* **a.** have a duty to; ought to. *I should study tonight.* **b.** expect to. *We should be able to come.* **c.** past tense of shall.

should·'ve /shood′ əv/ contraction of **should have**.

shout /shout/ *v.* to call out loudly. *We shout into the tunnel to hear the echo.*

show•er /shou′ ər/ *n.* **a.** a short fall of rain. *During the afternoon there was a shower.* **b.** a bath in which water comes down in a spray. *I take a shower every morning.*

shut•ter /shŭt′ ər/ *n.* a movable cover or screen for a window. *We need to replace our front window shutter.*

sigh[1] /sī/ *v.* to let out a long, deep breath. *If Todd wins, he will sigh with relief.*

sigh[2] /sī/ *n.* the act of sighing. *She gave a sigh of sadness.*

sight /sīt/ *n.* **a.** the power or ability to see. *A pilot's sight must be good.* **b.** something that is seen. *The sunset last night was a lovely sight.*

sign /sīn/ *n.* **a.** something that stands for something else; a symbol. *The sign for adding is "+."* **b.** a board or space used for advertising or for information. *The traffic sign says "No Parking."*

sil•ly /sĭl′ ē/ *adj.* (**sil•li•er, sil•li•est**) foolish; not sensible. *It's silly to go out in the cold without a coat.*

since[1] /sĭns/ *conj.* **a.** because. *Since I bought a new catcher's mitt, I'd like to give you the old one.* **b.** after the time that. *I haven't seen him since he moved away.*

since[2] /sĭns/ *prep.* ever after. *We've lived here since 1997.*

sit /sĭt/ *v.* (**sits, sat, sit•ting**) to rest on the lower part of the body. *Dad always likes to sit in this chair.*

size /sīz/ *n.* **a.** the amount of space that a thing takes up. *Look at the size of that elephant!* **b.** one of a series of measures. *Which size paintbrush do you need?*

skate[1] /skāt/ *n.* **a.** a shoe with a blade for moving over ice. *If the pond is frozen, we can use our skates.* **b.** a shoe with four wheels; a roller skate. *You can rent skates at the arena.*

skate[2] /skāt/ *v.* (**skates, skat•ed, skat•ing**) move along on skates. *Don't skate so fast.*

skill /skĭl/ *n.* the ability to do something well as a result of practice. *His skill in playing the violin may someday make him famous.*

Pronunciation Key

ă	pat	ŏ	pot	th	**th**in
ā	pay	ō	toe	*th*	**th**is
âr	care	ô	paw, for	hw	**wh**ich
ä	father	oi	n**oi**se	zh	vi**si**on
ĕ	pet	ou	**ou**t	ə	**a**bout,
ē	be	o͝o	t**oo**k		item,
ĭ	pit	o͞o	b**oo**t		penc**i**l,
ī	pie	ŭ	c**u**t		gall**o**p,
îr	p**ier**	ûr	**ur**ge		circ**u**s

skip /skĭp/ *v.* (**skips, skipped, skip•ping**) **a.** to move by hopping on one foot and then the other. *When I feel happy I skip down the street.* **b.** to bounce over. *I can skip this stone over the water.*

skirt /skûrt/ *n.* **a.** the part of a dress that hangs below the waist. *She wore a dress with a long skirt.* **b.** a garment that hangs from the waist. *Many girls wear a sweater and a skirt in the fall.*

sky /skī/ *n.* (**skies** *pl.*) **a.** the air over any given point on the earth. *See the bird in the sky.* **b.** The appearance of the air overhead, often used in the plural to refer to the weather. *The skies showed it was going to pour.*

sled[1] /slĕd/ *n.* a low platform on runners that slides over ice and snow. *It is fun to coast down a hill on a sled.*

sled[2] /slĕd/ *v.* (**sleds, sled•ded, sled•ding**) to travel on a sled. *We went sledding after the first snowfall.*

sleep[1] /slēp/ *v.* (**sleeps, slept, sleep•ing**) to rest the body and the mind by closing the eyes and losing awareness. *Did you sleep through the movie?*

sleep[2] /slēp/ *n.* a state of rest; not being awake. *Most people need at least eight hours of sleep each night.*

slice[1] /slīs/ *n.* a thin, flat piece cut from something. *Give everyone a slice of bread.*

slice[2] /slīs/ *v.* (**slic•es, sliced, slic•ing**) to cut into slices. *Mom sliced the watermelon.*

slide[1] /slīd/ *v.* (**slides, slid, slid•ing**) to move smoothly and easily over a surface. *The skiers slide over the snow.*

slide[2] /slīd/ *n.* a smooth surface on which a person can slide. *Children like to go down the slide at the playground.*

slight /slīt/ *adj.* not big; small; slender. *Although it looks sunny, there's a slight chance it will rain later today.*

slim /slĭm/ *adj.* (**slim•mer, slim•mest**) thin; slender. *The wind blew over the slim tree.*

slip•pers /slĭp′ ərz/ *n.* (**slip•per** *sing.*) low, comfortable shoes that can be slipped on and off easily. *Slippers keep your feet warm on cool nights.*

slow /slō/ *adj.* (**slow•ly** *adv.*) **a.** not fast or quick. *The turtle makes slow but steady progress.* **b.** behind time. *Your watch is slow.*

smile[1] /smīl/ *v.* (**smiles, smiled, smil•ing**) to look happy or amused by turning up the mouth at the corners. *The teachers smile as we sing our songs.*

smile[2] /smīl/ *n.* the act of smiling; a smiling expression. *A smile can make your day brighter.*

smoke[1] /smōk/ *n.* a cloud that rises from something that is burning. *The smoke from the fireplace smells good.*

smoke[2] /smōk/ *v.* (**smokes, smoked, smok•ing**) to give out smoke. *The chimney is smoking.*

smooth /smōōth/ *adj.* having no bumps or rough spots. *The smooth highway made driving a pleasure.*

smooth•est /smōō′ thəst/ *adj.* the superlative form of **smooth**. (**smooth•er**) having the most even surface; the least rough or lumpy. *This is the smoothest blanket I have ever felt.*

snacks /snăks/ *n.* (**snack** *sing.*) small amounts of food eaten between meals. *Mom packed snacks of fruit and nuts for the long road trip.*

snow[1] /snō/ *n.* frozen water crystals that fall to the earth as soft white flakes. *Snow falls in winter.*

snow[2] /snō/ *v.* to fall as snow. *It has started to snow.*

snow

soak /sōk/ *v.* **a.** to wet through; to make or become wet. *The heavy rains will soak the dry land.* **b.** to let stay in water or other liquid. *The baseball player will soak his sore arm in hot water.*

soap /sōp/ *n.* a substance used for washing. *Use plenty of soap when you wash your hands.*

sock•et /sŏk′ ĭt/ *n.* a hollow opening into which something fits. *The lamp flickered because the bulb was loose in the socket.*

soft /sôft/ or /sŏft/ *adj.* (**soft•ly** *adv.*) **a.** not hard. *We can dig easily in this soft ground.* **b.** smooth; not rough. *The baby has soft skin.* **c.** quiet; gentle; mild. *She has a soft voice.*

soft•ware /sôft′ wâr′/ or /sŏft′ -/ *n.* the programs and information used on a computer. *The new game software is fun to use.*

soil /soil/ *n.* ground; earth; dirt. *Plants grow in rich, dark soil.*

so•lo /sō′ lō/ *n.* a piece of music performed by one person. *Jim played a trumpet solo at the concert.*

some•one /sŭm′ wŭn′/ or /sŭm′ wən/ *pron.* somebody; some person. *Someone ought to fix that front door.*

some·thing /sŭm′ thǐng/ *pron.* a certain thing that is not specifically named. *Give the dog something to eat.*

some·where /sŭm′ hwâr′/ or /sŭm′ wâr′/ *adv.* at some place; to some place. *There is a pond somewhere in the park.*

song /sông/ or /sŏng/ *n.* a tune; a piece of music to be sung. *The principal asked us to sing another song.*

sor·ry /sŏr′ ē/ or /sôr′ ē / *adj.* (**sor·ri·er, sor·ri·est; sor·ri·ly** *adv.*) feeling regret; full of sorrow or sadness. *I'm sorry; I didn't mean to bump you.*

sound¹ /sound/ *n.* anything that is heard; a noise. *The sound of the bells came softly on the breeze.*

sound² /sound/ *v.* to make a noise. *His snores sound all through the house.*

south /south/ *n.* the direction to the left when a person faces the sunset. *A warm wind blew from the south.*

space /spās/ *n.* **a.** the area in which the planets and stars exist. *Earth travels in space around the sun.* **b.** room; a place. *There is no more space for passengers in the crowded train.*

speech /spēch/ *n.* (**speech·es** *pl.*) a talk given in public. *The President made a speech on television.*

spend /spĕnd/ *v.* (**spends, spent, spend·ing**) **a.** to pay out money. *Never spend more than you earn.* **b.** to pass time. *We spent the weekend at the beach.*

spent /spĕnt/ past tense of **spend**.

spice /spīs/ *n.* a seasoning used to add flavor to food. *Pepper is a spice.*

spin·ning /spǐn′ ǐng/ *v.* (**spins, spun, spin·ning**) twirling something. *The woman was spinning cotton on the spinning wheel.*

splash¹ /splăsh/ *v.* **a.** to scatter and fall in drops. *Raindrops splash on the pavement.* **b.** to make wet or dirty. *The cars splash me with mud as they speed past.*

Pronunciation Key

ă	pat	ŏ	pot	th	thin
ā	pay	ō	toe	th	this
âr	care	ô	paw, for	hw	which
ä	father	oi	noise	zh	vision
ĕ	pet	ou	out	ə	about,
ē	be	ŏŏ	took		item,
ĭ	pit	ōō	boot		pencil,
ī	pie	ŭ	cut		gallop,
îr	pier	ûr	urge		circus

splash² /splăsh/ *n.* (**splash·es** *pl.*) a scattering or throwing of a liquid. *The children made a splash as they jumped into the water.*

sponge /spŭnj/ *n.* a porous mass used for cleaning and washing. *I always wash my car with a sponge.*

sport /spôrt/ or /spōrt/ *n.* any game involving exercise; recreation. *Swimming is a common summer sport.*

spot¹ /spŏt/ *n.* a small mark of a different color. *There's a spot of paint on the rug.*

spot² /spŏt/ *v.* (**spots, spot·ted, spot·ting**) to see; to locate; to catch sight of. *How can we spot him in this big crowd?*

spot·ted /spŏt′ ĭd/ *adj.* having spots. *Heather wore a spotted blouse.*

sprain¹ /sprān/ *n.* a sudden twist of a joint with stretching or tearing of ligaments. *I couldn't run because of my ankle sprain.*

sprain² /sprān/ *v.* to injure by a sudden or severe twist. *You will sprain your ankle if you don't wear the right shoes.*

spray /sprā/ *n.* water or another liquid flying through the air. *The spray of the water got my shirt wet.*

spring[1] /sprĭng/ v. (**springs, sprang, sprung, spring•ing**) **a.** to jump; to leap. *The fox will spring at the rabbit.* **b.** to snap back into position. *A rubber band will spring back instantly.*

spring[2] /sprĭng/ n. **a.** a coil of wire or a strip of metal that goes back into shape after pressure is released. *Does your watch have a spring?* **b.** the season of the year that begins about March 21 and ends about June 21. *The weather begins to get warm in spring.*

spy[1] /spī/ n. (**spies** *pl.*) **a.** an agent employed by a state to get secret information. *The spy was hired to photograph the secret factory.* **b.** someone who secretly watches another person or persons. *Is she a spy from the other team?*

spy[2] /spī/ v. (**spies, spied, spy•ing**) **a.** to observe secretly. *He will spy on the other company's plans.* **b.** to catch sight of. *I spy Mom's car in the driveway.*

stamp /stămp/ n. a small, printed piece of paper for sticking on letters and packages to show that the postage has been paid. *You can buy a stamp at the post office.*

stamp

stand /stănd/ v. (**stands, stood, stand•ing**) **a.** to be or place upright. *Can you stand on one leg?* **b.** to endure; to put up with. *How can you stand such a mess?*

stare /stâr/ v. (**stares, stared, star•ing**) to look at with a steady gaze. *Mei Li stared at the painting, fascinated by the bright colors.*

state /stāt/ n. **a.** the condition of. *The old house was in a bad state.* **b.** one of the fifty separate divisions of the United States. *Rhode Island is the smallest state.*

sta•tion /stā′ shən/ n. the place from which a service is provided or operations are directed. *The local radio station will broadcast the game.*

steam /stēm/ n. the vapor into which water is changed by heating. *We could see steam rising from the iron.*

stew /sto͞o/ or /styo͞o/ n. a thick soup that is cooked slowly. *This stew has beef, potatoes, and carrots in it.*

stick /stĭk/ n. a long, thin piece of wood or other material. *We used a stick to stir the paint.*

stitch[1] /stĭch/ n. (**stitch•es** *pl.*) one complete movement of a threaded needle through cloth or other material. *Tie a knot after the last stitch.*

stitch[2] /stĭch/ v. (**stitch•es, stitched, stitch•ing**) to sew. *Can you stitch these quilt squares together?*

stone /stōn/ n. **a.** rock; hard mineral matter. *Our house is built of stone.* **b.** a small piece of this material; a bit of rock. *I threw a stone into the water.* **c.** a gem. *Diamonds are precious stones.*

stop[1] /stŏp/ v. (**stops, stopped, stop•ping**) to halt or come to a halt. *This bus will stop at all railroad crossings.*

stop[2] /stŏp/ n. a halt or a short visit. *We made a stop at the grocery store.*

store /stôr/ or /stōr/ n. a place where things are sold. *Salim bought a hammer in the hardware store.*

storm /stôrm/ n. strong winds often accompanied by heavy amounts of rain, snow, hail, or sleet. *In summer a storm can bring thunder and lightning.*

stor•y /stôr′ ē/ or /stōr′ ē/ n. (**stor•ies** *pl.*) a tale or account of an adventure or happening. *Mr. Lee told us a story about his grandfather.*

strange /strānj/ *adj.* unusual; odd. *We were startled by the strange noise.*

straw[1] /strô/ *n.* **a.** the hollow stalks or stems of grain, such as wheat or oats, after the grain has been removed. *Straw is used to make baskets.* **b.** a thin hollow tube of plastic or paper. *Karen drank her milk through a straw.*

straw[2] /strô/ *adj.* made of straw. *She wore a straw hat.*

straw•ber•ry[1] /strô′ bĕr′ ē/ *n.* (**straw•ber•ries** *pl.*) a low-growing plant that has white flowers and a red, fleshy fruit that can be eaten. *I put a strawberry on each cupcake for decoration.*

straw•ber•ry[2] /strô′ bĕr′ ē/ *adj.* having the flavor of strawberries. *I use strawberry toothpaste.*

stray /strā/ *v.* (**strays, strayed, stray•ing**) to wander or roam. *My dog will stray if he isn't wearing his leash.*

stream /strēm/ *n.* a brook, creek, or small river. *The stream bubbled over the rocks.*

street /strēt/ *n.* a road in a city or town. *This street is always crowded during rush hour.*

stretch /strĕch/ *v.* **a.** to hold out; to extend. *Rachel stretched her hand across the table.* **b.** to draw out to full length; to extend to full size. *Jeff stretched after he woke up.*

string /strĭng/ *n.* a thin cord; a thick thread. *How much string do you need for your kite?*

strong /strông/ or /strŏng/ *adj.* **a.** not weak; powerful. *We need someone strong to lift this box.* **b.** hard to break or knock down; lasting; tough. *You will need a strong rope.* **c.** not mild; sharp. *Some people like strong cheese.*

stud•y[1] /stŭd′ ē/ *v.* (**stud•ies, stud•ied, stud•y•ing**) to try to learn by thinking, reading, and practicing. *We study many subjects in school.*

stud•y[2] /stŭd′ ē/ *n.* (**stud•ies** *pl.*) an investigation; an examination. *Our school nurse made a study of our health habits.*

stuff[1] /stŭf/ *n.* things; objects of any kind. *Don't put any more stuff in the car.*

Pronunciation Key

ă	pat	ŏ	pot	th	**th**in
ā	pay	ō	toe	*th*	**th**is
âr	care	ô	paw, for	hw	**wh**ich
ä	father	oi	n**oi**se	zh	vi**s**ion
ĕ	pet	ou	**ou**t	ə	**a**bout,
ē	be	ŏŏ	t**oo**k		it**e**m,
ĭ	pit	ōō	b**oo**t		penc**i**l,
ī	pie	ŭ	c**u**t		gall**o**p,
îr	pier	ûr	**ur**ge		circ**u**s

---

stuff[2] /stŭf/ *v.* to fill by packing things into. *We stuffed the box with old newspapers.*

sud•den /sŭd′ n/ *adj.* (**sud•den•ly** *adv.*) **a.** not expected. *We got caught in the sudden rainfall.* **b.** quick; hasty. *Mr. Parker made a sudden decision.*

sug•ar /shŏŏg′ ər/ *n.* a sweet substance from sugar cane or sugar beets. *I like one teaspoon of sugar in my tea.*

sum•mer[1] /sŭm′ ər/ *n.* the warmest season of the year. *Summer comes between spring and fall.*

sum•mer[2] /sŭm′ ər/ *adj.* of summer; for summer. *Some summer days are very hot.*

sum•mit /sŭm′ ĭt/ *n.* the top of a mountain. *The climbers hope to reach the summit.*

sun•shine /sŭn′ shīn′/ *n.* the light from the sun. *Our cat loves to nap in the sunshine.*

sup•per /sŭp′ ər/ *n.* the last meal of the day. *We hurried home for supper.*

sure /shŏŏr/ *adj.* (**sur•er, sur•est; sure•ly** *adv.*) certain; positive. *Are you sure the clock shows the correct time?*

swal•low /swŏl′ ō/ *v.* (**swal•lows, swal•lowed, swal•low•ing**) to pass from mouth to throat to stomach; to gulp. *Swallow your food carefully.*

sweet /swēt/ *adj.* **a.** having the taste of sugar. *We ate sweet rolls for breakfast.* **b.** pleasing. *I think roses have a sweet smell.*

swim /swĭm/ *v.* (**swims, swam, swum, swim•ming**) to move in water by moving arms, legs, fins, etc. *Fish swim, but so do people.*

swim

switch[1] /swĭch/ *n.* (**switch•es** *pl.*) in an electrical circuit, a device for making a connection. *When we turn the switch, the light goes on.*

switch[2] /swĭch/ *v.* **a.** to turn on or off. *Please switch the fan off.* **b.** to change. *Let's switch places; you stand here.*

switch•es /swĭch' əz/ *n. pl.* (**switch** *sing.*) devices used for making, breaking, or changing electrical connections. *The light switches are on the front wall.*

tai•lor /tā' lər/ *n.* a person whose job is making or altering clothing. *I took my dress to a tailor for alterations.*

take /tāk/ *v.* (**takes, took, tak•en, tak•ing**) **a.** to accept or receive. *Take one; they're free.* **b.** to carry. *We take three suitcases.* **c.** to travel on. *Let's take the bus.* **d.** to take up; to require; to use. *Boxes take up too much space.*

teach•er /tē' chər/ *n.* a person who teaches. *Who is your piano teacher?*

tear /târ/ *v.* (**tears, tore, torn, tear•ing**) to rip or pull apart. *We made shapes by tearing pieces of paper.*

tell /tĕl/ *v.* (**tells, told, tell•ing**) **a.** to say; to talk about. *Tell us a story.* **b.** to make known. *Don't tell the answer to anyone.*

tent /tĕnt/ *n.* a portable structure of canvas or other material supported by a pole or poles. *We sleep in tents when we go hiking.*

test[1] /tĕst/ *n.* an examination or trial, often consisting of a series of questions or problems. *There were twenty problems on the arithmetic test.*

test[2] /tĕst/ *v.* to try; to examine; to put to a test. *Our teacher will test us in history next week.*

thank /thăngk/ *v.* to say or show you are pleased and grateful. *I want to thank Grandfather for my game.*

that•'ll /thăt' əl/ contraction of **that will**.

their /thâr/ *adj.* of, belonging to, or relating to them. *Is that your cat or their cat?*

➤ **Their** sounds like **there**.

there[1] /thâr/ *adv.* **a.** in or at that place. *Put the flowers over there.* **b.** to that place; into that place. *I went there last week.*

there[2] /thâr/ *pron.* used to introduce a sentence or clause in which the subject follows the verb. *There is a new student in our class.*

➤ **There** sounds like **their**.

they'd /thād/ contraction of **they had** or **they would**.

they'll /thāl/ contraction of **they will**.

they've /thāv/ contraction of **they have**. *They've left you plenty of food.*

thick /thĭk/ *adj.* **a.** large in size from one side to its opposite; not thin. *The old castle door was very thick.* **b.** measuring in distance through; in depth. *The geography book is one inch thick.*

thing /thĭng/ *n.* (**things** *pl.*) **a.** any object; anything that exists and can be seen, heard, felt, etc. *He took his clothes and some other things to summer camp.* **b.** an action; a matter; an affair. *That was a good thing to do.*

think /thĭngk/ *v.* (**thinks, thought, think•ing**) **a.** to use the mind to reach decisions, form opinions, etc. *I can't think when there is noise all around me.* **b.** to have in mind as an opinion, idea, etc.; to believe. *They think they know the answer.*

thin•ner /thĭn′ ər/ *adj.* (**thin, thin•nest**) being more slender or less thick than something or someone else. *This bed sheet is thinner than the comforter.*

thin•nest /thĭn′ ĭst/ *adj.* (**thin, thin•ner**) being the most slender or least thick of anything or anyone. *That is the thinnest book I have ever seen!*

thirst /thûrst/ *n.* a desire for something to drink caused by a dry feeling in the mouth or throat. *The horses satisfied their thirst by drinking from a stream.*

though¹ /thō/ *adv.* however. *You must admit, though, that she was partly right.*

though² /thō/ *conj.* in spite of the fact that; although. *Though it was getting late, we kept playing for a while longer.*

threw /thrōō/ past tense of **throw**.

throw¹ /thrō/ *v.* (**throws, threw, thrown, throw•ing**) to toss or cast through the air. *Throw the ball to Angie.*

throw² /thrō/ *n.* an act of throwing; a toss. *The player made a bad throw to first base, and the runner was safe.*

thun•der /thŭn′ dər/ *n.* the loud noise caused by the violent expansion of air heated by lightning. *Thunder often comes before rain.*

ti•ger /tī′ gər/ *n.* a large cat with yellowish fur and black stripes. *Tigers live in Asia.*

time•ly /tīm′ lē/ *adj.* (**time•li•er, time•li•est**) happening at a good time; well-timed. *She planned her timely arrival so she didn't miss dinner.*

Pronunciation Key

ă	pat	ŏ	pot	th	thin
ā	pay	ō	toe	*th*	this
âr	care	ô	paw, for	hw	which
ä	father	oi	noise	zh	vision
ě	pet	ou	out	ə	about,
ē	be	ōō	took		item,
ĭ	pit	ōō	boot		pencil,
ī	pie	ŭ	cut		gallop,
îr	pier	ûr	urge		circus

---

ti•tle /tīt′ l/ *n.* the name of a book, movie, painting, etc. *When I had finished reading the story, I couldn't remember its title.*

toad•stool /tōd′ stōōl′/ *n.* a particular type of mushroom, oftentimes poisonous. *The truffle is an edible toadstool.*

toast¹ /tōst/ *v.* to make crisp, hot, and brown by heat. *Would you like me to toast your bread?*

toast² /tōst/ *n.* sliced bread that is browned by heat. *I like toast for breakfast.*

to•ma•to /tə mā′ tō/ *n.* (**to•ma•toes** *pl.*) a commonly grown reddish fruit. *Please add a tomato to my salad.*

toot /tōōt/ *n.* a short, sharp sound made by a horn or whistle. *They heard the toot of the tugboat whistle.*

tore /tôr/ or /tōr/ past tense of **tear**.

track /trăk/ *n.* (**tracks** *pl.*) **a.** a mark or a series of marks left by an animal, person, wagon, etc. *We saw the tire tracks on the snow.* **b.** a special path or course set up for racing. *A mile is four times around the track.* **c.** the metal rails on which trains run. *The railroad track runs through a tunnel.*

trac•tor /trăk′ tər/ *n.* a large machine on wheels, used for pulling trucks or farm equipment. *The farmer drove the tractor into the barn.*

trade¹ /trād/ *n.* **a.** the business of buying and selling goods. *Our company carries on trade with people all over the world.* **b.** an exchange of goods; a bargain. *I made a trade with him.*

trade² /trād/ *v.* (**trades, trad•ed, trad•ing**) **a.** to buy and sell goods. *Some companies trade with foreign countries.* **b.** to exchange. *I'll trade my pen for that book.*

train /trān/ *n.* a line of connected railroad or subway cars. *Many people take a train to work every day.*

train

trash /trăsh/ *n.* something that is no longer valuable; a useless thing; rubbish. *These old toys are trash; throw them out.*

tray /trā/ *n.* a flat holder or platform with a rim, used for holding or carrying something. *Put the dishes on a tray.*

treat¹ /trēt/ *v.* **a.** to handle; behave toward. *You must treat animals gently.* **b.** to try to cure or relieve. *I hope the doctor can treat me for the pain in my stomach.*

treat² /trēt/ *n.* anything that pleases or gives pleasure. *Seeing a movie at school was a special treat.*

trip¹ /trĭp/ *n.* a journey; a voyage. *They took a trip around the world last year.*

trip² /trĭp/ *v.* (**trips, tripped, trip•ping**) to lose one's balance by catching a foot on something. *Be careful not to trip on the edge of the rug.*

trout /trout/ *n.* (**trout** or **trouts** *pl.*) a freshwater fish that is closely related to salmon. *The rainbow trout has black speckles on its back and a pink stripe along each side.*

trunk /trŭngk/ *n.* **a.** the main stem of a tree apart from limbs and roots. *After they cut down the tree, all that was left was the trunk.* **b.** a large, hard box for moving clothes or other items. *My grandparents used this trunk when they came from Greece.* **c.** the luggage compartment of a car. *The stroller is in the trunk of the car.*

trust /trŭst/ *v.* **a.** to believe in; to depend or rely on. *We trust the doctor to do what is best for us.* **b.** to expect; to assume. *I trust you have finished your homework.*

try¹ /trī/ *v.* (**tries, tried, try•ing**) to attempt. *Try to answer all of the questions.*

try² /trī/ *n.* (**tries** *pl.*) an attempt; an effort to do something. *She hit the target on her first try.*

tube /to͞ob/ or /tyo͞ob/ *n.* a long, hollow cylinder used to carry or hold liquids and gases. *A drinking straw is a tube.*

tur•key /tûr′ kē/ *n.* a large North American bird covered with thick feathers. *Turkeys can weigh more than thirty pounds.*

turn¹ /tûrn/ *v.* **a.** to move or cause to move around a center; to rotate. *Wheels turn.* **b.** to change directions. *Turn left at the post office.*

turn² /tûrn/ *n.* **a.** a change in direction or condition. *Make a right turn at the next street.* **b.** a time to do something. *Whose turn is it to bat?*

twirl /twûrl/ *v.* to turn rapidly. *The ice skater will twirl on one skate.*

twitch /twĭch/ *v.* (**twitch•es, twitched, twitch•ing**) to pull or move with sudden motion. *We watched the leaf twitch and then fall from the tree.*

ug·ly /ŭg′ lē/ *adj.* (**ug·li·er, ug·li·est**) unpleasant to any sense. *His mask was very ugly and scary.*

un·cle /ŭng′ kəl/ *n.* **a.** the brother of one's father or mother. *I have two uncles on my mother's side.* **b.** the husband of one's aunt. *We visited our aunt and uncle last spring.*

un·der /ŭn′ dər/ *prep.* **a.** below; beneath. *I found money hidden under a rock.* **b.** less than. *You can repair the broken window for under forty dollars.*

un·friend·ly /ŭn frĕnd′ lē/ *adj.* not friendly. *I stayed away from the unfriendly dog.*

un·hap·py /ŭn hăp′ ē/ *adj.* (**un·hap·pi·er, un·hap·pi·est; un·hap·pi·ly** *adv.*) not happy; sad; full of sorrow. *When Maria was unhappy, we tried to cheer her up.*

un·til[1] /ŭn tĭl′/ *prep.* **a.** up to the time of; till. *I slept until noon today.* **b.** before the time of. *He could not stop working until midnight.*

un·til[2] /ŭn tĭl′/ *conj.* **a.** up to the time that. *We waited for you until the show was about to begin.* **b.** before. *She would not serve dinner until everyone was seated.*

up·on /ə pŏn′/ or /ə pôn′/ *prep.* on. *Place the book upon the table.*

ver·y /vĕr′ ē/ *adv.* greatly; extremely. *He was very unhappy when he lost his dog.*

voice /vois/ *n.* **a.** a sound made with the mouth, especially by talking or singing. *We heard her voice above all the others.* **b.** the type or quality of sound made with the mouth. *That singer has a pleasant voice.*

Pronunciation Key

ă	pat	ŏ	pot	th	thin
ā	pay	ō	toe	*th*	this
âr	care	ô	paw, for	hw	which
ä	father	oi	noise	zh	vision
ĕ	pet	ou	out	ə	about,
ē	be	o͞o	took		item,
ĭ	pit	o͞o	boot		pencil,
ī	pie	ŭ	cut		gallop,
îr	pier	ûr	urge		circus

wag·on /wăg′ ən/ *n.* a four-wheeled vehicle for carrying loads usually pulled by a tractor, a horse, or a person. *Dad pulled us in the red wagon.*

waist /wāst/ *n.* the narrow part of the body between the ribs and the hips. *Belts are worn around the waist.*

wal·rus·es /wôl′ rəs əz/ or /wŏl′ rəs əz/ *n. pl.* (**wal·rus** *sing.*) large, arctic sea animals, related to seals, and having large tusks. *Walruses can live to be forty years old.*

war /wôr/ *n.* a fight or struggle, usually between countries or parts of a country. *There are great losses of life and destruction of property in a war.*

➤ **War** sounds like **wore.**

warm[1] /wôrm/ *adj.* **a.** having a small amount of heat; neither hot nor cold. *Blankets keep us warm.* **b.** affectionate. *They gave us a warm greeting.*

warm[2] /wôrm/ *v.* to make warm; to heat. *Warm the food before you serve it.*

warn /wôrn/ *v.* to tell of coming danger. *The sirens will warn us of a tornado.*

warp /wôrp/ *v.* to bend or buckle from dampness. *Cover the wood so the rain doesn't warp it.*

wash•cloth /wŏsh′ klôth′/, /wŏsh′ klŏth′/, or /wôsh′ klôth′/ *n.* a cloth used to wash a person's face or body. *Use a washcloth to wash your face.*

watch¹ /wŏch/ *v.* **a.** to look at. *Did you watch television after school?* **b.** to pay attention to; to be careful. *Watch where you are going.*

watch² /wŏch/ *n.* (**watch•es** *pl.*) a small clock that is worn on the wrist or carried in a pocket. *I checked my watch before I left the house.*

watch

wa•ter /wô′ tər/ or /wŏt′ ər/ *n.* the clear liquid that falls as rain. *Water becomes ice when it freezes.*

wave¹ /wāv/ *n.* **a.** a rising swell of water moving across the surface of a body of water. *The waves splashed against the rocks.* **b.** a signal made with the hand. *He gave a wave as he passed us.*

wave² /wāv/ *v.* (**waves, waved, wav•ing**) **a.** to move up and down or from side to side. *The branches wave in the wind.* **b.** to give a signal or greeting by moving the hand. *We wave good-bye.*

way /wā/ *n.* **a.** a path, road, or course. *The way was blocked by a fallen tree.* **b.** direction. *Come this way.* **c.** distance. *It's only a short way from here.* **d.** a manner. *She has a funny way of talking.* **e.** a detail or feature. *In many ways his plan seemed good.*

wear /wâr/ *v.* (**wears, wore, worn, wear•ing**) **a.** to have on the body. *People wear clothes.* **b.** to make or produce gradually as a result of rubbing, scraping, etc. *He wore a hole in the sleeve of his sweater.*

➤ **Wear** sounds like **where**.

weav•ing /wē′ vĭng/ *v.* (**weaves, wove, wov•en, weav•ing**) making by lacing threads, yarns, or strips under and over each other. *She is weaving a basket out of straw.*

we'd /wēd/ contraction of **we had** or **we would**.

weigh /wā/ *v.* **a.** to determine the weight of by using a scale. *Weigh the package before you mail it.* **b.** to have weight of a certain amount. *She weighs eighty pounds.*

wel•come /wĕl′ kəm/ *v.* (**wel•comes, wel•comed, wel•com•ing**) to greet with pleasure. *The flight attendant will welcome us on the plane.*

we'll /wēl/ contraction of **we will**.

➤ **We'll** sounds like **wheel**.

were /wûr/ past tense of **be**.

west¹ /wĕst/ *n.* the direction in which the sun sets. *East and west are opposite directions.*

west² /wĕst/ *adj.* **a.** in the west; of the west; toward the west. *Cindy lives in the west part of town.* **b.** from the west. *A west wind was blowing.*

west³ /wĕst/ *adv.* toward the west. *We walked west.*

we've /wēv/ contraction of **we have**.

wheel /hwēl/ or /wēl/ *n.* (**wheels** *pl.*) a round frame that turns on a central axis. *A bicycle has two wheels.*

➤ **Wheel** sounds like **we'll**.

wheel•chair /hwēl′ châr′/ or /wēl′-/ *n.* a chair with two large and two small wheels for use by a disabled person. *The wheelchair helped him get around after he broke his leg.*

where¹ /hwâr/ or /wâr/ *adv.* **a.** in or at what place. *Where will you be?* **b.** to what place. *Where did you go?*

where² /hwâr/ or /wâr/ *conj.* to the place that; in the place that. *Stay where you are.*

➤ **Where** sounds like **wear**.

whirl /hwûrl/ or /wûrl/ *v.* to move in a circle with great force or speed. *The wind made the pinwheel whirl.*

whisk•ers /hwĭs′ kərz/ or /wĭs′ kərz/ *n. pl.* (**whisker** *sing.*) **a.** short hairs growing on the side and chin of a face. *My dad's whiskers feel rough.* **b.** long, stiff hairs that stick out near the mouth of a cat or other animal. *My pet mouse has black whiskers.*

whit•er /hwīt′ ər/ or /wīt′ ər/ *adj.* being more white than something else. *This paint makes the wall look whiter than before.*

whit•est /hwīt′ ĭst/ or /wīt′ ĭst/ *adj.* being the most white of anything else. *You have the whitest shirt I have ever seen.*

who'd /hood/ contraction of **who would** or **who had.**

who'll /hool/ contraction of **who will.**

who've /hoov/ contraction of **who have.**

wide /wīd/ *adj.* (**wid•er, wid•est; wide•ly** *adv.*) **a.** covering or having much space from side to side; broad; not narrow. *Our new car has wide seats.* **b.** having a certain distance from side to side. *My room is ten feet wide.*

wild /wīld/ *adj.* not tamed; not cultivated; living or growing in a natural condition. *Wild flowers grew along the side of the road.*

wild•cat /wīld′ kăt′/ *n.* a large cat that is not tame. *The wildcat growled at the people at the zoo.*

win /wĭn/ *v.* (**wins, won, win•ning**) **a.** to gain a victory. *Do you think our team can win?* **b.** to get or earn. *Nina's pig may win a ribbon at the fair.*

win•dow /wĭn′ dō/ *n.* an opening in the side of a house, automobile, etc., usually covered with glass. *The window lets in light and air.*

wish¹ /wĭsh/ *v.* (**wish•es, wished, wish•ing**) to want; to desire. *She wishes she could have that watch.*

wish² /wĭsh/ *n.* (**wish•es** *pl.*) thing wanted. *The genie granted the young boy three wishes.*

with•out /wĭth out′/ *prep.* **a.** not having; with no. *I left without my umbrella.* **b.** with a lack or neglect of. *I sometimes speak without thinking.*

Pronunciation Key

ă	pat	ŏ	pot	th	**th**in
ā	pay	ō	toe	*th*	**th**is
âr	care	ô	paw, for	hw	**wh**ich
ä	father	oi	n**oi**se	zh	vi**si**on
ĕ	pet	ou	**ou**t	ə	**a**bout,
ē	be	ŏŏ	t**oo**k		it**e**m,
ĭ	pit	ōō	b**oo**t		penc**i**l,
ī	pie	ŭ	cut		gall**o**p,
îr	pier	ûr	**ur**ge		circ**u**s

wit•ty /wĭt′ ē/ *adj.* (**wit•ti•er, wit•ti•est; wit•ti•ly** *adv.*) showing wit; clever and amusing. *The witty speaker made the audience laugh.*

won't /wōnt/ contraction of **will not.**

wool•ly /wŏŏl′ ē/ *adj.* (**wool•li•er, wool•li•est**) consisting of wool. *He sheared the woolly sheep.*

word /wûrd/ *n.* a group of letters that make sense because they stand for a certain thing. *We use words when we speak and write.*

wore /wôr/ or /wōr/ past tense of **wear.**
➤ **Wore** sounds like **war.**

work¹ /wûrk/ *n.* **a.** the use of strength or skill to make or do something; labor. *Building the dam was hard work for the beavers.* **b.** job; occupation; the thing one does to earn a living. *Her work is modeling clothes.*

work² /wûrk/ *v.* **a.** to have a job for pay in order to make a living. *We work in a big office.* **b.** to operate; to do as it should. *Does that machine work?*

worm /wûrm/ *n.* a slender animal with a soft, segmented body and no vertebrae. *An earthworm is a popular worm used for fishing bait.*

wor•ry¹ /wûr′ ē/ or /wŭr′ ē/ *v.* (**wor•ries, wor•ried, wor•ry•ing**) to be or cause to be restless, disturbed, or anxious about something. *I am worried about getting to the airport on time.*

wor·ry[2] /wûr′ ē/ or /wŭr′ ē/ *n.* (**wor·ries** *pl.*) a cause of anxiety or trouble. *Money is a constant worry to him.*

would /wŏŏd/ *v.* **a.** used to express what could have happened or been true. *I would have come if I had known you were sick.* **b.** used to make a polite request. *Would you carry this for me?* **c.** past tense of **will**.

would·'ve /wŏŏd′ əv/ contraction of **would have**.

wrap /răp/ *v.* (**wraps, wrapped, wrap·ping**) **a.** to enclose in something by winding or folding. *Wrap the baby in warm blankets.* **b.** to cover with paper. *Did you wrap the gift for your mother?*

wrapped /răpt/ *v.* (**wraps, wrapped, wrap·ping**) covered an object with paper or another material and taped or tied it up. *She wrapped the gift with pink paper.*

wrin·kle[1] /rĭng′ kəl/ *n.* a small crease or fold. *Rosa ironed the wrinkles out of her skirt.*

wrin·kle[2] /rĭng′ kəl/ *v.* to crease or crumple. *Your forehead wrinkles when you frown.*

write /rīt/ *v.* (**writes, wrote, writ·ten, writ·ing**) **a.** to form letters or words with a pen, pencil, or other instrument. *Most people learn to write in school.* **b.** to be the author of. *He wrote a story for the school newspaper.*

➤ **Write** sounds like **right**.

wrote /rōt/ past tense of **write**.

yawn·ing /yô′ nĭng/ *v.* opening the mouth wide as an involuntary reaction to being tired or bored. *Matt was yawning during the long movie.*

yel·low /yĕl′ ō/ *n.* the color of a lemon or of butter. *Yellow is a bright, sunny color.*

yoke /yōk/ *n.* a wooden frame that connects two work animals at the neck. *The farmer put the yoke on the oxen.*

➤ **Yoke** sounds like **yolk**.

yolk /yōk/ *n.* the yellow part of an egg. *Linda added one yolk to the cake mix.*

➤ **Yolk** sounds like **yoke**.

yolk

you'd /yŏŏd/ contraction of **you would**.

you'll /yŏŏl/ contraction of **you will**.

your /yŏŏr/ or /yôr/ or /yōr/ *adj.* of or belonging to you. *Is this your coat?*

your·self /yŏŏr sĕlf′/, /yôr sĕlf′/, /yōr sĕlf′/, or /yər sĕlf′/ *pron.* (**your·selves** *pl.*) the pronoun referring to you. *Please help yourself to some snacks.*

you've /yŏŏv/ contraction of **you have**.

zip·per /zĭp′ ər/ *n.* a fastening device with two rows of tiny teeth that can be closed together by a sliding tab. *My boots close with a zipper.*

The **Writing Thesaurus** provides synonyms—words that mean the same or nearly the same—and antonyms—words that mean the opposite—for your spelling words. Use this sample to identify the various parts of each thesaurus entry.

- **Entry words** are listed in alphabetical order and are printed in boldface type.
- The abbreviation for the **part of speech** of each entry word follows the boldface entry word.
- The **definition** of the entry word matches the definition of the word in your **Spelling Dictionary**. A **sample sentence** shows the correct use of the word in context.

- Each **synonym** for the entry word is listed under the entry word. Again, a sample sentence shows the correct use of the synonym in context.
- Where appropriate, **antonyms** for the entry word are listed at the end of the entry.

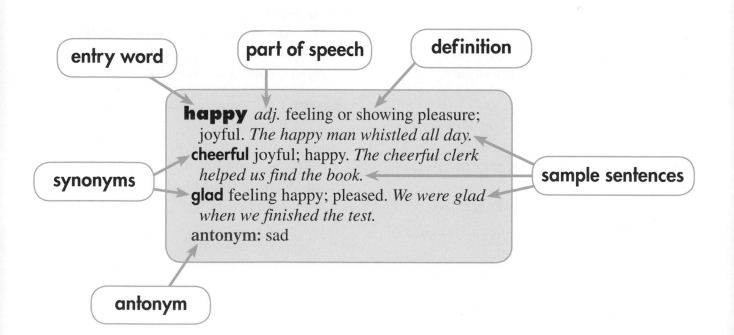

entry word

part of speech

definition

happy *adj.* feeling or showing pleasure; joyful. *The happy man whistled all day.*
cheerful joyful; happy. *The cheerful clerk helped us find the book.*
glad feeling happy; pleased. *We were glad when we finished the test.*
antonym: sad

synonyms

sample sentences

antonym

about *adv.* somewhere near. *She guessed it was about seven o'clock.*
almost nearly; just about. *That bus is almost on time; it is only two minutes late.*
nearly almost; not quite. *We were nearly finished with our homework.*
roughly somewhat like. *The houses looked roughly alike.*

afraid *adj.* frightened; filled with fear. *Some people are afraid of falling from high places.*
alarmed filled with sudden fear. *The man was alarmed by the loud noise.*
fearful showing fear. *The fearful kitten raced to its mother.*
frightened full of fright. *The frightened child hid from the very scary creature.*

after *prep.* following. *Don't forget that you come after me in the parade.*
behind farther back. *We will march behind the clowns.*
following coming after. *The parade will take place the following day.*
next following at once. *You will have the next turn.*

always *adv.* all the time; constantly. *At the North Pole, it is always cold.*
ever at any time. *Have you ever traveled to Europe?*
forever for always. *People want to be healthy forever.*

badly *adv.* poorly; in a bad manner. *He plays the piano well but sings badly.*
awfully in an awful manner; terribly. *Usually the clowns are funny, but they acted awfully rowdy today.*
dreadfully in a dreadful manner. *The actor played his part dreadfully.*
poorly in a poor manner. *The football team played poorly today.*

band *n.* any flat strip of material used for holding something together. *Put a rubber band around each newspaper.*
sash long, broad strip of cloth worn around the waist. *The dress has a red flowered sash.*
strap a thin strip of leather or another type of material. *I put a strap around the suitcase.*

better *adj.* higher in quality; more excellent; finer. *Does anyone have a better place?*
improved made better. *The mayor told about the improved condition of the city budget.*
superior very good; above average. *She did superior work as an officer.*

blow *v.* to move rapidly. *We could hear the wind blow.*
blast to blow up; tear apart. *They had to blast the rocks for the new roadway.*
toot to give a short blast. *The horn will toot at lunchtime.*

bright *adj.* shining; giving light; reflecting light. *See how bright the car is when it is polished.*

brilliant sparkling; shining brightly. *A brilliant light shone in the sky.*

clear bright; light. *You could see the plane fly across the clear sky.*

light clear; bright. *It is as light as day in here.*

shiny bright; shining. *The shiny vase sparkled in the sunlight.*

C

care *n.* protection; close attention. *A baby needs loving care.*

concern interest; attention. *Our main concern was using the right words.*

interest a feeling of taking part in or wanting to know. *The students had an interest in space travel.*

worry a cause of anxiety or trouble. *Money is a constant worry to him.*

carry *v.* to take from one place to another. *Will you carry this package home?*

conduct to carry or transfer. *The wires conduct electricity from the wall to the lamp.*

transport to carry from one place to another. *A truck was used to transport the new cars.*

catch *v.* to get; take and hold onto; seize. *Watch the boy catch the ball!*

capture to take by force. *The zookeeper will capture the runaway animal.*

seize to grasp; take hold of. *The happy child tried to seize the big balloon.*

change *v.* to make or become different. *She will change her mind.*

alter to make different. *We can alter our plans for the trip to the zoo.*

vary to change; become different. *I will vary the colors in the picture.*

choose *v.* to pick out. *Choose the kind of toy you want.*

elect to choose for an office by voting. *Who did the group elect as class president?*

pick to make a choice. *I will pick the winner of the contest.*

select to choose; pick out. *The teacher will select a book about the stars.*

close *v.* to shut. *Close the door when you leave.*

bolt to fasten with a bolt. *She will bolt the door each night.*

seal to close tightly; shut. *He tried to seal the box with tape.*

shut to close; to prevent entrance. *We shut the door to the gym.*

convert *v.* to change into another form, substance, or condition. *Jim's dad plans to convert their basement into a playroom.*

change make different; replace. *We need to convert our dollars into pesos when we arrive in Mexico.*

transform change in appearance; alter. *He could transform his car into a robot.*

translate put into another language; change from one form to another. *She will translate the Spanish words into English for us.*

cost *n.* price that is to be paid. *The cost of meals in restaurants is going up.*

amount the value; sum. *The amount on the bill was twenty dollars.*

charge price for service; cost. *A delivery charge will be added to the furniture bill.*

price the cost in money; the amount of money for which something is sold. *The price should be clearly labeled.*

dawn *n.* the first appearance of light in the morning. *Dawn came at six o'clock this morning.*
  daybreak time when light appears in the morning. *The rooster crowed at daybreak.*
  sunrise time when the sun appears in the sky. *The campers got up at sunrise.*

digging *v.* making a hole in the ground; breaking up the soil. *The dog was digging in the backyard.*
  burrowing making a hole in the ground. *We caught a rabbit burrowing under the fence.*
  tunneling making a way under the ground. *Moles are tunneling under the whole backyard!*

draw *v.* to make a design, picture, etc. *The artist will draw an outline before he paints the picture.*
  design to make a sketch or a plan. *She will design a new skirt.*
  outline to give a sketch; plan. *We must outline our ideas for the report.*
  sketch to make a rough drawing. *The builder will sketch the plans.*

dream *n.* the thoughts, feelings, and pictures that occur in a person's mind as he or she sleeps. *Her dream was about flying in an airplane.*
  nightmare a very troubled dream. *The terrible nightmare made him scream.*
  vision something seen in one's imagination, dreams, or thoughts. *He had a vision that he was the new captain.*

drop *v.* to fall or let fall. *I will try not to drop a dish as I dry it.*
  fall to drop from a higher place. *The leaves fall from the trees.*
  lower to put down. *Use the rope to lower the flag.*

dull *adj.* uninteresting; boring. *It was such a dull book that I fell asleep reading it.*
  boring dull; tiresome. *The boring play had no exciting action in it.*
  tiresome tiring; boring. *Without any good jokes, the clown's act was very tiresome.*
  uninteresting not interesting. *With no points scored, it was a very uninteresting game.*

early *adv.* sooner than usual; before the usual time. *I will have to get up early to go fishing tomorrow.*
  shortly before long. *The parade will start shortly.*
  soon in a short time; before the usual time; early. *The bus arrived much too soon.*
  antonym: late

earn *v.* to deserve as a result of performing a service, doing work, etc. *After we study for two hours, we will earn a break.*
  merit to earn; deserve. *The careful workers merit the award for their excellent safety record.*
  rate to consider, regard; put a value on. *We rate the movie the best science show of the year.*

fair *adj.* in keeping with the rules; according to what is accepted as right. *If you want to play on the team, you must learn fair play.*
equal of the same value, size, rank, amount, etc. *The two boys are of equal weight.*
just right; fair. *She received a just reward for her heroic deeds.*
reasonable not asking too much; just. *We paid a reasonable price for the bookcases.*
antonym: unfair

fight *v.* to try to overcome by force. *Boxers wear padded gloves when they fight.*
battle to take part in a fight or struggle. *The team will battle for first place.*
clash to disagree strongly; fight. *The reporter's viewpoint always seems to clash with ours.*

find *v.* to look for and get back a lost object. *We will find my watch.*
discover to find out; learn for the first time. *The hikers want to discover a new trail in the woods.*
locate to find the specific place. *The museum guide helped us locate the dinosaur display.*
antonym: lose

finish *v.* to come or bring to an end; complete or become completed. *The movie will finish at 9:30.*
complete to finish; get done. *We will complete the job before we go home.*
conclude to come or bring to an end. *The speaker will conclude by asking everyone to help with the book fair.*
end to stop; to come or bring to its last part. *Our story will end with a very clever surprise.*
antonyms: start, begin

flash *n.* a light that appears suddenly and briefly. *A flash of lightning appeared in the distance.*
gleam a flash or beam of light. *You could see the gleam of the car's lights through the fog.*
sparkle shine; glitter; flash. *The sparkle of the jewels caught my eye.*

float *v.* to stay or move in or on top of air, water, or liquid. *Ice will float in water.*
drift to carry or be carried along by air or water. *The wind made the balloons drift toward the trees.*
antonym: sink

flow *v.* to move in a stream, as water does. *A river can flow to the ocean.*
run to flow. *Water will run downhill.*
stream to flow, move. *The tears seemed to stream down his face.*

fool *v.* to trick or attempt to trick someone. *Her costume could not fool me into thinking she was someone else.*
deceive to mislead; trick. *The magician tried to deceive us with his magic tricks.*
trick to fool; cheat. *We will trick them into thinking the painting was real.*

fresh *adj.* newly made, grown, or gathered. *Mother baked fresh bread.*
new not having existed before. *We played with the new computer game.*
unusual not ordinary. *The book was an unusual size.*
antonym: stale

friend *n.* a person one likes. *Julio is a good friend.*

  companion someone close to another; someone to share with. *Jane's dog is her favorite companion.*

  comrade a close friend. *The officer and her comrade directed traffic.*

  mate a fellow worker or companion. *My trusted mate helped with the work.*

  pal a friend; comrade. *My pal and I like to play baseball.*

funny *adj.* strange; unusual; peculiar. *That is a funny way to act.*

  curious odd; unusual. *We heard the curious noises from the haunted house.*

  odd strange; peculiar. *The music was odd because it had no melody.*

  peculiar unusual; strange. *Having a snake for a pet is somewhat peculiar.*

furry *adj.* covered with fur. *A mouse is a small furry animal.*

  bushy thick; spreading. *The pirate's beard was very bushy.*

  hairy covered with hair. *The dog has a hairy body.*

  woolly covered with wool or something like it. *The sheep had a woolly coat.*

give *v.* to hand over to another as a present. *Please give me the watch.*

  award to give; present. *He will award a prize to the best writer.*

  donate to give help or money; contribute. *We will donate our time to clean the park.*

  present to offer; give. *The track coach will present ribbons to the winning teams.*

  antonym: take

grand *adj.* large; beautiful; impressive. *The queen lived in a grand palace.*

  magnificent stately; grand. *The royal family lived in a magnificent castle by the river.*

  majestic noble; grand. *The queen rode in a majestic carriage.*

  splendid brilliant; grand. *The picture showed a splendid view of the palace.*

great *adj.* large in size or number; big. *A great crowd of people was at the carnival.*

  enormous huge; very large. *The enormous crowd clapped for the clowns.*

  immense very large; huge. *The immense elephant stood by the tiny mouse.*

  large big. *A whale is large.*

  vast very great; large. *The animals roamed through the vast jungle.*

hair *n.* the mass of thin threadlike strands that grow on a person's or animal's skin. *Elizabeth has beautiful hair.*

  curl a lock of hair forming a ring. *She tucked a curl behind her ear.*

  locks the hair on one's head. *She tied a ribbon around her curly locks.*

happy *adj.* feeling or showing pleasure; joyful. *The happy man whistled all day.*

  cheerful joyful; happy. *The cheerful clerk helped us find the book.*

  glad feeling happy; pleased. *We were glad when we finished the test.*

  antonym: sad

high *adj.* tall; far above the ground. *Walnuts fell from a high branch.*
  tall having great height. *The tall building could be seen for miles.*
  towering very high. *They climbed up the towering mountain.*
  antonym: low

hop *v.* to move by jumping. *Rabbits hop from place to place.*
  bound to leap or spring. *The sheep bound from rock to rock.*
  leap to jump. *The tiger can leap over the fallen tree.*
  spring to jump; to leap. *The fox will spring at the rabbit.*

hurry *v.* to act quickly; move fast. *Hurry or you'll be late.*
  fly to move quickly, swiftly. *We were so busy that the time seemed to fly.*
  hustle to move fast; hurry. *We had to hustle to get to the bus stop on time.*

hurt *v.* to cause pain to. *The sting of the bee hurt his arm.*
  ache to be in pain; hurt. *His arm must ache after he fell off his bike.*
  pain to suffer; hurt. *The sore finger seemed to pain her when she wrote.*
  smart to feel sharp pain. *His eyes will smart from the dust in the air.*

ice *n.* water that has been frozen solid by cold. *Ice keeps food and drinks cold.*
  glaze a smooth, glossy coating. *The glaze is what makes the dishes shine.*
  hail small pieces of ice falling like rain. *The hail beat on the windows.*
  sleet snow or hail mixed with rain. *The sleet covered the town with a shiny coat of ice.*

jelly *n.* a food made by boiling fruit juices and sugar. *I like grape jelly.*
  jam food made by boiling fruit and sugar until thick. *The jam was full of purple grapes.*
  preserves fruit cooked with sugar and sealed in containers. *We put strawberry preserves on our toast.*

join *v.* to put together; to connect. *They will join the caboose to the last car of the train.*
  combine to put two or more things together. *The chef will combine the meat and vegetables for the stew.*
  link to connect or join. *The chain will link the gate and the fence.*

kind *adj.* gentle and caring. *They are always very kind to animals.*
  gentle kindly; friendly. *The teacher spoke with a gentle voice.*
  good-hearted caring; generous. *The good-hearted neighbor helped.*

last *adj.* coming after all others; final. *The last train leaves at six o'clock.*
  concluding bringing to an end. *The concluding question asked for the name of the president.*
  final at the end; coming last. *The final act of the play was exciting.*

lastly *adv.* at the end; finally. *Lastly, pour the batter into a cake pan and put it into the oven.*
  finally at last; at the end. *We finally found the missing ring.*

learn *v.* to gain skill or knowledge in. *We learn spelling in school.*
  acquire to obtain. *She wants to acquire the skills to read another language.*
  master to become skillful; to learn. *He can master the addition facts.*
  study to try to learn by thinking, reading, and practicing. *We study many subjects in school.*

leave *v.* to go away; to go from. *The train will leave in ten minutes.*
  abandon to leave and not return. *The people were told to abandon the ship.*
  desert to leave without notice. *The officer will not desert her post.*
  antonym: arrive

lesson *n.* something to be taught or learned. *My brother is taking his violin lesson.*
  exercise something that gives practice. *The assignment was a math exercise.*
  lecture a planned speech on a topic. *The lecture was on safety.*

letter *n.* a symbol for a sound. *Z is the twenty-sixth letter in our alphabet.*
  character letter, mark, or sign used in writing. *What is the Chinese character for "happy"?*
  symbol something that stands for something else. *The + sign is a symbol used in math.*

lift *v.* to raise from a lower to a higher position. *This box is too heavy for me to lift.*
  elevate to raise up; lift. *The worker used the crane to elevate the heavy beam to the top of the building.*

  hoist to raise; lift up. *The sailors will hoist the sails to begin the trip.*
  raise to put up; lift up. *We had to raise our hands if we wanted a turn.*

list *v.* to write or print in a column. *List the spelling words on your paper.*
  enter to write or print in a book. *You need to enter the addresses by the names.*
  record to write or put in some form. *The scorekeeper will record each score.*

little *adj.* small. *An elephant is big and an ant is little.*
  brief lasting a short time; little. *A brief meeting was held.*
  small not large; little. *The hummingbird is a very small bird.*
  tiny very little; wee. *The tiny ladybug sat on the leaf.*
  antonyms: big, large

load *n.* something that is carried. *The load was too heavy for the small car.*
  cargo goods sent by plane or ship. *The cargo was unloaded from the plane.*
  freight goods carried by plane, truck, ship, or train. *The dock worker sent the freight by truck.*
  shipment goods sent together to a company or person. *The shipment arrived this morning.*

mail *v.* to send by mail; to place in a mailbox. *Did you mail my letter?*
  send to cause or order to go. *The principal might send the children home early because of the storm.*
  transmit to send; to pass along. *The clerk will transmit the order by computer.*

maybe *adv.* perhaps. *Maybe he hasn't left the train yet, and we can still find him.*
perhaps could be; maybe. *Perhaps you will get the first ticket.*
possibly perhaps; by a possibility. *Possibly that is the winning number.*

mild *adj.* not harsh; not severe; warm rather than cold. *We had a mild winter last year.*
calm still; quiet. *Without any wind, the water was calm.*
easy smooth and pleasant. *Her quiet, easy way made everyone around her feel comfortable.*
gentle not rough or violent; mild. *A gentle breeze blew through the trees.*

morning *n.* the earliest part of the day, ending at noon. *We eat breakfast every morning.*
forenoon part of day from sunrise to noon. *We spent the forenoon in the park.*
antonym: evening

news *n.* information; things that a person has not heard about. *What is the news about your brother's new job?*
information knowledge about some fact or event. *The information contains a description of the space launch.*
report information about something seen, heard, done, or read. *The report had many interesting details.*

night *n.* the time between evening and morning; the time from sunset to sunrise when it is dark. *The stars shine at night.*
evening early part of night. *Each evening we eat dinner.*

nighttime time between sunset and morning. *Nighttime begins at dark.*
antonym: day

oil *n.* a greasy liquid obtained from animals, plants, or minerals. *Olive oil is used for salads.*
lubricant oil or grease put on parts of machines to help them move or slide easily. *The mechanic put a lubricant in the engine.*
petroleum a dark liquid found in the earth's crust. *Gasoline is made from petroleum.*

page *n.* one side of a sheet of paper in a book, magazine, newspaper, or letter. *Kurt knew from the first page that he would like the book.*
leaf one sheet of paper. *Each side of a leaf is called a page.*
sheet one piece of paper. *He used one sheet of paper.*

pail *n.* a round bucket with a handle. *He put water in the pail.*
bucket a pail made of plastic, metal, or wood. *The water was in a big bucket.*
scuttle a bucket for carrying or storing coal. *A scuttle was used to store the coal by the old cookstove.*

paint *v.* to cover a surface with paint. *They will paint the fence.*
color to give color; put color on. *He wants to color the fire engine red.*
draw to make a design, picture, etc. *The artist will draw an outline before he paints the picture.*

pair *n.* two things of the same kind that go together; a set of two. *Carlos has a new pair of shoes.*

couple two of anything; a pair. *We saw a couple stumble during the lively dance.*

double person or thing like another. *A person who looks like and can act for an actor is called a double.*

mate one of a pair. *He could not find the mate to his glove.*

peace *n.* quiet and calm; stillness. *We like the peace of the country.*

calm stillness; quiet. *There was a strange calm before the storm hit.*

quiet stillness; peace. *I need quiet to be able to study.*

serenity calmness; peace and quiet. *We enjoyed the serenity of the countryside.*

antonym: war

people *n.* human beings; persons; men, women, boys, and girls. *People of all ages attended the fair.*

folks people or group of people. *The city folks come to work by bus.*

population number of people in a specific place. *The population of our town is 3,500 people.*

public all the people. *The public was invited to the free concert.*

place *n.* a certain point; a spot. *The coolest place is near the river.*

location place or position. *This is a good location for a repair shop.*

point place or spot. *The race starts at this point.*

spot place. *This is the spot where we can set up the tent.*

place *v.* to put in a particular position; to set. *Place your pencil on the desk.*

put to set at a particular place. *I put the books back on the bookshelf.*

rest to set or place. *He can rest the ladder against the tree.*

set to put in some place or position. *I set the dishes in the sink.*

plain *adj.* simple; not fancy in appearance. *Tracey wore a plain dress.*

modest humble; not bold. *The modest child did not brag about her talent.*

point *v.* to aim. *He meant to point his arrow at the target.*

aim to point or direct. *We tried to aim the telescope at the moon.*

beam to send out; direct. *The machine will beam the light at the sign.*

direct to point or aim. *Direct the light at the sign.*

level to keep even; to aim. *The soldier will level his weapon at the target.*

train to point or aim. *He tried to train the light on the actor.*

pool *n.* a tank filled with water and used for swimming. *Peter swam across the pool.*

basin very shallow water area. *The boats docked in the basin of the harbor.*

lagoon pond or small lake. *The boat was anchored in the lagoon.*

pond a very small lake. *The ducks swam across the pond.*

pretty *adj.* lovely; pleasing; pleasant to look at or to hear. *The garden was filled with pretty flowers.*

attractive pleasing; lovely. *The attractive person modeled new fall clothes.*

beautiful very pretty; pleasing. *The beautiful queen wore a blue dress.*

lovely very pretty; beautiful. *The lovely flowers filled the room with color.*

prize *n.* a thing won in a contest. *Tony won the prize for spelling the most words correctly.*

award prize; something given after careful selection. *The award went to the student with the best test score.*

medal prize; award. *The best swimmer won a gold medal.*

reward payment offered for the return of property or a person. *We got a reward for finding the ring.*

proud *adj.* having satisfaction and pleasure. *The proud mother watched her daughter graduate.*

exalted filled with pride and joy. *Everyone was exalted by the victory of their beloved king.*

lofty very high; proud. *The group had set lofty goals for the safety project.*

real *adj.* actual; true; not imagined; not made up. *My uncle told us a real story about his trip to Brazil.*

actual real; made of facts. *The book tells of actual events in history.*

factual true; consisting of facts. *She wrote a factual report.*

true real; genuine. *This is a true story of the life of the queen.*

ribbon *n.* a narrow strip of fabric, especially one used as a decoration. *She wore a yellow ribbon in her hair.*

braid a narrow band of fabric used to trim clothing. *The uniform is trimmed with a gold braid.*

tape a narrow strip of material. *The seams had tape on the edges.*

right *adj.* correct; true; accurate. *Allan's answers were all right.*

accurate exact; correct. *The man gave a very accurate description of the football game.*

correct right; without errors. *I gave you the correct answer.*

proper fitting; right for the occasion. *This is not proper behavior at a wedding.*

round *adj.* shaped like a circle. *Our swimming pool is square, but theirs is round.*

circular round like a circle. *The building has a circular tower.*

ringlike like a circle. *The bracelet had ringlike links in it.*

sad *adj.* unhappy. *We were sad when our team lost.*

joyless sad; without joy. *The joyless group waited for news about the fire.*

unhappy sad; without cheer. *The clown wore a very unhappy face.*

sail *v.* to move swiftly, especially in air or on the water. *The ship can sail down the river.*

boat to go in a boat. *We want to boat down the river to fish.*

cruise to sail from place to place. *The ship will cruise to the islands.*

sand *n.* tiny bits of stone in large amounts, found in the desert and on shores along oceans, lakes, and rivers. *This beach has smooth sand.*

dust fine, dry earth. *The dust settled all over the road.*

grit fine bits of sand or gravel. *The boat was covered with grit.*

powder dust made from grinding, crushing, or pounding a solid. *The rocks were ground into fine powder.*

scent *n.* an odor; a smell. *The dogs followed the scent of the wolf.*
  aroma strong odor; fragrance. *The aroma of flowers filled the air in the garden.*
  fragrance pleasant odor or smell. *The new fragrance smelled like fresh flowers.*
  smell an odor; a scent. *The smell of fresh bread filled the air.*

sharp *adj.* having a fine point or a thin edge for cutting. *The knife blade is sharp.*
  fine sharp. *The scissors had a very fine cutting edge.*
  keen sharp; cutting. *The knife had a keen edge.*

shoot *v.* to send out swiftly. *The archer will shoot an arrow at the target.*
  bombard to attack. *The children always bombard us with questions.*
  fire to shoot; discharge. *The officer tried to fire his gun at the target.*
  launch to send out; throw. *NASA will launch the rocket on schedule.*

sight *n.* something that is seen. *The sunset last night was a lovely sight.*
  scene view; picture. *The snow on the mountain peaks made a pretty scene.*
  spectacle sight; something to see. *The fireworks were a beautiful spectacle.*
  view something seen; scene. *She painted a scenic view of the hillside.*

sign *n.* something that stands for something else; symbol. *The sign for adding is +.*
  mark a symbol. *Writers put a question mark at the end of a question.*
  symbol something that stands for something else. *The + is a symbol used in math.*

sled *n.* a low platform on runners that slides over ice and snow. *It is fun to coast down a hill on a sled.*
  bobsled a long sled on runners with steering wheel and brakes. *He won an Olympic medal as brakeman for the second American bobsled.*
  sleigh cart on runners. *The horse pulled the sleigh over the snow.*

slow *adj.* not fast or quick. *The turtle makes slow but steady progress.*
  leisurely without hurry. *We took a leisurely stroll around town.*
  poky moving slowly. *The poky old camel took forever to get there.*
  antonym: fast

smooth *adj.* having no bumps or rough spots. *The smooth highway made driving a pleasure.*
  even level; flat. *The road is even with no holes or ruts.*
  level flat; even. *The grass was level as far as we could see.*
  antonym: rough

soft *adj.* quiet; gentle; mild. *She has a soft voice.*
  gentle low; soft. *He has a gentle way of playing the piano.*
  mild not harsh; not severe. *She had a very mild manner.*
  antonym: hard

soil *n.* ground; earth; dirt. *Plants grow in rich, dark soil.*
  dirt earth; soil. *We put some dirt into the flowerpot.*
  earth ground; soil. *Plant these seeds in black earth.*
  ground soil; earth. *The ground in the field is rich and fertile.*

splash *v.* to make wet or dirty. *The car tried to splash me with mud as it sped past.*
  splatter to splash. *The rain will splatter the windows.*
  sprinkle to scatter or spray with small drops. *Use the can to sprinkle water on the flowers.*

stick *n.* a long, thin piece of wood or other material. *We used a stick to stir the paint.*
  pole a long piece of wood. *The wires went to the telephone pole.*
  rod a thin stick. *The clothes were hung on a metal rod.*
  stake a stick pointed at one end. *The stake held up the corner of the tent.*

stop *v.* to halt or come to a halt. *The car will stop if we don't get more gas.*
  cease to come to an end; stop. *The treaty meant all fighting would cease.*
  halt to stop. *They had to halt the parade until the mayor arrived.*
  pause to stop for a short time. *We will pause for a short rest.*
  quit to stop. *The men quit working because of the rain.*

story *n.* a tale or account of an adventure or happening. *Mr. Lee told us a story about his grandfather.*
  account a detailed statement about an event. *Each witness gave an account of the accident.*
  legend a story of the past that might be based on real events. *The story of Robin Hood is a legend of old England.*
  tale a made-up story. *The tale was about the magic of the sea creatures.*

street *n.* a road in a city or town. *This street is always crowded during rush hour.*
  avenue a wide street. *Trees lined both sides of the avenue.*
  boulevard a broad street. *The boulevard was named after a president.*
  road a way for cars, trucks, etc., to travel. *The road went from town to the farm.*

summer *n.* the warmest season of the year. *Summer comes between spring and fall.*
  midsummer the middle of the summer season. *The fair always came to town midsummer.*
  summertime summer; the summer season. *We loved to swim in the summertime.*

sunshine *n.* the light from the sun. *Our cat loves to nap in the sunshine.*
  sunlight the light of the sun. *The plants needed sunlight to grow.*

T

take *v.* to accept or receive; to grasp. *Take one; they're free.*
  grab to seize suddenly; to take. *The man tried to grab the paper before it could fly away.*
  grasp to hold; to seize. *She had to grasp the railing to walk down the stairs.*
  seize to take hold of; to grasp. *He tried to seize the paper before we could read what it said.*
  antonym: give

test *v.* to try; to examine; to put to a test. *Our teacher will test us in history next week.*
  check to examine; to prove true or right. *The quiz will check how well we add numbers.*
  examine to test skills or knowledge. *This assignment will examine your understanding of today's math lesson.*
  quiz to give a short test. *The teacher needed to quiz the students on the chapter they had read.*

think *v.* to have in the mind as an opinion, idea, etc.; to believe. *She tried to think of the answer.*

believe to think something is true or real. *I believe you know the rules.*

expect to think something will occur. *I expect our team to win the game.*

imagine to picture in one's mind. *I like to imagine that elves did the work.*

track *n.* a mark or series of marks left by an animal, person, wagon, etc. *We saw a bicycle track in the snow.*

mark a line, spot, or dot made by something on an object. *That mark was made by the cat's claws.*

pattern a guide to make something. *Use the pattern to make the star.*

treat *v.* to handle; behave toward. *You must treat animals gently.*

handle to touch or use with the hands. *He meant to handle the vase carefully.*

manage to guide or handle. *She can manage the workers very well.*

under *prep.* below; beneath. *I found the money hidden under a rock.*

below lower than; under. *The sign is hanging below the branches.*

beneath below; under. *The light was placed beneath the window.*

until *prep.* up to the time of; till. *I slept until noon today.*

till until; up to the time of. *The game lasted till five o'clock.*

very *adv.* greatly; extremely. *He was very unhappy when he lost his dog.*

exceedingly unusually; greatly. *The report was done exceedingly well.*

extremely greatly; strongly. *She was extremely busy at work today.*

greatly in a great manner. *She was greatly pleased by the award.*

war *n.* a fight or struggle between countries or parts of a country. *There are great losses of life and destruction of property in a war.*

fight a struggle; contest. *The fight was scheduled for Tuesday.*

struggle a conflict; fight. *The struggle for freedom took many years.*

warm *v.* to make warm; to heat. *Warm the food before you serve it.*

cook to prepare with heat. *The stew must cook for several hours.*

heat to make or become warm. *The furnace will heat the house.*

wave *v.* to move up and down or from side to side. *The branches began to wave in the wind.*

flap to move up and down. *The bird needed to flap its wings to get off the ground.*

flutter to wave back and forth quickly. *The flag will flutter in the wind.*

wide *adj.* covering or having much space from side to side; broad; not narrow. *Our new car has wide seats.*

broad large across; wide. *The broad road had four lanes in each direction.*

extensive far-reaching; large. *There were extensive changes in the plans for the new building.*

antonym: narrow

without *prep.* not having; with no. *I left without my umbrella.*

less without; with something taken away. *The group was less two people.*

minus less; decreased by. *Five minus two leaves three.*

work *n.* job; occupation; the thing one does to earn a living. *Her work is modeling clothes.*

business work; occupation. *Their cleaning business can be found in the shopping mall.*

job piece of work. *The plumber did a good job of fixing the shower.*

occupation job; work. *Her occupation was bank manager.*

work *v.* to have a job for pay in order to make a living. *He likes to work in a big office.*

labor to work hard; toil. *The gardener will have to labor many hours in the spring.*

toil to work hard. *The farmer needs to toil in the field for many long hours.*

worry *n.* a cause of anxiety or trouble. *Money is a constant worry to him.*

anxiety fears about what might happen; worries. *She felt great anxiety over her test.*

nervousness anxiety; jumpiness. *His nervousness was caused by his fear of heights.*

wrap *v.* to enclose in something by winding or folding. *Wrap the baby in warm blankets.*

bundle up to wrap up. *He needed to bundle up in a heavy coat.*

envelop to wrap, cover, or hide. *The caterpillar will envelop itself in a cocoon.*

D

E

F

Credits